Praise for *You Are an Ironman*

"For anyone who dreams of doing a triathlon or needs to find motivation, *You Are an Ironman* is a fantastic read! Steinberg follows six ordinary athletes on their individual odysseys, he illuminates their courage and commitment and inspires readers to boldly pursue their dreams."

—Lynn Cox, author of *Grayson* and *Swimming to Antarctica*

"[A] compelling and inspirational read for obsessive exercisers and couch potatoes alike."

—The Associated Press

"Anyone dreaming of completing a triathlon or just seeking to get off the couch and into better shape will find inspiration here."

—*Kirkus Reviews*

"Readers will surely want to carry on and experience the excitement that leads to the finish line in Tempe, Ariz., [*sic*] where the race announcer proclaims to each entrant who comes across that 'you are an Ironman.'"

—*Winston-Salem Journal*

PENGUIN BOOKS

YOU ARE AN IRONMAN

Jacques Steinberg is a senior editor for *The New York Times* where he has worked for more than two decades, covering education and the media. He is the author of the bestselling *The Gatekeepers*. He lives outside New York City.

YOU ARE AN
IRONMAN

HOW SIX WEEKEND WARRIORS
CHASED THEIR DREAM OF FINISHING
THE WORLD'S TOUGHEST TRIATHLON

JACQUES STEINBERG

PENGUIN BOOKS

PENGUIN BOOKS

Published by the Penguin Group

Penguin Group (USA) Inc., 375 Hudson Street, New York, New York 10014, U.S.A.

Penguin Group (Canada), 90 Eglinton Avenue East, Suite 700, Toronto, Ontario, Canada M4P 2Y3
(a division of Pearson Penguin Canada Inc.)

Penguin Books Ltd, 80 Strand, London WC2R 0RL, England

Penguin Ireland, 25 St. Stephen's Green, Dublin 2, Ireland (a division of Penguin Books Ltd)

Penguin Books Australia Ltd, 250 Camberwell Road, Camberwell, Victoria 3124, Australia
(a division of Pearson Australia Group Pty Ltd)

Penguin Books India Pvt Ltd, 11 Community Centre, Panchsheel Park,
New Delhi – 110 017, India

Penguin Group (NZ), 67 Apollo Drive, Rosedale, Auckland 0632, New Zealand
(a division of Pearson New Zealand Ltd)

Penguin Books (South Africa) (Pty) Ltd, 24 Sturdee Avenue, Rosebank,
Johannesburg 2196, South Africa

Penguin Books Ltd, Registered Offices: 80 Strand, London WC2R 0RL, England

First published in the United States of America by Viking Penguin,
a member of Penguin Group (USA) Inc. 2011
Published in Penguin Books 2012

1 3 5 7 9 10 8 6 4 2

Ironman® and Ironman Triathlon® are trademarks of World Triathlon Corporation.

"Tri-Mantra" by Olivier Blanchard. Used by permission of the author.

E-mail message from Paul Huddle to Seth Cannello. Used by permission of Paul Huddle.

Photograph credits
Page 273: Photo by Debbie Reece
276: Photo by Steven T. Norman
278: United States Air Force
279: Photo by Scott and Leanne Johnson
283: Courtesy Tracy Tucker-Georges
284: Photo by Robert Bonnette

THE LIBRARY OF CONGRESS HAS CATALOGED THE HARDCOVER EDITION AS FOLLOWS:
Steinberg, Jacques.
You are an ironman : how six weekend warriors chased their dream
of finishing the world's toughest triathlon / Jacques Steinberg.
p. cm.
ISBN 978-0-670-02302-8 (hc.)
ISBN 978-0-14-312207-4 (pbk.)
1. Ironman triathlons.   2. Triathlon.   3. Triathlon—Training.   4. Athletes—Biography.   I. Title.
GV1060.73.S84 2011
796.42'57—dc22   2011015195

Printed in the United States of America

For Ali, Jordan, and Sharon
who make me feel like an IronDad, every day
and
For Paul Epstein, Gary Rodbell, and Will McCurdy
who put the "will" (and "can") in Team Will

Contents

CONTENTS

YOU ARE AN IRONMAN

Introduction

Nell Martin loped between the glass towers of downtown Tempe and at last broke through the wide band of tape that had been stretched taut in front of her, snapping it as if she were popping the cork from a bottle of champagne. The watch on her left wrist read 10:34 P.M.—more than three hours after the sun had set over this gateway to the Arizona desert. High above her head the numbers 15:34:36 were illuminated in neon yellow, as bright as a Times Square billboard, signifying the 15 hours, 34 minutes, and 36 seconds she had taken to complete her day's journey. Her skin was caked white with salt, the result of a continuous sweat that had long ago dried in the cool night air. Willing herself to a stop a few steps past the finish line, Nell allowed a volunteer whose hands were sheathed in latex gloves to wrap her in a foil blanket. He then escorted her toward a table piled high with pizza, of all things. There she could begin restoring her body to normal—including tending to the leg muscles that would soon begin to throb uncontrollably—a process that would ultimately take more than a week.

An anesthesiologist and married mother of three teenagers, Nell was in better shape than many of those recovering around her. Nearby, as if at a makeshift Red Cross disaster tent, several dozen men and women laid out on cots were receiving sugar water and other intravenous fluids through needles tethered to clear plastic bags. Occasionally a wheeled stretcher would be summoned to take someone by ambulance to a nearby emergency room for more intensive attention. But Nell needed no such intervention. For five years she had trained diligently for this day, as a way to mark her fiftieth birthday, which she had celebrated only a few days before. As her heart rate slowed, her mind kept returning to the ten words the announcer had said to the crowd assembled in makeshift bleachers on either side of the finish line.

"Nell Martin of Grand Junction, Colorado," he had boomed, "*you* are an Ironman."

On that Sunday before Thanksgiving 2008, as much of the nation contemplated gorging itself on turkey and stuffing with family and friends, Nell and more than two thousand others swam, cycled, and ran longer and farther in one day than many of us will do in a lifetime. Ranging in age from eighteen to seventy-six, they were competitors in the Ford Ironman Arizona, one of twenty-three officially sanctioned, 140.6-mile Ironman triathlons staged around the world that year. Eight were in the United States, including the Ford Ironman World Championship in Kona, Hawaii, the original and best known of such races. In an Ironman, the already formidable elements of a typical triathlon (known as an Olympic-distance)— 0.9-mile swim, 26-mile bike ride, 6-mile run, all of which was sufficient to kill at least eight participants in 2008 alone—are supersized.

An Ironman triathlon consists of a 2.4-mile open-water swim (the equivalent of about 175 lengths across a community lap pool), followed by a 112-mile bike ride (imagine pedaling from New York City past Philadelphia), and then, as if some kind of cruel joke, a 26.2-mile marathon run. No physical exam is typically required, nor is any previous experience— other than for Ironman Hawaii, which is open mainly to top finishers in various age groups in prior qualifying races. Those who choose to put their bodies and minds through such a gantlet, nearly all weekend warriors with jobs and families, must complete the entire event in no more than seventeen hours—which includes any time spent recovering from the swim or changing from biking gear into running shoes. Nell Martin, for example, had emerged from Tempe Town Lake shivering so profoundly that it took sixteen minutes before she could mount her bike.

With the swim beginning at 7:00 A.M. sharp, the deadline that looms is the stroke of midnight. Even someone crossing the finish line ninety seconds late, as one woman did at Ironman Arizona 2008, is branded with the scarlet letters every Ironman triathlete dreads: DNF, or "did not finish." Mike Reilly, the announcer whose hoarse voice has welcomed nearly 200,000 successful Ironman competitors across the finish line in more than a hundred such races since 1989, has a special message for those who have come up painfully short.

"You are an Ironman," he tells them over the public address system, "in our hearts."

At the previous Ironman Arizona, staged on an April day when temperatures soared well over ninety degrees, nearly 15 percent of the participants—about 300—had quit well before they were within range of Reilly's voice. Even now, with Ironman Arizona having been moved to the cooler confines of November (the high temperature, just after midday, was eighty), 121 people had withdrawn mid-race.

Nell Martin, who had run a marathon at forty-three but had otherwise not considered herself much of an athlete for the first four decades of her life, had become a first-time Ironman with nearly ninety minutes to spare (and, no, the powers that be who preside over the Ironman culture, some of them women, have yet to accede to a gender-neutral designation). Like the more than fifty thousand others who completed an Ironman-distance triathlon somewhere in the world in 2008—and the hundreds of thousands of others who participated in triathlons of lesser intervals that year—Nell's early-morning swims and runs and midday bike rides had paid off. Little surprise, then, that in her hotel room afterward she found she could not sleep—not because of the various aches she was feeling, and not even because of the adrenaline that still coursed through her veins, but because she was so filled with the sense of pride and satisfaction.

At five o'clock the next morning, she left her room, climbed into her rental car, and headed back toward the park adjacent to the finish area to celebrate her accomplishment in the only way that seemed appropriate. Taking her place in a line that was already about one hundred people long before sunrise—and would snake to nearly five hundred as the sun came up—Nell waited patiently for nearly two hours. Just after 7:00 A.M., barely twenty-four hours after she had descended into the sixty-two-degree waters of Town Lake to begin her odyssey—and less than nine hours after she completed it—she strode up to a volunteer seated in front of a laptop.

Yes, Nell Martin said as she handed over her credit card, she was there to sign up for next year's race.

After the race organizers had accommodated those who had shown up in person to register—including other 2008 participants and race volunteers, as well as some who had flown cross-country just to ensure they got a place—the registration process was opened to a national audience online. The computer system promptly crashed. Long before sundown, Ironman Arizona 2009, which was a year away, had sold out—and at no small cost to the participants. Though the stock market was still in the midst of its historic plunge that fall, each of the would-be competitors in Ironman Arizona had paid $525 apiece to enter. Some had withdrawn the money from the saving accounts of their college-bound children to reserve a slot, while others had deferred expenses like house repairs. The fee, they knew, was nonrefundable.

Why would so many people choose to put themselves through so much agony and effort in pursuit of a single goal? What toll does their training, often upwards of fifteen hours a week for months on end, exact on their families, their friends, their jobs? To what extent does engaging in such a grueling endeavor endanger their health, in the short term and beyond?

On the other hand, consider that one participant who completed Ironman Arizona minutes after Nell Martin was Ed Wolfgram, a seventy-six-year-old psychiatrist from St. Louis. Less than a year earlier, Wolfgram had undergone an aortic valve replacement. He was also recovering from prostate cancer. I caught up with him just a few moments after he finished that race, out of breath and steadying himself on his wife's shoulder near the food tables set up in a nearby park. Why, I asked him, would he embark on an endeavor as potentially life-threatening as an Ironman, having just emerged from so serious a medical ordeal? (At least five participants have died during Ironman competitions in North America in the last decade.)

"It has everything to do with how long you live and how healthfully you live," Wolfgram said. "And if that's not enough," he added quickly, in reference to his rationale for swimming, biking, and running on a regular basis, "it has a lot to do with how you function sexually!"

Wolfgram's accomplishment raises these questions, among others: To what extent is the role of the mind as important as that of the body, if not more so, in someone's completing an Ironman? What is the payoff, psychologically and otherwise? For those willing to put in the enormous time and training, does it represent, in the words of Jimmy Riccitello, the head referee of the Arizona race, a "poor man's Everest"—a feat of remarkable endurance that is for many people actually attainable? And what does it say about our society—three decades after we became a nation of runners—that for tens of thousands of Americans, a standard marathon no longer presents a sufficient challenge?

To feel fulfilled athletically and in other ways, these Ironmen (and would-be Ironmen) insist, they need to train simultaneously in three sports. More than a few participants in Ironman Arizona could be heard dismissively referring to the marathon portion of their race as "our cooldown."

In this book I examine the phenomenon of Ironman triathlons (and, by extension, triathlons in general) through the eyes of those who have chosen to participate in them. More specifically, I follow a small group of people from across the country as they prepare for—and then compete in—Ironman Arizona in November 2009, the year after Nell Martin became an Ironman.

Like her, each of the main competitors I profile in the pages that follow selected Arizona as the setting for his or her first Ironman attempt. The hurdles they face in attempting to cross that finish line are substantial. These include not only getting into sufficient shape and staying free of injury in the months leading up to the race, but also completing the first two legs of the Ironman event before the cutoffs imposed by the race directors. Those interim benchmarks, which if missed result in automatic disqualification, are 2 hours 20 minutes, for the swim portion, and 10 hours 30 minutes (timed from the beginning of the swim) for the bike.

Though several dozen athletes in each Ironman race are professionals who live off their prize money and sponsorships, their stories are not my focus. Instead, the pages here will be given over primarily to the experiences of so-called age-groupers, people who, like most triathletes, regard the sport as a hobby, albeit for some of them an all-consuming one. One woman waiting in line to register for Ironman Arizona 2009 told me her triathlon training had contributed to the dissolution of her marriage, prompting knowing nods from others standing around her.

While I have attempted to convey to readers the virtual experience of swimming laps alongside the participants in their health club pools, and cycling with them for miles near their homes, *You Are an Ironman* is not intended as a how-to or training book. The athletes I shadow certainly impart much advice on how to gear up for an Ironman—as well as, by example, some mistakes to avoid—but readers seeking a week-by-week plan of attack in preparation for such an event would do well to consult books like *Your First Triathlon*, by Joe Friel, or *Start to Finish: Ironman Training*, by Paul Huddle and Roch Frey, the co-directors of the Arizona race. There is also the Web site BeginnerTriathlete.com.

While the stories recounted here should ring true to those who may have already completed such an adventure themselves, I also hope this book will prove illuminating and entertaining to a broader audience—including those readers who may have idly wondered what it takes to embark on such a journey, as well as others who, however curious, have no intention of ever lacing up a pair of running shoes, let alone clipping into the pedals of a bike traveling in excess of thirty miles an hour.

In the end, this is a book that attempts to bore deep into the lives, minds, and souls of these athletes—people who could be our neighbors—to capture what this experience feels like, not just for the participants themselves but for their spouses and children.

While relatively few of us will ever experience an Ironman as a participant, the number of Americans who have set about tackling a triathlon—including at the entry-level sprint distance—has risen dramatically in recent years. In 2000, for example, 21,341 people purchased memberships in USA Triathlon, a nonprofit organization that sanctions such events. By 2007 that figure had more than quadrupled, to 100,674. Over the same period, the number of sanctioned triathlons in the United States more than doubled, to more than 1,200. And that figure does not take into account the hundreds of other triathlons organized each year not by any official body but by small towns, gyms, and charitable organizations, which draw tens of thousands of other competitors. In an effort to combat the sharp rise in obesity among young people tethered to their PlayStations and iPhones, countless communities have begun staging kiddie triathlons—the one in my community, open to 250 children as young as six, now has a waiting list—including some branded by the Ironman organization as IronKids.

These days the competition just to register for such races is often as intense as that within the races themselves. One minute after midnight on November 1, 2008, a Sunday, the organizers of the New York City Triathlon used their Web site to make available the several thousand slots in the following year's race. Like tickets to a Bruce Springsteen concert, the event—which would not take place until the following July—was sold out in less than a half hour. (The prior year's race had sold out in eight hours.)

The increase in the number of people who have sought out the challenge of an Ironman is even more striking. Just fifteen men participated in the first Ironman, in Hawaii in 1978. Plans for that original Ironman competition had been hatched during the awards ceremony for a Hawaiian running relay race in February of the previous year. As the beer flowed, a group of friends, some of them in the military, gathered around a table and began arguing about who was more fit: swimmers, cyclists, or runners. To resolve their dispute, the participants imagined chaining together the routes for the Waikiki Roughwater Swim (2.4 miles), the Around-Oahu Bike Race (112 miles), and the Honolulu Marathon (26.2 miles). At some point before the end of that fateful awards ceremony, one of the kibitzers, a navy man named John Collins, ascended the stage and grabbed the microphone to make an impromptu announcement.

"I suggested we put all three Oahu events together," Collins later recalled in an article published in 2001 on the Ironman Web site. "I said the gun would go off and the clock keep running and whoever finished first, well, we'd call them the Ironman."

"It got a really good laugh at the time," he added.

What had inspired Collins to use the name Ironman, by all accounts a term that had come off the top of his head?

His inspiration, he later said, came from a runner stationed at the Pearl Harbor Naval Shipyard, "a man who could run 2 or 20 miles—all at the same pace," according to Nick Munting, an Australian journalist who profiled Collins for the Ironman Web site.

When the first-ever Ironman eventually took place, a year later, twelve of the fifteen participants completed it—some of them fueled not just by the beer they consumed along the way but by chili, too.

As one of those pioneers, Tom Knoll, wrote in *Triathlete* magazine in July 2009:

> The goal for most of us was just to finish, hopefully in 24 hours or less. Little did we realize that what we were now attempting would someday become an Olympic event and captivate the dreams of competitors around the world, including millions of spectators who would view these triathlons in person or on TV.
>
> We had all paid a $5 entry fee, and there was no prize money or trophies awarded to the top finishers. There was no traffic control, no aid stations and most of us did not have helmets on for the 112-mile bike ride around the island.

The following year, another fifteen participants, including the first woman, competed. The records of their participation were dutifully kept by Collins—in a shoebox. But the race, which in 1981 was relocated from relatively crowded Oahu to Kona, on the less populous Big Island, would quickly vault in popularity, recognition, and stature in the years that immediately followed. One reason was national media attention, including a ten-page feature by a *Sports Illustrated* reporter who had stumbled onto the race in 1979 while on assignment to cover a golf tournament. A year later, producers of *Wide World of Sports*, on ABC, approached race organizers for permission to film the event. Collins said yes, though he did warn them, "Watching the race is about as exciting as watching a lawn-growing contest."

That may have been true initially, but not after several million television viewers were transfixed by the odyssey and determination of Julie Moss, who competed in the fifth installment of the race, in February 1982. A college student who had entered the Ironman as a research project for her studies in exercise physiology, Moss could be seen approaching the finish line in first place (among women) despite obviously suffering from fatigue and dehydration. "In the homestretch," according to the official history of the race on the Ironman Web site, "she staggers like a punch drunk boxer." Just yards from the finish, she fell to the ground. Though the eventual winner, Kathleen McCartney, would pass her, Moss crawled across the finish line. "Her courage and determination," according to the official recounting of her performance that day, "creates the Ironman mantra that just finishing is a victory."

In 2006, less than three decades after the staging of the original Ironman, 75,000 men and women competed in either an Ironman (at the same 140.6-mile distance as its namesake) or a so-called half Ironman (now known as a "70.3") in the United States and around the world. Two years later, that figure had risen to 100,000, according to World Triathlon Corporation, the organization that eventually trademarked the Ironman brand (including on those ubiquitous Timex Ironman digital watches) and that sponsors more than sixty full- and half-distance races, including Arizona. In 2010, participation in Ironman-branded events exceeded 140,000. (World Triathlon Corporation is a story in and of itself; it was founded by a Florida eye doctor and Ironman enthusiast who purchased the Kona race in 1990 from a health club manager; she, in turn, had taken it over from Collins when the Navy transferred him from Hawaii.) By the mid-2000s, more than three million viewers were tuning in each fall to NBC's broadcast of the Hawaii race, according to the Nielsen Company.

In the summer of 2011, World Triathlon Corporation announced that Ironman was ready to take its act to one of the world's biggest stages: New York City, which would host an Ironman triathlon in August 2012. Specifically, the organizers said the swim course would be in the Hudson River, the bike ride would wind through New Jersey into New York State's Rockland County, and the run would cross the George Washington Bridge before concluding in Manhattan's Riverside Park. When, a year before the starting cannon was scheduled to sound, the three thousand competitors' slots were offered for sale, they sold out online in fewer than ten minutes, according to John Korff, who organizes New York City Triathlon and lured Ironman to New York. The non-refundable price: $895 per person ($1,500 for those participating on behalf of charities).

Race officials told *The New York Times* they expected the economic impact on the tristate region to be about $50 million.

As is the case with triathlons of lesser distances, the percentage of women who are participants in Ironman and half-Ironman races—particularly women in their thirties and forties—is rising at an even faster rate than that of men. While 27 percent of the members of USA Triathlon in 2000 were women, that figure had risen to 37 percent by 2007.

Little wonder that cottage industries made up of apparel manufacturers, magazine publishers, bicycle makers, and custom trainers have sprouted up to meet the needs of this fast-growing, deep-pocketed group. Even the most casual of triathletes can easily spend in excess of $5,000 preparing for a race, once the price of a modestly outfitted road bicycle was added to the cost of clip-on bike shoes, running sneakers, a wetsuit, waterproof bike clothing sleek enough to fit under that wetsuit (the better to facilitate the transition from water to bike), and swim lessons. Moreover, for those participants who take their weekend sports as seriously as their jobs—and who have the discretionary cash to do so—the cost of a custom-fitted triathlon bike alone could approach $10,000.

That same individual might spend several thousand dollars more to be videotaped swimming, biking, and running, and having that footage analyzed professionally by a cadre of trainers, as if he or she were preparing for the Olympics. Based on how quickly triathlons of various distances were selling out that year, the growing community of swimmers, cyclists, and runners appeared to represent one sector of the economy that may well be recession-proof. Just before the economic downturn took hold, Providence Equity Partners, a private investment firm worth an estimated $21 billion (its holdings include Warner Music and the MGM brand), bought World Triathlon Corporation and the Ironman name. Soon afterward it acquired NA Sports, the licensee that organized many of the North American Ironman and 70.3 races. The purchase price was not disclosed.

Readying oneself for an Ironman, and then competing in one, can be viewed from at least some angles as a selfish act. The would-be participant chooses to opt out of many of the ordinary moments of everyday life to train for several thousand hours in a year. And even when that person is not training, she might not be fully engaged in the recital, Little League game, anniversary dinner, or conference call going on at the time, because she's daydreaming about the miles ahead, or just plain exhausted. Others become preoccupied and distracted nursing pulled muscles, torn ligaments, or broken bones. And as with so many activities in which a burst of endorphins is among the rewards, some people get addicted and compulsive. One man proudly passed out fliers on the eve of Ironman Arizona in 2009 boasting that he was putting himself through an additional Ironman-distance swim, bike ride, and run on each of the two days prior to the actual race, in which he would also compete. The year before, at Arizona, I was introduced to Joe Bonness, a fifty-three-year-old contractor from Naples, Florida, who had just completed his fifty-seventh Ironman, representing at least two a year for more than a quarter-century. "I'm always after the bigger challenge," he told me.

Some Ironman triathletes, to say nothing of their families, have paid the ultimate price for their participation in a sport that is far more dangerous than tennis or golf. Bernard P. Rice, a thirty-five-year-old man from Kalispell, Montana, lost consciousness at some point during the swim portion of the November 2006 Ironman Florida, in Panama City, which was patrolled by volunteers in kayaks. He never awoke, and passed away three days later. Mr. Rice's family later sued the race organizers, claiming he had died as a result of their negligence. While the race organizers had said Mr. Rice died of "a massive heart attack," his family countered that he "went into cardiac arrest after having been medically unattended for a significant period of time after being brought to shore by volunteers out in the water." The race organizers prevailed, at least partly because Ironman participants must sign an exhaustive two-page waiver in which they agree in advance to take full responsibility for whatever might happen to them on the course.

Others have died in the swim portions of Ironman competitions in Utah (2002) and British Columbia (2009, just a few weeks before Ironman Arizona), as have participants in the swim portions of lesser-distance triathlons having nothing to do with Ironman. These include the death of a thirty-two-year-old man who was pulled unconscious from the Hudson River in July 2008 during the New York City Triathlon. An autopsy was inconclusive, but a jellyfish sting was thought to have contributed to his death. While triathletes have certainly perished during the cycling and running portions of their races—the first Ironman death, in California in 2001, involved a cyclist who lost control on a steep downhill, crashing into a metal railing—a disproportionate number appear to perish during the swim. (In marathons, by contrast, the deaths appear more evenly distributed across all twenty-six miles of the race.)

And yet, for all the media attention surrounding such fatalities, relatively few of those who participate in triathlons—including those of the epic Ironman distance—die as a result of doing so. To the contrary: Many competitors say that their participation (and the training leading up to it) are essential to keeping them physically and mentally healthy, if not alive. The banquet that precedes every Ironman competition always features testimonials from those who describe how their triathlon training put their cancer in remission or seemingly cured their depression.

At one such banquet, at an open-air pavilion on the shore of Tempe Town Lake before Ironman Arizona in 2008, my eye was drawn to a man who appeared to be in his thirties who was listening intently to the speeches. He sat not on a folding plastic chair but in a wheelchair. His name was Anthony Pedeferri, and he told me that he had been rendered a quadriplegic in the line of duty as a California highway patrolman during a routine traffic stop eleven months earlier. After he'd walked to the passenger side of the vehicle, as is customary in California, that car was struck by a second driver, who was traveling seventy-four miles per hour in a Chevy pickup, high on PCP. The impact of the accident killed the driver of the first car, which burst into flames, and sent Officer Pedeferri flying through the air, landing in a ditch seventy feet away. His back, neck, and collarbone were broken, along with all the ribs on his left side, and his spinal cord was completely severed. Once Officer Pedeferri, a father of two young daughters, had been airlifted to a nearby trauma center, one of the doctors called his wife and urged her to rush to the hospital to say goodbye. The doctor explained to her that her husband had "only ten minutes to live." And yet he survived.

The reason? Ironman training.

Just weeks before his accident, Officer Pedeferri had completed Ironman Hawaii in Kona—his eleventh such race. "The doctor said the fact that I was an endurance athlete saved my life," Pedeferri told me. "I could deal with the lack of oxygen better than the average person." At the time of his accident, he had already registered for the race that was to be his twelfth: Ironman Arizona 2008. He explained that he was not yet sufficiently recovered to begin to train as a so-called challenged athlete (who must finish an Ironman in the same seventeen hours as able-bodied competitors). But as we sat talking that night, the sun setting in front of us on the lake in which the swim portion of the race would begin thirty-six hours later, Officer Pedeferri told me he had set an even more ambitious goal for himself. "I just turned thirty-eight," he said. "My goal is when I turn forty to get back to Kona."

While Officer Pedeferri's story may be among the more gripping to ever intersect with Ironman, every participant in every race, whether he finishes or not, serves to inspire someone—whether it's the members of his own family or perfect strangers. Joe Bonness, who, as I mentioned earlier, has finished more than fifty Ironmans, is an example of someone you might say has taken triathlon to the extreme. But the reader may wish to reconsider that judgment when taking into account the fact that waiting for him at the finish line of every race is his wife, Susan, who is confined to a wheelchair as a result of complications from diabetes. She proudly told me that, like a NASCAR pit crew boss, she was responsible for plotting the itinerary of each trip.

And then there's the philanthropic side of all this. Ironman athletes have formally raised nearly $50 million for various charities, many of them seeking to cure life-threatening illnesses, through a matching donor program called the Janus Charity Challenge. But the Janus program has been in operation only since 2000, and the fund-raisers who've raised $50 million through it represent just 2 percent of Ironman participants. Though nearly every Ironman dedicates her race to some cause larger than herself, most raise money informally and on their own, a gesture of quiet largesse known only to a select few.

Bryan Reece, a fifty-year-old investment manager from San Antonio whose story is among those showcased in this book, spent the year before his inaugural Ironman dutifully collecting the names of cancer victims from anyone he encountered: clients of his firm, the person riding next to him on the stationary bike in a spin class, the waitress in a restaurant. Some of the names he was given were of those who were still alive; others, like Reece's father, had long since died. His plan, he told anyone who would listen, was to find some way to carry all those names somewhere on his body during Ironman Arizona. He even thought seriously about writing the name of each on a white swim cap that would go below his official Ironman cap.

Such training alone has also been known to enable people to rewrite their long-standing definitions of themselves. Many of those who set themselves on the path toward Ironman will tell you they did not grow up thinking of themselves as athletes, but do so now, in middle age. An Ironman triathlete might not be fast, but she can endure. A cancer patient setting about training for an Ironman may no longer think of himself or herself as sick, or sickly. Those who have lost children or spouses to illness can find a haven in Ironman, where they can change the subject for a few hours while still celebrating their loved ones and spreading the word of the indelible imprint they left behind.

Others who participate in triathlons have used such contests to embrace parts of themselves they may have previously sought to conceal. Let's face it: Few sports outside the world of triathlon provide so many rewards to those who have been forever told by friends and colleagues that they have classic "Type A," if not anal, personalities. Indeed, triathlons literally reward points for such behavior. In addition to timing how fast one completes the swim, bike, and running courses, race organizers also clock the transitions between those events. Thus, the time it takes one to strip out of a wetsuit and pull on a bike shirt and shoes is part of the official result—and, in the case of Ironman, tallied en route to the seventeen-hour time limit. So is the time it takes someone to transform from biker to runner. In preparation, athletes (and their families) are sent scurrying in the days and hours before a race, executing endless to-do lists and filling various bags with what they think they might need along the way, including clothing and sustenance.

One of my favorite spots in the area of transition from swim to bike at Arizona 2009 was the eyeglass table—on which were arrayed dozens of pairs of prescription lenses, carefully sealed in zip-lock bags marked with names and bib numbers. Soon their owners would emerge from the water and, in some cases, feel their way to that table, so that they might better see the road that lay ahead.

Nearby was another table of athletes' critical possessions. On it were displayed more than a dozen insulin pumps and diabetic testing kits, a testament to the challenges their owners must have faced in advance of descending into the water before dawn that day.

The reader should know at the outset that I am no Ironman. I am a journalist. And the approach I am taking here is modeled on that of other sportswriters who may have been far less gifted as athletes than their main characters. Still, the most valuable background I bring to this project may well be my brief firsthand immersion in the triathlon world. Four years ago, my friend Paul asked me to join him and his friend Gary for an early-morning swim on a cold winter Sunday at a nearby YMCA. Paul told me not to be intimidated but also warned me that Gary was a bit of a hard-ass. After graduating from high school in New York City in the early 1970s, Gary had relocated to Israel and enlisted in the Israeli army. Before long, Gary was recruited to join an elite paratrooper unit that came under fire in Lebanon.

I, by contrast, wasn't exactly ready for boot camp.

At the time I met Gary, I was a father of two young children and on the precipice of forty, tipping the scale about ten pounds overweight. (My wife would say I'm being generous.) My most recent athletic experience had not ranged much beyond the StairMaster at the local gym. Never much of an athlete, I had last crisscrossed a pool in a lap of freestyle in college. And my last formal swimming lesson was surely years before that, at summer camp. Little wonder that, as Gary and Paul glided back and forth for forty-five minutes without a break, I could barely make it across the pool and back without stopping to gulp for air. And yet, I was somehow hooked.

Before long I was joining Paul and Gary several mornings a week for swims of nearly a mile. They were also dragging me along to early-morning classes at a local spin studio run by their friend Laurie, where a dozen of us would pedal stationary bikes to classic rock tunes by the Who and Van Morrison. When the weather warmed, we took to the roads of Westchester County, New York, for Sunday morning rides that soon lasted nearly four hours and traversed nearly fifty hilly miles. At Gary's urging, I bought a Trek bike for $1,300. I considered it an expensive, almost luxurious purchase, but I was told I had gotten off relatively cheap, in part by buying a model discontinued from an earlier year.

It was Gary, who was in his early fifties and had already competed in four Ironman-distance races, who first suggested that I might put all this experience to use in a more formal setting. In the spring of 2007 he grabbed me after spin class with a modest proposal: that I join a relay team that would be competing in an upcoming triathlon in Rye, New York. Knowing I had yet to take up running, he said I could swim the 0.9-mile swim portion of the race (it would require a wetsuit, in Long Island Sound), followed by a 24-mile bike ride. Someone else we knew would do the run. Though he had phrased his approach as a question, he also made clear that it was an offer I was not entitled to refuse. He said he knew I was ready, even if I didn't.

Only a handful of the three thousand people who competed that day swam slower than I did. I climbed out of the salty sound after 34 minutes. I didn't fare much better on the bike course, clocking in at 1 hour and 45 minutes, or about 15 miles an hour, which sounds impressive until you consider that the second half of the course was mostly downhill. Thanks to the slow start I had given her, the runner to whom I handed off the equivalent of an electronic baton—an ankle strap with a chip that recorded our times—had little chance of moving out of the back of the pack.

But that wasn't the point. I had accomplished my mission, such as it was, and felt like a combination of Michael Phelps and Lance Armstrong. When I went for my annual physical a few weeks later, my doctor pronounced himself amazed: My blood pressure and cholesterol, and even my weight, had seemingly reversed course, registering where they had six years earlier. Told at my previous physical that I might soon need to consider going on a cholesterol-lowering drug, at the rate those numbers had been climbing, I was now informed that such a remedy no longer appeared necessary.

The following year, I did the swim-bike portion of two more triathlons. And at Gary's insistence I completed the 1.2-mile swim and 56-mile bike ride of my first half-Ironman relay, in and around Lake Winnipesaukee, New Hampshire. As I write this, I have begun, for the first time, to add the run to my repertoire, and have set a goal of completing a sprint-distance triathlon in 2011. Gary says an Ironman is in my future, but I'm inclined to disagree. It is at times like this that I gently remind Gary, to whom this book is dedicated, that I have titled it *You Are an Ironman*, not *I Am . . .* For now I have just tried to stay in sufficient shape to keep up with my friends and the training of those I profile here.

Moreover, for the first time in my life, as I celebrate my forty-fifth birthday, I feel like I'm part of a team. Supported by a rotating cast of weekend warriors, Gary has used the various races in which he has competed to raise hundreds of thousands of dollars for a rare and little-understood disease called Barth Syndrome. Sapping nearly all energy from the body and racking it periodically with heart failure and infections that require hospitalization, Barth has afflicted a young man in our town named Will McCurdy since he was born. Will is now in his early twenties, and Gary, a friend of his family, has made raising money for research a personal quest. Nearly a dozen of us who have been privileged to get to know Will and his family through Gary have made his cause ours as well.

But nothing has bound Team Will together quite as much as the announcement that Gary made during the celebration at Will's house following the annual Rye triathlon in October 2008. At fifty-five, Gary obviously had been hurting that day as he grimaced through the three segments of the race. His knees were racked with arthritis and cartilage tears. His left shoulder still throbbed from a fall he had taken a few weeks earlier. His back ached. And yet, he told us that day, he felt he had one more big event in him: He had decided to sign up for what he described as his "retirement race," the following November. It would be Ironman Arizona 2009, which he favored, in part, because it was among the flatter Ironman courses and would give him a year to train.

As he spoke, tears streamed down the cheeks of his wife, Colette, who had watched the toll Gary's training had taken on his body over the years. She knew this Ironman would probably be his hardest, even if she had seen him in worse shape. (He had completed his fourth Ironman, in Florida in 2006, a year after a car collided with his bike, leaving him with three hundred stitches in his cheek and a fractured shoulder.)

In announcing his intention to compete in Ironman Arizona, Gary also had a request: He wanted as many of us as possible from Team Will to join him. While I was clearly not yet ready, Paul and several of our other friends, all over forty, would ultimately decide to accompany Gary in what would be their first Ironman.

To get a sense of what they were getting themselves into, and with a hunch that there was a larger story to tell, I traveled to Ironman Arizona 2008, which I took in as a spectator, just a few weeks after Gary's announcement. That the competitors had transformed their bodies, and often their lives, in pursuit of such a monumental accomplishment was obvious from that opening dinner. The dry air of the day still hot, Mike Reilly asked those in the audience who had lost more than twenty pounds through their training to stand. Maybe seventy-five did. He then asked those who had lost thirty pounds to continue standing, and about forty of them remained. By the time he called out those who had lost more than fifty pounds, a handful still stood, including a man from Las Vegas with a shaved head who had shed more than sixty pounds and a woman from Austin who had dropped more than seventy. Both were called onto the stage, to thunderous applause. In an impromptu interview with Reilly, the man told the crowd that his weight had been so high—304 pounds—that his kidneys had begun to fail. He estimated his current weight at a sleek 212.

Reilly also invited up the oldest competitors, who included Ed Wolfgram and a woman in her early seventies who had competed in four previous Ironman races, none of which she'd finished. He also paid tribute to the youngest, who included an eighteen-year-old girl from Texas who told the audience that her asthma had been so severe that she could barely swim a year earlier. (She would wind up finishing the Arizona race, with several hours to spare.) A man in his thirties from Arizona spoke about getting into shape following a heart attack, an experience that was chronicled in a short video shown on a big screen. He finished the Arizona race, too.

One of the marquee competitors introduced that Friday night was German Silva, whom some in the audience remembered well as the winner of the New York City Marathon in 1995 and 1997. From the stage, Reilly, who had never attempted an Ironman himself, taunted Silva good-naturedly, telling the audience that the marathon champion likely had no idea what he was getting himself into. A modest man, Silva, who had entered the race as a dare from a friend, appeared nonplussed.

During the race two days later, Silva would finish with enviable times in the swim (1 hour, 15 minutes, 22 seconds) and bike (5 hours, 42 minutes, 59 seconds). Only the marathon, the event for which he was best prepared, stood between him and the finish line of his first Ironman. He had almost ten hours still on the clock, enough time to practically walk it. And yet, after jogging the first eight hundred meters, he informed race organizers that he was done for the day—a DNF. His back ached, and he would later say that he had simply run out of steam that day.

"I laid down to stretch, but couldn't stand up anymore," he told me. "So I decided to step out, and enjoy a lunch afterwards."

He may have won the New York City Marathon, but he was not yet up to the challenge of an Ironman.

CHAPTER 1

Left, Right, Repeat

he sun had not yet risen over Glendale, a suburb of Phoenix, as Tom Bonnette placed his hand on the gearshift of his family's gold Dodge minivan and slowly backed the vehicle out of the driveway. It was just after five on a Monday morning in late November 2008, a time when Tom, a forty-two-year-old high school English teacher, might ordinarily be going out for a run or a bike ride before school. But he had taken this morning off, not just from working out but from work. He had arranged for a substitute to cover his class for a few hours so that he might embark on a special mission. He was signing up for his first Ironman.

But as he pulled onto the palm-lined street in front of his stucco-sided home, whatever excitement he was feeling was suddenly dashed by a loud, grinding *grrrrrr* emanating from the steering column of the ten-year-old minivan. Sensing that the problem was potentially serious, Tom thought about going back into the house and grabbing the keys to the family's other car, but he knew that his wife, Shannon, a public school teacher who was training to become an administrator, needed it. Moreover, he thought, she had already sacrificed enough, with all the time Tom had been away from his family exercising. And so Tom continued on his day's journey, anxiously steering his hobbled minivan toward Interstate 17 for the half hour drive south to the race sign-up in Tempe. Mindful that Ironman Arizona 2009 was likely to sell out quickly, he wondered if his Ironman odyssey might be over before he'd gotten to the sign-up, let alone the starting line.

Since he was a young boy growing up in Arizona, Tom had been watching the nationally televised broadcasts of the original Ironman in Hawaii, and he dreamed about competing in one himself. Three decades later he would still remember the names of the pros he saw complete the Hawaii course well under the seventeen-hour time limit—guys like Scott Tinley and Mark Allen—as well as Julie Moss's legendary crawl across the finish line in 1982. Through elementary school and middle school, at least, his own Ironman dreams had seemed decidedly unrealistic. Tom's frail body was so wracked by asthma that he could pretty much count on at least one trip to the emergency room (followed by a hospital admission) each fall and winter as the brittle, dead grass of the Arizona desert took flight and constricted his airways.

His health problems had begun almost immediately after his family moved from West Virginia to Arizona in 1974, when Tom was in second grade. Soon after his arrival, he experienced an asthma attack during a pickup soccer game that was severe enough to send him to the hospital for the first time. He was placed on a regimen of as many as five medications, which included one delivered by a frightening-looking inhaler. Twice a week he received injections from a local allergist.

"As much as I loved sports," he recalled, "I couldn't fully participate."

Photos of him as a Little Leaguer at the time show a boy who was as pale as he was gaunt. As he prepared to graduate from middle school, he weighed just eighty pounds.

In high school, though, Tom began to outgrow his asthma, so much so that he tried out for the cross-country team and made it. Like so many boys his age, Tom had been inspired during the 1976 Olympics by the gold-medal decathlon performance of Bruce Jenner, whose accomplishments were memorialized on the fronts of countless boxes of Wheaties. As a runner, Tom wouldn't be winning any medals and didn't even win any meets; this may have had less to do with his asthma than the training meal he typically consumed just before a race: a Hostess apple pie. Still, Tom recalls, his coach assured him that he had more talent than he thought he did.

As an adult, Tom had progressed so much as a recreational runner that he had been able to complete five marathons. By now his six-foot frame was packed tight with 180 pounds. Though he still retained the soft-spokenness and gentle bearing of the asthmatic youngster he once

was, he had shaved his head, making him look a bit menacing—as impos-
ing as some of those professional Ironman athletes he'd admired so much
on TV. A broad, toothy smile was overshadowed by fierce blue eyes. Tom
certainly didn't look like the prototypical English teacher.

With those races from TV at the back of his mind—and with the belief
that being able to swim, bike, and run, ideally on the same day, was a lot
less boring than just running—Tom had also completed several Olympic-
distance triathlons (less than one-quarter the Ironman distance) in his
thirties. In October 2008, at forty-two, he finished his first half-Ironman;
known as the Soma Triathlon, and located in Tempe, it featured the same
lake as Ironman Arizona and much of the same bike and run course. Now,
Tom felt confident, he was ready for the full distance. In fact, while many
Ironman participants will refrain from setting a time by which they hope
to finish their race—at least publicly—Tom had such a target, and was not
shy about sharing it: 12 hours—5 hours under the 17-hour limit and
within striking distance of those early pros.

"Not everybody can do an Ironman in under 12 hours," he explained,
"and that's what I plan on doing."

While Tom could have chosen to sign up for any of eight Ironman-
distance races in North America that year—including those that would
have entailed climbing the steep hills in Lake Placid, New York, or Coeur
d'Alene, Idaho, or swims through the choppy ocean of Panama City,
Florida—he decided to stay close to home. Ever since the Ironman organization had added a race in Tempe to its schedule in April 2006, Tom
had stood in the crowd each year, watching in amazement and taking
mental notes on the course and on what seemed to propel the participants
forward. At this year's Ironman Arizona, which had taken place the previous day and ended only a few hours earlier, Tom had served as one of
more than two thousand volunteers. After donning an official Ironman
volunteer T-shirt—which featured the Ironman symbol, with its dot
over the *m* making that mere *m* appear to be an *im*—Tom was stationed
at the corner of Rio Salado and McClintock in downtown Tempe, near
the beginning of the run course. For five hours in the dry heat, he directed one athlete after another to turn right—never mind that they already knew to do so.

And next year, he hoped, there would be someone standing on the same corner to tell him to make that very turn.

At that moment Tom had no doubt why he wanted to compete in such an event. Not only did he wish to prove to himself that he was capable, but he intended to set an example for his three daughters, ages five to fifteen. And he wanted to be a role model for his students at Central High, an inner-city public school, all of whom were learning English as a second language from him. He wanted all the children in his life to know that, whatever other responsibilities they might have, they should allow themselves the time and space to pursue a passion, to do something they loved. As he explained:

> The primary reason for me doing this is that I want to show my daughters and students that we can all do what we set out to do if we prepare ourselves AND NOT GIVE UP. I never give up, and this is just a fun way to prove it. I want them to see the pained expression on my face as I run by and know that I am suffering but not giving up.

But as much as he was thinking about inspiring others, Tom was also pursuing an Ironman to prove something to himself. As he put it:

> I'm also doing it because I need outward validation for all the training I do in the wee hours of the mornings to mentally prepare for my day. I want to see how far all that training can take me physically and mentally. That, and swimming, biking and running on a regular basis is damn fun. And, I can eat a lot of chocolate and not feel like a slob.

As Tom continued on the nail-biting drive to registration, he could not ignore the vibrating sound of metal grinding deep inside the dashboard, now coupled with a sluggishness in the steering wheel itself. After five miles on the interstate, he pulled off the road—no easy task, as he sensed, rightly, that the power steering was going—and turned around, his destination now his local mechanic.

As he pulled into the parking lot of the repair shop, Tom decided to throw in the towel on his dream of becoming an Ironman—at least on a course set so close to his hometown, in 2009—before dawn had even broken.

It was, in the end, a matter of money.

One reason Tom had not attempted Arizona (or any other Ironman, for that matter) in previous years was the $525 registration fee. As a father of three, he felt he simply could not justify that extravagant expense on an annual teacher's salary of $53,193. That morning, Tom was still gnawed by guilt over the $800 he had spent a few years earlier on a triathlon bike frame, one that would position his body in more of an aerodynamic crouch than his old road bike. Though he had bought it at a discounted price, negotiated through a local triathlon club, and had saved several hundred dollars more by transferring the pedals, chain, and other parts from his old bike to his new one, he still felt bad. For that matter, he continued to regret the $185 registration fee he had spent to enter that half-Ironman race a month earlier.

Anyone watching an Ironman as a spectator might assume, from the sophisticated gear on display, that it is a sport for the well-off; in many instances it is, in fact, a hobby for those willing to devote seemingly endless financial resources to the purchase of top-of-the-line biking, swimming, and running gear and accessories, with the hope that those tools might give them maximum advantage in finishing the race as fast as possible. Still, there are plenty of men and women competing at every Ironman who, like Tom Bonnette, have had to sacrifice any number of dinners or movies out to save for a basic wetsuit (starting price, about $100) or padded Lycra bike shorts (maybe $50) or cleated bike shoes (at least another $100). Over the years, Tom's wife and daughters had encouraged him to make these purchases, knowing how much he loved training for and participating in triathlons.

He had finally decided to enter an Ironman as a reward to himself for inching toward the completion of another marathon-like journey. The following May, if all went according to plan, Tom would earn his master's degree in teaching English as a second language. To do so, he had completed nearly two years of online courses offered through the district and had composed a stack of term papers that, when laid atop one another, were as thick as a phone book. The tuition for his graduate degree was $14,000, all of which he had borrowed in loans. The Phoenix Union High School District, where he worked, promised a $6,000 bump in annual salary to teachers who earned a master's, and Tom's was set to kick in during the 2009–10 school year, just in time for Ironman Arizona. With that pending raise, he felt he could rationalize carving out a few hundred dollars for the race entry fee.

Now, however, as he sat outside the mechanic's shop, Tom calculated in his head how much this latest car repair might cost. The figure that immediately came to mind was $500. He immediately pulled out his cell phone and called home, waking his wife to tell her about the car problem and the decision he had made.

"I'm not doing it," he said of the race, clicking off the phone before she could even try to get him to change his mind. As he prepared to get out of the car and bring the keys to the mechanic, though, he had a realization: He had set out so early in the day, mindful of the 6:00 A.M. start for race registration, that he had beaten his mechanic to work by at least an hour.

As he settled in to wait for someone who worked at the shop to show up, Tom started to have second thoughts about the snap decision he had made and soon called Shannon back.

"What do you think," he asked, "if I still do the race and we get this taken care of some other time? It still runs."

She was immediately encouraging, reminding him of all he had done to prepare and of how obviously important the race was to him. The family would somehow make it work; he needn't worry. Tom then called his father, who had been a mechanic himself. His father quickly rendered his prognosis of the problem: However hobbled, the power steering might last a year before becoming permanently disabled. By then Tom could figure out some way to pay for the parts and repair.

His guilt sufficiently assuaged, Tom once again put the van in gear and headed out in search of his dream. The digital clock on the dashboard showed that it was not yet 5:30 A.M. If the van stayed in one piece, he could still make it to Tempe Town Lake in time.

———

The pain in Bryan Reece's back and sides was excruciating.

It was a Saturday morning in January 2007, and Bryan, who had endured a sleepless night inside his Spanish-style home, safe behind the locked gates of a residential enclave outside San Antonio, was convinced he had a kidney stone. Bryan, then forty-seven, had never had a kidney stone before, nor, as a manager at a local branch of a financial services firm, did he have any particular qualifications to make that diagnosis. At the urging of his wife, Debbie, Bryan reluctantly called her brother, an oncologist, to give him a rundown of his symptoms. Debbie's brother was inclined to agree with Bryan's diagnosis, but believed he should go immediately to the emergency room so that the pain might be mitigated. An appointment with a urologist could then be arranged, ideally as soon as Monday.

Bryan toughed it out for another hour before he finally told Debbie that her brother was right: He had to go to the ER. Bryan even let Debbie drive the mile or so to North Central Baptist Hospital, which was a sure sign of how lousy he was feeling.

After administering a generous shot of morphine, the doctor on call ordered a battery of X-rays. Sometime later, after the doctor had granted Bryan's request for a second dose of the drug, he placed a series of films on a backlit board and gave Bryan and Debbie his preliminary diagnosis.

"You ever see a swollen disk?" the doctor asked, as Bryan recalled.

"No," said Bryan, although now that he thought about it, he had been experiencing back pain for some months. He'd even tried to address the problem by buying a new pillow and mattress, all to no avail.

"Your spine is supposed to look like this," the doctor said, the fingers of his hand tight against one another.

"But yours," the doctor added, "looks like this." Bryan noted that his fingers were spread apart, like the webbed foot of a duck.

"You'll need an MRI," the doctor concluded. "You'll probably need back surgery, too."

Bryan and Debbie left the hospital dejected but not entirely surprised. They'd been telling each other for the past three or four years that they each needed to get in better shape. Now the day of reckoning, at least for Bryan, appeared to be at hand.

The following Thursday, Bryan arrived at the office of a general physician who was new to him. Since moving to San Antonio from Dallas two years earlier, he had yet to get around to finding a regular doctor. The nurse began by taking his blood pressure and pulse, and after reading the meter cuffed to Bryan's arm, she met his eyes with an uneasy glance.

"I'm going to take your pressure again," she said, "and this time, don't talk."

This was no easy assignment for Bryan, whose father had been an amiable used car salesman. Bryan had inherited his dad's loquaciousness, as well as his powers of persuasion.

And yet, sensing the looming gravity of the situation, he kept silent as the nurse checked the pressure on the same arm again, before switching the cuff to his other arm.

"The doctor will be in in a few minutes," she said.

Bryan figured he was in for a wait, but less than a minute later the doctor rushed in and immediately took the blood pressure reading himself.

Later, Bryan would have trouble remembering the specific results he got that day, but he recalled the doctor's telling him they were "ridiculously high."

He had to admit to the doctor that he had not had a physical in at least five years. For that matter, he said, he probably had not stepped inside a gym or had an aerobic workout for nearly thirty years, since not long after college.

In truth, he looked it. The top of his head was nearly bald, and the close-cropped hair that remained on the sides of his head had turned prematurely white. While his usually smiling, hazel eyes twinkled with the mischievousness of a man much younger than his late forties, Bryan's six-foot-three-inch frame—currently packed with more than 250 pounds—had, at times, a pronounced stoop.

Bryan had grown fat on a diet of dinners that featured too many steaks accompanied by too many beers (four was not unusual) or martinis (at least a few) and glasses of red wine.

As the examination continued, Bryan was given an EKG and could tell from the doctor's demeanor that it had gone no better than the reading of his blood pressure. But he was not prepared for the prognosis.

"You're a heart attack waiting to happen," the doctor said, as Bryan recalled. "I'm surprised you haven't had one already."

"You're going to have to take better care of yourself," he continued. "Or you're going to die."

The doctor said he didn't need to await the analysis from the laboratory of the blood he had just drawn—he was putting Bryan on a blood pressure drug called Benicar. He instructed Bryan to monitor his own blood pressure twice a day and return in a month.

Still reeling from the diagnosis, Bryan was preparing to get dressed when he remembered that he had originally come to see the doctor for a very different reason.

"What about my back?" Bryan asked. "Do I need to have an MRI?"

"Bryan," the doctor responded, "your back is the least of your worries right now."

Less than two years after that life-altering appointment, Bryan boarded a plane with Debbie for a three-hour flight that would have seemed unthinkable only a few months earlier. Their destination: Tempe, Arizona. It was the week before Thanksgiving 2008, and Bryan was signing up for the Ironman race that would be staged there a year later. A colleague in his early seventies had recently been diagnosed with an advanced form of cancer, and Bryan had decided to dedicate his race to raising money for the disease through Lance Armstrong's LiveStrong foundation.

"That's why I know I'll finish," he said matter-of-factly, though without any audible Texas swagger.

While they would never meet Tom Bonnette, Bryan and Debbie were, it turned out, just a few spots ahead of him on the line for registration on the morning of Monday, November 24.

For Bryan, it was not enough to register online from the comforts of his home or office, as most of the entrants would do. He felt he needed to be there in person, to ensure that he got a slot. He and Debbie also wanted to volunteer at Ironman Arizona 2008—not only so he would earn a priority registration for the 2009 race, but so that he could scope out every inch of what he would be getting himself into. The couple had been assigned to the finish line of the 2008 race during prime time—from 7:00 P.M. to midnight, when most athletes would come across—and would serve as "catchers," a responsibility that, just as it sounds, entails catching the competitors as they cross the finish line and invariably go weak in the knees.

At first glance, it would appear that Bryan Reece, once hopelessly sedentary and on the brink of cardiac arrest, had set himself a goal that might well take his life.

In the months since the doctor's wake-up call, however, he had carefully and methodically built himself up, taking part in races of increasing difficulty. These efforts had culminated, however improbably, in Bryan's first half-marathon and half-Ironman. He had even started a blog for family, friends, and fellow triathletes to follow him on this unlikely path. He called it *Left, Right, Repeat*—the phrase he repeats to himself, continuously, as he runs.

In an attempt to pass on the gifts that his new life as a triathlete had given him, Bryan also served as a mentor on the Web site BeginnerTriathlete.com, introducing himself there in early 2008:

> My name is Bryan—aka left, right, repeat. I am a 48-year-old business person who is busy at work, was overstressed, overweight, oversedentary and overwhelmed last year at this time. Since March of 2007 I have lost 27 pounds, completed 2 sprint triathlons, 2 indoor triathlons, one 50 mile organized bike tour, a couple of 5ks and a 10k. I do triathlon to save my life . . . more on that another time but suffice to say I am off all medication and healthier than I have ever been in my life.

How had he managed to turn his health around in such a relatively short time?

His is a story that begins, like those of so many baby boomers who have gotten a stern lecture from a doctor, at the gym.

By early March 2007 Bryan had responded sufficiently to the blood pressure medication that his doctor had cleared him—in fact, ordered him—to join a gym. Bryan and Debbie quickly narrowed their list of candidates to two choices: a new YMCA and a local branch of the Life Time Fitness chain. Both were sprawling, state-of-the-art, and close to home, but Bryan ultimately ruled out the Y for a simple reason: To get there from his office, he would have passed his home.

"I just knew I would stop at home," he explained, "and I'd never make it to the gym."

On March 8 of that year, Bryan strode into Life Time and promptly submitted to what it calls a metabolic assessment. He was fitted with an oxygen mask, to monitor his respiration, and a heart monitor and placed on a treadmill for a slow twelve-minute walk. When the gym trainer conducting Bryan's assessment walked him over to a stationary bike, he noted that Bryan's heart rate immediately spiked.

"All I had to do was look at the stationary bike and I was getting a cardiovascular workout—from fear, I guess," Bryan recalled. Eventually he got on the bike, however gingerly.

That day Bryan made a pledge to himself: "You always hear the story: the person who joined the gym, went for six months, and didn't lose a pound, nothing changed. I was not going to be that person."

"I wouldn't say it happened overnight," he added, "but going to the gym quickly became a way of life. I knew it had to be."

Two months later, sufficiently adept at the stationary bike, Bryan signed up for his first spin class, which he'd seen listed on the club's roster of offerings. He walked into the windowless studio, with its tan hardwood floors and several dozen gleaming stationary bikes, and had three goals in mind: "not to throw up, not to fall off, and to last the whole hour." Not only did he make it, but he was immediately hooked, and not just on the classic rock sound track that served to distract him from the task at hand. "I thought it was the greatest thing ever."

Afterward the instructor came over to congratulate him and collect his initial observations. "I told her," Bryan recalled, "there are people in here that wear those bike shoes, clipped to the pedals. Isn't that a little over the top? I'll never have those shoes."

"Be careful what you say," the teacher told him.

Later, he would laugh when recalling how sure he was of the artificial limits he'd imposed, however temporarily and arbitrarily, on his road to fitness.

The signal moment on his path to becoming a triathlete—and to attempting to become an Ironman triathlete—came after a spin class about a month later. By then Bryan was spinning three or four times a week, sometimes arriving fifteen minutes before class to warm up at some length on his own in the quiet, empty studio. After a rigorous "hills" class one morning—in which a lever on the bike was fastened tight against the front wheel, to simulate a climb—Bryan went downstairs to the locker room to change.

"I look over," Bryan recalled, "and this guy from the class is putting on a pair of swim trunks."

"I said to him, 'What are you doing?'"

"He said, 'I'm getting ready to go swim.'"

"I said, 'After *that*?'"

"He said, 'I do some triathlons. I *need* to swim today.'"

"I said, 'Dude, that's the craziest thing I've ever heard.'"

But, Bryan later acknowledged, "he had planted a seed."

That night at home, Bryan began Googling the word "triathlon." He quickly came upon references to the Ironman, which evoked memories of the races he had seen years earlier on television—including Julie Moss's memorable crawl across the finish line, her muscles giving out. Bryan remembered that race, and soon found a clip of it on YouTube. He watched it that night, not for the last time.

I can't imagine that anyone would ever do a race like that, Bryan thought. *But it's cool.*

Bryan learned that there were triathlons of varying distances leading up to the Ironman. He even read about a sprint-distance triathlon—typically a quarter-mile swim, a 13-mile bike ride, and a 3-mile run. Right then, he said, "I started toying with the idea that maybe I could do something like that."

The only bike he'd been on in the past thirty years, however, was one that not only didn't move but was almost hermetically sealed inside a climate-controlled bubble. Though he'd always enjoyed being in pools as a kid, he was not sure he'd ever had a swimming lesson, or even swum an entire lap.

And running? Though he'd played linebacker on his high school football team, he always hated the running drills. "I only ran when people yelled at me," he said. "There was nothing about it that I even remotely liked."

Over the next few days, Bryan did more and more research on the many facets of the sport of triathlon. "Finally, one day I screwed up the courage to say something to Debbie," he said. "We were sitting in the den and I said to her, 'What would you think if I told you I was thinking of doing a triathlon?'"

Bryan recalled that moment as a turning point, adding: "This could have all ended right there. If, when I said that to her, she had laughed, it would have been over. I was at that moment of truth."

"I think that'd be cool," she told her husband, calmly.

Later Bryan would say that he was confident he knew what Debbie was really thinking: *Let's make sure the life insurance is paid up.*

As a first step toward his first triathlon, Bryan found a twelve-week training plan online. If he followed it, he would, at least theoretically, be ready for his first triathlon by September 2007. As luck would have it, there was a triathlon in September, right in San Antonio. Bryan read that the swim was even shorter than in a typical sprint—400 yards, or about sixteen lengths in a community pool—followed by a 15-mile bike ride and a 3.1-mile (or 5K) run. Bryan decided to sign up. Soon after, he found another triathlon, in nearby Corpus Christi, that was even shorter: a 200-yard swim (eight lengths back and forth across a typical pool) followed by a 12-mile bike ride and 1.25-mile run. This one was in late August, still leaving Bryan plenty of time to complete most of his training plan.

It would, however, require a bit of humility on his part: The reason the course was so short was that it was intended for young children. Adults (presumably their parents) were invited to do the course afterward. Taylour, Bryan and Debbie's daughter, was already in college by that point.

There were a number of logistics he needed to square away. He still needed to buy a bike, but that seemed simple enough. More important, though, he needed to learn to swim.

Bryan remembered the man from the spin class—his name was Jim Counce ("rhymes with bounce," he liked to say.)—and the invitation he had extended to Bryan to swim with him one day. Bryan decided the time had come to at least dip a toe into one of the pools at Life Time Fitness, which seemed as wide as a football field was long. However much he appreciated Jim's invitation, Bryan decided that he would go it alone. *If I'm going to struggle, I'm going to struggle without anyone I know watching me*, he thought. He also decided that his first swim, such as it was, would be on a day on which he did no other exercise. After ensuring that no one he knew was within sight, he slipped into the far left lane of the indoor pool and began making his way across. He was swimming the front crawl, as best he could remember from his boyhood, making sure to breathe on his right after each full stroke. As the far wall came into view, he lunged for it. He couldn't seem to catch his breath and didn't think he'd ever be able to let go.

Bryan had a decision to make. He could get out of the pool right there, which his body seemed to be ordering him to do. But somewhere in the recesses of his memory, he remembered someone's telling him that you never got out of a pool on the side opposite the one you entered.

And so, after his breathing and heart rate had returned to an approximation of normal, he set out for the other side of the pool. By the time he reached the halfway point, he could do little more than walk to the end. He quickly got out, grabbed a towel, and headed for the showers.

How, he wondered, nearly inconsolable, *am I ever going to get into shape for those two races?*

Now, two years later, as he stood on the line to register for Ironman Arizona 2009, twelve months before the race, Bryan motioned me over. He said he wanted to amend something he had told me a day earlier, when we had first met and he was brimming with bravado.

Since then, he told me, he and Debbie had worked their five-hour shift as "catchers" at the finish line, ending at midnight. During that time, one athlete after another had crossed the line and proceeded to collapse into the volunteers' arms as if they were suits sliding off hangers. The entire time, Bryan had been unable to erase the thought that a year from now, somebody would be catching him—if he were fortunate enough to make it to that finish line.

"You asked me earlier if I was scared," he said, his eyes fixed on mine. "I lied when I said no.

"Here's my real answer," he said. "Hell, yeah!"

As Bryan and Debbie were working their late-night shift at the finish line, a woman named Tracy Tucker-Georges was milling nearby. She was at

Ironman Arizona 2008 in a different capacity: It was her job to hold the clear plastic tape tight as the participants in the race sprinted, staggered, or stumbled across the line. Working with a partner, she would then cut that piece free and stretch another across, in anticipation of the next finisher's arrival.

A nurse from the San Fernando Valley, in Southern California, Tracy, who had just turned forty-four, was married and had two daughters, ages fourteen and seventeen, and a husband, Chris, who was in the commercial real estate business. She stood five foot six, with brown eyes, and though she liked to think of herself as a double for Cameron Diaz, she was probably more likely to be mistaken for the actress Mary Stuart Masterson (who co-starred in the movie *Fried Green Tomatoes*, among others). She liked to change her hair color from red to blond to brown to suit the season, or her mood. She was sassy, impish, and quite often foul-mouthed. She was also loud, and her daughters periodically found themselves slinking away from her in the supermarket whenever she struck up a conversation with, well, pretty much anyone. Before long she would invariably be telling that person she was a Scorpio, which was probably no surprise to someone who might inadvertently tick her off and get an earful in response.

Tracy had traveled to that year's race solely to support six friends who were competing in it. All would cross the finish line at Ironman Arizona 2008, most of them breaking through that tape as Tracy held it. They were "my boys," as Tracy called them affectionately on a blog about their exploits that she had set up for an exclusive readership of family and close friends. She couldn't have been prouder about how they'd done.

The "poking and prodding," as Tracy referred to it, began soon after the last of her group had completed the race. The sign-up for the following year's competition would begin the next morning, her friends told her; she should go for it. Tracy just laughed them off. While she had done a handful of sprint-distance triathlons with her friends in recent years— as well as a race, a month earlier, that was slightly longer than an Olympic but far short of a 70.3—an Ironman was nearly four times longer than the longest triathlon she'd ever completed. Not to worry, her boys said. She probably could have handled the swim and bike portions of that day's race, having ridden more than a hundred miles a week with the group in the weeks leading up to it and swimming several miles a week on her own. And while she considered herself more a fast walker than a slow runner, the boys were confident that Tracy could get herself up to speed between now and Ironman Arizona 2009. The only promise she would make to her friends was that she would think about it.

Growing up in Southern California in the 1970s, Tracy Tucker had hardly considered herself athletic. She was the oldest in a family of three children, and her father, who worked for the Southern California Gas Company, and mother divorced when she was four. While other kids her age might be taking part in sports, Tracy had been forced, by necessity, to grow up a bit faster. Her mother had been only nineteen when her first child was born, and it sometimes fell to Tracy to take care of her two younger brothers. (Her mother would go on to marry a second time, a relationship that produced Tracy's half sister and half brother; her father and his girlfriend also had a son.)

"We didn't have a lot of money," Tracy remembered. "My brother, Tommy, was the one who always played baseball, Little League. I didn't do anything. I wasn't athletically inclined at all. It was always about my brother. In high school, I remember my phys-ed teacher telling me I should try out for the volleyball team. I didn't. I was shy, completely different than now. You didn't know I was there."

Tracy's path toward confidence and self-assurance—as well as, not coincidentally, toward participating in triathlons—began at Los Angeles County Hospital in the late 1980s. By then she had become a nurse, a profession to which she'd aspired since she was in middle school. Assigned the night shift in the burn ward at County Hospital, she says, she "learned that I could handle stress" and that she was "pretty levelheaded and cool about it." In the process, "I became a stronger person."

It was around this time that one of her colleagues told Tracy that he liked to spend his weekends taking part in organized group bike rides known as centuries—so named because they were typically about 100 miles—and that she should consider joining him sometime. She said she was game but didn't have a bike. Soon she would spend $600, a lot to her at the time, on a Cannondale with an aluminum frame. After a few warm-up rides at 10, 15, and 20 miles, she joined her colleague—as well as his girlfriend and a friend—for something called the Los Angeles River Ride. It was 75 miles, far longer than anything Tracy had ever attempted. The day before the race it had rained, leaving the course slick. "I had an absolute blast," Tracy recalled. "I was covered in mud, and afterward we all went to the all-you-can-eat Soup Plantation. I was filthy dirty, ate a bunch of food and loved it. It was a thrill."

A few more "fun rides," including informal ones that benefited organizations like the National Multiple Sclerosis Society, followed, as did Tracy's first race against the clock, a 26-miler in nearby Fontana. "I hated it," Tracy said. "I didn't like having to go so fast. It was windy. It was ugly. My nose was running like crazy." In time, Tracy came to realize that she preferred going longer and farther on a bike than going fast. Her first century, in Solvang, California, fit the bill. On the morning of the race, though, she awakened with bronchitis. As Tracy remembered:

> To ease the symptoms of my bronchitis, I put Vicks Vapo-Rub all over my chest. I washed my hands. Then I put "crotch cream" all over the chamois in my bike shorts, so I wouldn't get chafed. Unfortunately, there was still some Vicks Vapo-Rub on my hands.
>
> My crotch burned for the first hour of that ride.

Somehow, Tracy managed to overcome that discomfort—regular readers of her blog would become intimately familiar with the impact riding had on her "girly bits"—to finish in seven and a half hours. She recalled being "deliriously happy" and hooked.

Marriage and motherhood, however, intervened. In the early 1990s, Tracy met Chris through a self-help workshop called Lifespring, an offshoot of the efforts of the founder of est. The themes of Lifespring were consistent with the goals Tracy had set for herself around that time: learning about herself, gaining confidence, finding serenity in meditation. In one exercise, the participants were encouraged to discuss "the strangest place you had ever had sex." Tracy told the group that hers "happened to be while hiking, outdoors, with an ex-boyfriend." Perhaps not surprisingly, Tracy told the group she liked rock climbing. Chris, a rock climber himself, wasn't there to hear that story, but a mutual friend decided to try to fix them up. (She left out the part about the outdoor sex.)

Tracy's first impression? "He was tall and nerdy and a total geek," she said. "He was not my type at all. But he was a nice guy, and we became friends." Chris wasn't especially interested in her, either, but eventually they did go rock-climbing together.

They got married in May 1993. Their daughter, Codi, arrived in June 1994, joining Caitlin, a daughter of Tracy's from a previous relationship. Tracy would not resume riding in earnest until 2007, a year before traveling to Ironman Arizona in support of her friends. In the interim, though, she had developed a passion for race-walking. In 2004, a friend had turned her on to the Avon Walk for Breast Cancer, which was 26 miles. She did that event by herself but soon fell in with a group training for the Los Angeles Marathon the following year.

"I'm not a runner," Tracy had told a friend who'd encouraged her to join the group.

No worries, her friend told her. "Just walk it."

She did, finishing the race in six and a half hours. "I would walk past people doing a slow jog," Tracy would marvel later. "They would say, 'You guys are walking faster than we're running.'"

In 2006 she fast-walked the L.A. Marathon again, her elbows swinging, the soles of her running shoes never totally leaving the road surface, her gaze fixed straight ahead. That same year, she also walked her way through the Disneyland Half Marathon in Anaheim. Surrounded by all those runners, "there were definitely times where I wanted to try it," she recalled. "I would say, 'Let me run a bit, see how it is.' But every time I would try running, I was like, 'Oh, forget it.' It was too hard."

The push that Tracy needed to turn her walking into running—and to couple it with biking and swimming—came that same year. By now she was working in an orthopedic sports medicine practice in Los Angeles. One of the doctors who joined the group as a fellow, Jason Kurian, told Tracy he had signed up for an Ironman. She was intrigued, and he told her she could follow the race online, from the comfort of home. His stats would be updated at regular intervals, he explained, and in all likelihood she'd be able to see live video of him crossing the finish line.

That day, Tracy settled in at her home in Northridge, in the northern part of the San Fernando Valley. From the outside it looked like a classic suburban haven, complete with a swimming pool and diving board out back. But inside, Tracy and Chris had cultivated a whimsical, brightly colored motif that was more evocative of hot dogs than anything Martha Stewart might have counseled. One room was painted mustard yellow, the dining room was ketchup red, and the TV room was green, like relish.

As Jason did his Ironman, Tracy booted up her Mac laptop and flopped on the couch—for the record, it is indeed as tan as a bun—to begin to monitor his progress. Throughout the day she would punch in his name and bib number and learn that he was off the swim course and onto the bike and, eventually, off the bike and on to the run. Nearly ten and a half hours after he started, she was able to watch him cross the finish line. "His arms were in the air," she recalled. "He looked so refreshed. I remember his head was shaved." His performance that day had been fast enough for him to qualify for Ironman Hawaii in Kona the following year.

Tracy's first thought was: *I want to do a triathlon.*

But that impulse was quickly mitigated by a second: *Ten hours—that's a long time.*

This was in October 2006, and when Jason returned to work, Tracy "just drilled him about the whole thing." He then told her about a race in Palm Desert, California, the following spring that was somewhere between the sprint and Olympic distances: The swim was 500 meters (about twenty lengths in a typical pool), the bike was 14 miles, and the run a 5K, or 3.1 miles. Tracy decided to sign up, knowing that over the course of the next six months she would not only have to coax herself from walking to running but would need a refresher course in how to swim.

One advantage she would soon learn she had in swimming was that she "wasn't afraid of it." As a kid, she had gone swimming in the ocean, though she had never really done laps there or in a pool. Chris, on the other hand, had played water polo in college, had once coached a swim team, and had even written for *Swimming World* magazine, for which he covered the 1984 Olympics. Recently the family had joined a country club (nothing fancy, and no golf, Tracy was quick to emphasize), where Caitlin, their older daughter, swam and where Chris helped coach a so-called masters group of swimmers, many of whom had swum years earlier for their respective colleges. Under Chris's tutelage, Tracy progressed from the breaststroke to the front crawl. He also taught her a key swimming technique for triathlon: sighting, in which the swimmer pops his or her head up periodically and uses buoys or trees to stay on course.

Tracy also bought a training manual, *Your First Triathlon*, by Joe Friel. Like a sprinter, she immediately skipped to the middle of the book, where she located what she considered "the meat." There she found strength-building routines (with light weights, mercifully) and tips on running in hot weather ("Put a little ice in your hat or shirt").

A few weeks before that Palm Desert race, she decided to run on a track with a friend's twelve-year-old daughter—a training session that seemed harmless enough. At one point the girl said to Tracy, "Let's take off from the runner's position." She then bent down low, as if she were readying for an Olympic fifty-yard dash, and encouraged Tracy to do the same. About ten steps into her sprint, Tracy pulled to a dead stop, feeling a pop in her left knee. An examination later at the orthopedic practice where she worked confirmed that she had partially torn the medial and lateral portions of her meniscus, which acts a cushion for the kneecap. She knew the injury could have been much worse, had it involved her ACL, or anterior cruciate ligament, which has ruined more than a few amateur triathletes' careers.

Tracy decided, in consultation with her colleagues, that she could still compete in the Palm Desert race. The wisdom of that decision was borne out by her performance: She completed the swim in just over 10 minutes, and the entire race in 1 hour, 35 minutes. She admitted later that she was in "a little bit of pain" but that "maybe the endorphins took over." Two months later, though, she required surgery to repair that left knee.

The following year, in August 2008, she was sufficiently recovered to do a race in Santa Barbara that could probably best be described as an Olympic-plus-distance: a mile swim, a 34-mile bike ride, and a 10-mile run. She recalled that the experience "absolutely changed me"—though in much the way that a young child is changed by putting his hand too close to an open flame. Prior to Santa Barbara, Tracy delighted in treating her bike on any downhill runs as if it were a bobsled, flying as fast as she could. But at Santa Barbara that year, where the downhills were long and steep, a woman in her sixties tumbled off her bike and hit her head. Afterward, everyone approaching the accident site was slowed to a crawl by the race officials.

"I saw them loading her body into an ambulance," Tracy recalled. "She was in cervical traction. I get goose bumps just talking about it." The woman, who was rendered a quadriplegic, eventually died.

"I've got to pay better attention," Tracy resolved that day. "If I don't know a hill, I've got to be real careful. I won't go balls out."

Chastened and newly cautious, she traveled several months later to Ironman Arizona 2008 to be a spectator, cheerleader, and volunteer. Curious about every aspect of the race, she volunteered initially as a "stripper"—helping peel the competitors out of their wetsuits, right there in the open on the side of Tempe Town Lake, as soon as they emerged from the water. She also worked in the women's change tent, where she helped participants who were obviously bleary and almost delirious from their swims to gather the socks and bike shoes they had stowed away for the transition to their next event. Tracy saw that some had swum with bike shorts under their wetsuits but that others stripped down completely, right there in full view of the other competitors, before making a complete change of clothes. "That was excessive," Tracy decided.

She awoke the following morning at 5:30 at her hotel near the race site, her head filled with the voices of her boys goading her to follow their lead and sign up herself for Ironman Arizona 2009. Reflecting on all the training she had already put in, and the races she had done so far, she decided they were right. She could do this. And so she drove to the park adjacent to the race site and took her place in line—not too far behind Bryan Reece and Tom Bonnette. She was by herself; her friends had decided to sleep off their own races.

"I was committed to signing up," she recalled later. "But I was very anxious."

She called her husband to give him a heads-up and warn him that "the commitment's going to be a big one." He was supportive. While the race fee was steep, Tracy and Chris agreed that they could find it "in the budget."

Still, after she gave her credit card to one of the volunteers registering participants for the following year, Tracy suddenly thought to herself, *Oh* *shit! I can't believe I just paid $500 to do that. Now they're going to hold me to it.*

Afterward she told the boys the good news as they shopped for IRON-MAN FINISHER T-shirts at a big white tent set up by the race organizers nearby.

"You should buy this," her friends kept telling her, holding up a tank top or mug.

"You only buy that stuff after you've done it," she told them. "I didn't do anything."

CHAPTER 2

Lance Armstrong's
Not My Hero Anymore—You Are

The two defense contractors were engaged in a boisterous conversation about the race that had become their life's passion: the Ironman. Each had done at least one before—perhaps none with more flourish than the former Air Force colonel, who had completed an Ironman in just over eleven hours. That would be a major accomplishment for just about anyone competing outside the ranks of the pros, but it was especially impressive considering that the colonel had been in his mid-sixties at the time. Few participants in their twenties or thirties, let alone their forties or fifties, had crossed the finish line ahead of him. This day's mission, which each had executed successfully, almost paled in comparison: a sprint triathlon in and around Colorado Springs that had begun with a swim in the pool at Peterson Air Force Base and continued with a bike ride and run at nearby Schriever Air Force Base.

While the men spoke, Seth Cannello couldn't help but eavesdrop. As the director of the fitness center at Schriever, Seth had overseen the planning of that sprint race, even if he couldn't really relate to the experience of those who had participated in it. Just shy of forty, he felt that his own efforts to stay in shape had fallen into a bit of a rut. Though he was surrounded all day by officers and enlisted men and women who exercised with relentless regularity, Seth's own workouts would ebb and flow. He might ride a stationary bike in the morning or run a few miles along the perimeter of the base's high barbed wire fence after work. But he wasn't particularly diligent.

At six foot three, he might fluctuate in his weight by as much as fifteen pounds, from 160 to 175, but even at his heaviest, he would never appear especially muscular. Seth was wiry—all legs, it seemed, though naturally athletic. His close-cropped, full head of brown hair, tight smile, and ramrod-straight posture were a reminder of the four years he'd spent in the Army; he'd been honorably discharged in 1995, as a sergeant, having served abroad in Seoul, South Korea.

The day before that sprint triathlon each year, Seth would swim, bike, and run the course, just to check it out. But he had never done so against the clock, or with other people. And though curious, he'd never attempted an organized triathlon at that distance, or any other. For that matter, he'd probably not run more than three miles at any given time or biked twenty-five miles at a stretch. He did like to swim, but using the breaststroke, as the front crawl made him tired and spiked his heart rate. While aware of the Ironman, Seth always considered it "so intimidating."

Still, on this Friday afternoon in August 2008, as the men traded Ironman war stories, Seth felt a switch flip deep within himself and a light suddenly go bright, its intensity clarifying. "I just got jazzed up," Seth recalled. "I don't know what it was, but what they were saying really intrigued me. And so I said to them, 'I'm going to do it. I'm going to do an Ironman.'"

His impromptu declaration was met with immediate pats on the back and words of encouragement. But Seth Cannello didn't have a clue what he had just gotten himself into, or how he would possibly set about meeting the seemingly Herculean goal he had just established.

The following morning, a Saturday, Seth awoke just after five, as he so often did. His wife, Robin, a dental hygienist, and their three young daughters, ages seven to eleven, wouldn't be up for several hours, which was just as well, as he didn't want to waste a minute in embarking on the task at hand. His destination was an unfinished room in the corner of the basement of the family's home, in a subdivision on the outskirts of Colorado Springs that hadn't even existed a decade and a half earlier.

Clad in a simple T-shirt and workout shorts, his feet bare, Seth padded down the stairs and, passing the portion of the basement he and Robin had furnished as a simple playroom, entered a room that looked like the storage closet it was. Exposed insulation dangled from the ceiling. Suitcases and books gathered dust on the metal shelves. In the back was a Schwinn stationary bicycle that had been purchased at least seven years earlier. While Seth imagined he'd be spending many early-morning hours on that bike in the weeks and months ahead, he was not yet ready to get started.

Instead he flipped on the computer at the front of the room and typed "Ironman" into Google.

His immediate task was to find a race he might enter the following year, in 2009. Those in Lake Placid, New York; Panama City, Florida; and Madison, Wisconsin, seemed so far away. Even the race in Coeur d'Alene, Idaho, 1,100 miles from Colorado Springs, would be a bit of a hike, considering that flying would be out of the question and Seth would have to drive. The family's finances were already too tight, as evidenced by the state of the Toyota Camry sitting in the driveway. Its odometer had ticked off more than 160,000 miles in ten years, and its gray finish was heavily caked with dirt, its last wash a distant memory. Seth quickly concluded that the closest Ironman to his home was Ironman Arizona, in Tempe, about 780 miles away. He could even break up the trip by stopping along the way in the mountains of New Mexico to fish, something he loved to do whenever he could. He printed out maps of the swim, bike, and run courses in Arizona and made a mental note of the date: November 22, 2009.

OK, he said to himself, *I'm really going to do it.*

At some point in the next few days, Seth would brief his wife on his plans. By her own recollection, she wasn't especially supportive. As it was, Seth would often leave for work before dawn—completely missing the daily routine of getting their daughters off to school—and not arrive home until early evening, well after the girls had been shuttled to and from activities like soccer and dance. In an effort to prepare his wife for what would transpire in the lead-up to the race, Seth said he imagined building toward workouts that would last five, six, and even seven hours in a single day. "That's really going to have an impact," he warned Robin, figuring it was better to be bracing than to sugarcoat. "By July, all my weekends are going to be shot. I'm going to be training. You're going to have to bear with me."

Robin didn't say no, but her yes was, at best, lukewarm.

"This," she told her husband, "is your one and only shot." And so, she advised him, he'd better make the most of it. If Seth failed in his attempt to conquer Ironman Arizona, he should not count on getting a second chance.

In the weeks that followed, Seth would periodically push himself away from the computer inside his office at the fitness center and walk the aisles separating the treadmills, free-weight benches, and exercise studios. To anyone he recognized he would announce, "I'm going to do an Ironman." Asked later to explain why he had put himself so far out on a limb—even before he had actually registered for Ironman Arizona—Seth explained that the reason was simple: "I wanted to hold myself accountable. I knew they would keep asking me about it and asking me about my training."

On Sunday, November 23, 2008, Seth traveled down to his basement once again and spent the better part of the day in front of his computer. This time he was tracking the progress of the retired colonel, who would wind up finishing that day's race in 11 hours, 9 minutes, 24 seconds. All the while Seth imagined what it would be like the following year to be on the same course, engaged in the same seemingly never-ending quest.

But unlike Bryan Reece, who would be called upon to steady so many of the competitors at the finish line that night, Seth didn't know enough to be scared. In fact, he was so laid-back that the following morning at work, one of the other Ironman veterans in his midst reacted with incredulity when Seth told him that, no, he had not yet gotten around to logging on to the Ironman Web site to register for Ironman Arizona 2009. The man told Seth that he had already signed up, hours earlier, and that he sensed from the time it took him to get onto the site that the 2,500 or so available spots must be filling up quickly.

Just after five, Seth arrived home and raced downstairs to log on. In his mind he had already set aside the $425 he had thought it would cost to register. That was certainly a lot—more than twice as much, in fact, as he had spent recently to refurbish his LeMond road bike, which was at least seven years old. But he felt sure it would be money well spent. When he finally reached the site, though, Seth saw that the registration fee was actually $525. *This is outrageous*, Seth thought.

"I knew it was going to cost me even more money to train," he told me later. "And then there would be gas to get to the race and the cost of a hotel." Now Seth was seriously questioning the wisdom of the decision he had made several months ago. *Why had I told so many people so early that I was going to do this?* Then again, there were those two guys, who had spoken with such ardor about their Ironman experiences.

After what seemed like an eternity spent staring at the screen, Seth fished in his pants pocket for his wallet and pulled out his credit card. Moments after entering his data, the screen flashed with a message: He was in.

Later he would learn that he had secured one of the last slots for Ironman Arizona 2009.

While Seth Cannello had signed up for an Ironman as a way to jump-start his fitness regimen, he also did it as a way to celebrate what he considered to be a second lease on life. Fourteen years earlier, as a twenty-six-year-old stationed in the Army at the 121st Evacuation Hospital in Seoul, South Korea, Seth had learned he had testicular cancer. This was right around the time that cyclist Lance Armstrong was waging a similar battle. As Seth described the immediate aftermath of his diagnosis:

> I think it was more frightening for me to be told I had to have my testicle removed than being told I had cancer. Especially when my doctor told me he was going to remove it through my stomach. There are lots of thoughts that enter your head about your "jewels." Will I be able to have sex/children? Will I lose my masculinity?
>
> Luckily I spoke to a doctor that I knew on my softball team the day I was told I had cancer. He told me that if he had to choose a type of cancer, he would probably choose testicular cancer. The survival rate is excellent, and he told me we really

don't need "two." The "good" testicle takes over full testosterone production and you can't tell the difference after a few
days.

This is all true. However, when I spoke to my friends it was
like dropping a bomb. At first they were sympathetic, then the
jokes came. It really didn't bother me that much, but people
look at you differently. When I tell people I had testicular cancer, the first thing they do is drop their eyes to my crotch. It's
a natural reaction. It's funny now, but back then it was strange.

Soon after his surgery, when he still had his post-chemo peach fuzz,
Seth met Robin, and they were married thirteen months later. The couple
would learn they were pregnant with their first daughter in 1997, but
whatever good feelings they were experiencing as they awaited the birth
of Amber were tempered by the bracing news Seth received around the
same time: Tests had detected evidence of cancer in several of his lymph
nodes. Another surgery, this one known as a lymph node dissection, was
ordered, and was deemed successful. A few scares would follow over the
years, including the removal of a lump, later determined to be benign,
from Seth's back in early 2009. But by the time he decided to embark on
his Ironman journey, Seth was cancer free.

Which is not to say that his path to Ironman would be the same as that
of someone who had never been treated for the disease. One of the lingering effects of his chemotherapy was Raynaud's syndrome, in which the
blood drains from the fingers and toes in response to cold temperatures.
The temperature in Tempe Town Lake at the start of Ironman Arizona
2008 had been about sixty-four degrees.

Seth knew that the race organizers not only recommended that participants in Arizona wear a wetsuit; they all but required it. Those suits
extended to the wrists and ankles, as well as right under the chin, which,
Seth felt, would compensate for the fact that he didn't have much body fat
on his lean frame. But that suit would do nothing to protect him from the
effects of Raynaud's, which had rendered his feet and hands pale and almost immobile even in swimming pools that were heated to temperatures
in the high seventies. Seth wondered how he could possibly withstand a

swim of even a few minutes in those conditions, let alone one that could take him nearly two hours to complete.

For now, though, he had far more immediate concerns—namely, that he would need to step up his training markedly and steadily in the weeks ahead. As a certified health and fitness instructor, he figured he could devise some sort of plan. But in sharp contrast to Tracy Tucker-Georges, who would rely on her "boys" to motivate her during those long bike rides in California, and Bryan Reece, who loved nothing more than being surrounded by fellow pedalers in spin class, Seth made a conscious decision early on: He would prepare for the Ironman entirely on his own.

In the weeks that followed he would make good on that pledge, logging more hours than he could possibly count pedaling to nowhere in that windowless room in his basement. Virtually his only company was an artificial Christmas tree and Internet videos of Lance Armstrong, rerun on a loop on his computer screen.

Eventually, though, Seth would learn that no Ironman aspirant can exist on an island—at least not one with any realistic hope of finishing such an epic undertaking.

On November 4, 2006, the same day on which the Montana man had gone into cardiac arrest during the choppy swim in the Gulf of Mexico, Leanne Esler stood near the final loop of the run course at Ironman Florida, in Panama City. Leanne, who was twenty-seven and anxiously watching her first Ironman, was there to support her boyfriend, Scott Johnson. Scott, thirty-four, was seeking to complete his first Ironman after two aborted attempts. He had failed in his bid to complete the same race a year earlier (he tore a leg muscle on the bike ride and had to pull out); he'd also been unable to finish Ironman New Zealand, running out of gas on the run portion. He had met Leanne only five months prior to this latest Ironman bid, through the dating Web site Match.com.

As Scott completed that first lap of the run that cold November evening, Leanne spied him from the crowd and stepped onto the road to give him a hug. She knew the day had gotten off to a rocky start, and not just because the air was thirty-eight degrees when the starting cannon fired. Scott had been stung in the face by a jellyfish and had dog-paddled to a kayak for several minutes to ensure he had no allergic reaction. Though he had persevered, Leanne could see now that he was in rough shape.

"My legs hurt so bad," he told her.

She would have none of it.

"You're going to do this," she told him.

Perhaps, he thought, but at that point all he could think was *I still have thirteen miles to go.*

From the outset, theirs was a match that had been rooted in sports—running in particular. Leanne, a nurse from Canada who had recently moved to the seaside town of Wilmington, North Carolina, had typed the word "running" into the dating Web site's search engine and Scott's profile had popped up. He called himself "slowesttriathlet," and in his profile he said he was five foot seven, that his body type was "athletic and toned," and that he was "spiritual but not religious." He left out any mention of the extensive tattoos, shaped almost like serpents, that crisscrossed his upper right shoulder, chest, and side. But he did say he had lived in Wilmington since 1999. Moreover, he wrote:

> I also love closing my eyes and then pointing on a map and then driving there to spend the weekend. I've met a lot of wonderful people that I would have normally never crossed paths with that way. I enjoy hiking, camping, and basically anything outdoors.

And then there was this teaser: "I have become extremely athletic within the past five years (long story that I'll share with you if you email me)."

Sufficiently curious, Leanne "winked" at Scott—striking a key on her computer that sent him the electronic version of a glance across a crowded restaurant. When Scott logged onto his account later that June day, he saw that wink.

While "Runner_GirlNC" had not posted a photo of herself, Scott saw that she described herself as five foot two and "slender," with "auburn/red" hair and green eyes.

"I was hedging my bets that she was probably pretty good-looking," Scott later recalled. And so he read further, including this passage:

Hey there! I thought I would give this a try to see if I could find someone with similar interests as myself. It's harder and harder to find single people out there who like to do the same things I do. I am not really sure who I am expecting to find here on Match. Mostly I am looking to meet someone who wants to be a friend.

I am looking for an athletic guy who likes to run, bike and play golf. I run regularly and try to run a few races each year. It gives me a goal and makes my running seem purposeful. I am already signed up for my first ½ marathon in September, the Rock and Roll ½ Marathon in Virginia Beach and I am quite excited.

And so, cautiously, he e-mailed the woman who would turn out to be Leanne, and they immediately fell into a spirited exchange. At one point Scott had mentioned in passing that he was a member of the YMCA's Wilmington Triathlon Club, and, as luck would have it, Leanne knew someone who was not only a member of the same group but worked at a company called PPD (Pharmaceutical Product Development), where, if she judged correctly by his e-mail address, Scott worked as well.

"Oh, my God, I know Scott," the woman told Leanne. "You need to meet him!"

And so they made a plan to get together. In the interim, each sent the other a photo, and Leanne shared it with her friend.

"That's not who I was thinking of," the woman said sheepishly.

But after looking at the photo Scott sent, she told Leanne she also recognized him—from work and that same triathlon club. "He's a good guy, too," she assured Leanne.

One night in June 2006, Scott and Leanne met at Elijah's, a restaurant on Wilmington's historic downtown wharf, and their attraction in person was as strong as it had been online. Their appetizers had barely arrived when Scott began singing the song of triathlon. Leanne was certainly intrigued by the running portion of the races he described, but she told Scott that she couldn't remember the last time she'd been on a bicycle, and she did not swim. The ocean, in particular, scared her. No matter, he told Leanne. He would be happy to train her.

"That was it," Scott recalled. They would be a pair from that moment forward.

Four months later, she was there to support Scott as he mounted his third attempt to hear Mike Reilly say those precious words: "Scott Johnson of Wilmington, North Carolina, you are an Ironman." By then Scott had made good on his promise and had gotten Leanne to the point in her own swimming and biking that she could compete in a sprint triathlon. She had done so in Chapel Hill in July, a month after they met, and proved a quick study: She won the age group for women twenty-five to twenty-nine. As Scott crossed that Ironman finish line for the first time—right in front of her in Florida, on the top floor of a parking garage—Leanne recalled that the experience "was overwhelming."

"To know he'd tried two other times—it was inspiring."

After Scott had sufficiently caught his breath at the finish line, Leanne buttonholed him with a prediction.

"Someday," she told him, "I will do that."

Not long after they met, Leanne got around to asking Scott about the line in his Match.com profile referring to the "long story"—the one about how he'd become a triathlete. It would turn out to be among the most compelling true-life yarns she had ever heard.

Scott had been born with cystic fibrosis. His father, a Marine, and his mother, a teacher, had received that heartbreaking diagnosis when their younger son was three months old. At the time, in the late 1970s, there was no genetic test for CF, an incurable disease that fills the lungs with thick mucus that increasingly restricts a person's breathing. Eventually the lungs harden with scar tissue, making it increasingly difficult to exhale. Many children died as young as two, and at the time few CF patients had survived into their teens. After an early bout with pneumonia, Scott had been given a sweat chloride test, which measures how much salt is in a person's circulation. A high concentration, like Scott's, was a telltale sign of CF.

While Scott would later describe his childhood as "fairly normal," it was anything but. He was always small for his age and had a cough that made it sound as if he had smoked several packs of cigarettes a day for thirty years. Though cystic fibrosis is not contagious, Scott's parents had a hard time convincing the parents of some of the children in their town of Jacksonville, North Carolina, of that fact. "I actually had parents who wouldn't let me play with their children," Scott recalled.

The "normal" part of his childhood included playing baseball and a little soccer, as well as skateboarding, surfing, and even some wrestling, in high school. Among the many lessons Scott says his parents taught him was that he was never to feel sorry for himself.

"No matter how bad I got," he said, "my parents instilled in me that there was somebody else worse off. I never was one of those 'woe is me, the world owes me a favor' kind of people."

Still, as far back as he can remember, Scott says his parents were honest with him about the seriousness of his disease—and the fact that it might well kill him.

"I've never been one to appreciate sugarcoating," he said. "I'd rather have someone tell me straight."

That said, Scott's parents assured him that they would do everything possible to mitigate the effects of CF. For a half-hour to an hour, once and sometimes twice a day, they would pound their hands lightly on and around his chest to break up the mucus that might otherwise choke him.

Those sessions literally prolonged Scott's life, to the point that he was able to enroll in college, a milestone that few afflicted with cystic fibrosis ever reach. He chose the University of North Carolina, Wilmington, not far from home. "I surfed and drank and did everything that normal college people do." By that point Scott had taught himself how to do the "percussions" to clear his chest on his own. In 1994, he graduated with a degree in environmental science, with a concentration in biology. Soon he was at work, in Raleigh, albeit a bit far afield as a department manager of a Toys "R" Us.

Because he was so active, Scott had managed to stave off for years the most debilitating effects of CF, but his doctors had warned him that his lungs could hold out for only so long. In his early twenties he "began to go downhill," becoming susceptible to infections and enduring several hospitalizations. In 1999, at age twenty-seven, he had deteriorated so much that his doctors placed him on the list for a possible double lung transplant—an increasingly available option for CF patients, but one that was nowhere near as common as liver and kidney transplants. The lungs can be more difficult to transplant than other organs because they are directly exposed to the outside environment and all the bacteria and toxins afloat in it. Around this time, Scott wondered how much longer he might live.

"When you grow up with a terminal disease," he said, "you don't make future plans. You don't say, 'When I'm thirty, I want to have a house, kids, all that stuff.' You always have death in the back of your head."

On the other hand, he would argue that cystic fibrosis had actually made his life more fulfilling. "You appreciate life," he said. "You appreciate the time you have."

By early September 2001, that time appeared to be growing short. By then Scott was unable to leave the University of North Carolina medical center in Chapel Hill, having been admitted Fourth of July weekend. At several points he went into so-called carbon dioxide comas, triggered by dangerously high blood levels of the gas, which would be expelled by healthy lungs. The comas lasted anywhere from a few hours to a few days, and eventually he was completely bedridden. The muscles in his arms, legs, and back shriveled. If the lungs he so desperately needed did not materialize soon, Scott was told, he would die.

At a certain point in early September, the doctors and nurses began the eight-hour process of preparing Scott for surgery. And then, for reasons unknown to him, that process was suddenly aborted. A few days later the process began again. Two healthy lungs had been located, and would soon be placed on a plane and flown to Chapel Hill. But the hopes of Scott and his family were soon dashed: Every plane in the country had been grounded.

It was September 11, 2001.

At that point Scott knew his death was imminent. At first he hatched a plan to begin hoarding painkillers and other drugs, should he choose to hasten the inevitable and take his own life. "I was bad, bad, bad off," he recalled. "I was in a very dark place."

One night, in an attempt to distract himself, Scott reached for a pad of paper and a pen that had been placed at his bedside and began to make a list. He wanted to make note of those things he had "always wanted to do in life" but had never gotten around to, either because he had "run out of time" or was physically incapable of doing so. His mind drifting far from his hospital bed, Scott scribbled the names of places he wished to surf someday and mountains he hoped to climb. He toyed with the idea of writing down the word "marathon" but thought better of it. He had never especially enjoyed running, because of his lungs. But since he did like swimming and bicycling, near the top of that list he wrote the word "triathlon"—before adding "just one."

For him that list was a motivator. "I made a promise to myself that if I ever pulled through, I would start doing these things. I wasn't really mad, I wasn't really sad. But I had a lot of regret. I made a vow to myself that the next time I was back in a hospital bed, I wouldn't have any regrets."

On September 15, four days after the terrorist attacks, the transplant team again prepared Scott for surgery, and this time the precious cargo arrived on schedule, not a moment too soon. The doctors would wind up working for the better part of nine hours to remove Scott's badly damaged lungs and replace them. The following day, in intensive care, one of the most critical steps in his recovery took place when he was removed from a respirator and his new lungs given the opportunity to fill with air. There was no guarantee that they would, and at first Scott was certain that they were not working. For his entire life his breathing had been accompanied by pops and crackles. Now there was no sound at all. So why were his doctors and nurses smiling so broadly?

This, they assured him, was what normal breathing sounded like.

The transplant was deemed a success, but it would be some time before Scott could be declared out of the woods. Among his first assignments would be teaching his atrophied legs to walk again. His friends were not surprised to learn that he had become the first transplant patient in the memory of anyone at the hospital to walk so many laps around the nurse's station and up and down the hallways—a course that the hospital actually measured—that he completed a mile in one day.

Two weeks later, Scott was discharged, though told to stay in the Chapel Hill area for a few weeks, as there was still a risk of infection or rejection. Having passed that test, he was sent home to Wilmington. A few months later, as he stepped into the shower, he felt stabbing pains in his abdomen that were so severe, he sat down on the shower floor and began to throw up. An ambulance was called and a diagnosis was rendered swiftly: Scott had been on so many painkillers that his colon had become obstructed and ultimately perforated.

After emergency surgery, he was airlifted to Chapel Hill, where the transplant team could pump his body with antibiotics for three weeks. With his immunity suppressed, his doctors tried desperately to save his lungs, and again their efforts were blessed with success. His doctor, as Scott recalls it, told him: "You're now one of only two people in the world who has survived a perforated colon after any kind of transplant surgery."

Scott received that news in the spirit with which it had been delivered. *I guess it's not my time* yet, he thought. But after cheating death so many times, he kindly told his doctor, "Stop telling me this stuff."

The road to an Ironman truly begins with someone deciding to place one hand in front of the other in a pool, or one foot before the other on a fast-walk that might progress into a jog or run. Scott Johnson's Ironman journey unofficially began on the handicap ramp leading to a CVS pharmacy in Wilmington.

Not long after being released from the hospital after his abdominal surgery, Scott summoned the strength to drive himself to the drugstore. Once he got out of the car, however, he discovered that his legs remained so weak that he could not step onto the curb. "Your body and mind know what you're supposed to be doing," he recalled, "but your body can't do it. It's frustrating." And so, grudgingly, he ambled up the ramp instead.

With intensive physical therapy and walks that gradually grew in distance, Scott was able to begin running about six months later. Neither his parents nor his doctors were especially pleased, but Scott was in a hurry, as he explained:

> It's hard for most people to imagine what it would feel like if you couldn't really breathe all your life. What if you were bound to a wheelchair for the first 25 years of your life, and then you could walk? Wouldn't you want to train for a marathon? Wouldn't you want to get up and do as much as possible?

A lot of people told me to relax, to take it easy. What they didn't understand was that I had a second lease on life. I wanted to do what I wanted to do. Luckily I had a physical therapist who was just as crazy as I was.

Scott certainly hadn't forgotten the bucket list he had drafted, which he kept on his nightstand. A friend in Wilmington who had just done a marathon told Scott he had prepared for that endeavor under the tutelage of a group called Team in Training, an organization with chapters throughout the nation whose members have raised tens of millions of dollars for leukemia through their participation in marathons and triathlons. Accompanied by his friend, Scott went to an information session, where he was paired with a coach. With his doctors kept close in the loop, Scott began his training.

By May 2003, he was finally ready to draw a line through the word "triathlon" on his list. The race he chose was a sprint in White Lake, North Carolina, about an hour from Wilmington. That Scott had gotten himself to the edge of the water for the start of that swim, twenty months after he nearly died, seemed nothing short of miraculous to those who knew him. As if the circumstances could not get any better, the race he had chosen was on Mother's Day. As a surprise for her son, Scott's mother had traveled to White Lake and stationed herself near the finish line, however anxiously.

Scott had no idea whether he could finish that day, but the pressure on him mounted when someone got hold of the announcer and told him a quick version of Scott's story. When Scott entered the short chute leading to the finish line, the announcer said something to the effect of "Everyone pay attention to this guy. He had a double lung transplant less than two years ago."

Scott, meanwhile, was focused on his mother.

"I could see her at the end of the finish," he said. "I hugged her and I said 'Happy Mother's Day.' We both just lost it. We never could have imagined I could do something like that."

Afterward, Scott thought: *I didn't realize how addictive these races are.*

Before long he would complete five more sprint triathlons and then two races at the Olympic distance—one in North Carolina and the other on Grand Cayman Island. While he had no yardstick on which to measure his performance—there was no other person with a double lung transplant competing in triathlons, at least as far as he knew—he had finished each of those Olympic-distance races in about 2 hours. Not bad, considering that they each entailed nearly a mile swim, a 26-mile bike, and a 6-mile run. That same year, Scott was invited to his coach's house to watch NBC's coverage of the twenty-fifth anniversary of the original Ironman, from Kona. Before showing highlights of that year's race, the network broadcast a one-hour special featuring all the great moments from years past. "That's kind of when the idea sparked in my mind," Scott recalled, "to do a full Ironman."

In May 2004, less than three years after his transplant, Scott literally got halfway to that goal when he completed a half-Ironman at White Lake, the site of his first sprint. His time: 7 hours and 50 minutes. "At that point," he said, "I became the first person with a double lung transplant to do a half-Ironman."

If Scott could maintain that pace for the span of an Ironman, he would finish it in slightly less than sixteen hours, more than an hour before the cutoff. This math was not lost on him at the time—though he knew that being able to complete a half-Ironman in less than eight hours was no guarantee that he could travel twice as far and take only twice as long.

Scott decided that he would train for an Ironman in 2005. In particular, he set his sights on Ironman Florida. Scheduled in the fall, it fell near the end of the triathlon season, giving him most of the year to train. Also, he learned, it is a relatively flat course.

Not long afterward, he received an e-mail from a friend at work with the message "Check this out." Scott read that a woman who would be competing in Kona in just a few weeks was raising money for cystic fibrosis. Her name was Tracey Richardson, and she was from New Zealand. She had been invited to Kona after completing Ironman New Zealand earlier that year, where she had raised a substantial amount of money for the disease. (By now Ironman-distance competitions had spread from North America to nearly every continent, including Ironman Australia, Ironman China, Ironman Spain, and Ironman South Africa.) The article Scott's friend had sent him included an e-mail address for Richardson, so Scott dashed off a note to her. Mindful that Tracey had two children with

CF, Scott added, "Tell your kids it's not a death sentence." He then provided a brief summary of his own story.

Not twenty minutes later, Richardson's response landed in Scott's inbox. The two wound up writing back and forth several times before Richardson popped a question: Would Scott be interested in competing in the next Ironman New Zealand, which would be held in March 2005? She told Scott she was about to leave for Hawaii, and that he should think about it.

He thought about it quite a bit. If he participated in the New Zealand race, he would have just six months to prepare—not the twelve months he'd have had if Ironman Florida were his first race. Moreover, he would have to train in the winter, and Scott knew he was not a cold-weather person. But then, Scott said, he thought about "the 'regrets' thing—that if I didn't at least try, I'd regret it later in life." And so, not long after that year's Ironman Hawaii, Scott told her he would travel to New Zealand in early spring.

Scott wound up spending more than two weeks there and was greeted with an acclaim theretofore reserved for celebrities. In the days leading up to the Ironman, Scott spoke in schools and to individual families about how close he had come to dying.

Five years after that trip, Scott still recalls a ten-year-old girl named Amber, who virtually attached herself to his hip during his travels. "Two days before the race," he said, "she looked up at me and said, 'Lance Armstrong's not my hero anymore—you are.'" Scott was flattered but also remembers thinking to himself, *I'm not ready for this.* As he put it:

> Up until that point, I'd done these races for me. It was me giving the finger to cystic fibrosis—sort of like, "You've ruled me for twenty-nine years, but you're going down." This was the first lightning bolt that made me realize, *This is bigger than me now. I'm not just doing these races for myself. People are paying attention.*

In the end, several factors conspired against his being able to finish Ironman New Zealand. One was the road surface for the bike ride. "The roads over there are horrible," Scott recalled. "They take volcanic rock and grind it up to gravel size. Then they put it out and put a clear coat over it." The course was also hilly. And it was hot. "I ended up being on the bike for eight hours," Scott said. "I wasn't prepared for it. I didn't have the right nutrition. By the time I began that run, I was cooked."

At about mile 6, Scott noticed that his peripheral vision had begun to go blurry. By mile 8 he could barely see. He surmised that he had not consumed enough calories—or, at least, enough salt.

One of the things he had always promised his doctors and family was that he would never risk his overall health for a race, so he quit for the day. He was frustrated but proud of the many people whose lives he touched and of the more than $200,000 he helped raise for cystic fibrosis while there.

Eight months later, in November 2005, Scott waded into the Gulf of Mexico off Panama City to begin his first attempt at Ironman Florida. At least initially, he was having what he recalled as "a great race," not just on the swim portion but on the bike. He noticed on his digital odometer that his average speed was as high as twenty miles an hour, probably two miles an hour faster than what he would typically train at back in North Carolina. But at mile 100, as he climbed a high-rise bridge, he realized that something in one thigh "didn't feel quite right." In fact, he said, "it felt like someone had stabbed me." He pulled over and tried to stretch the muscle, to no avail. "The ambulance came by," he said. "They pulled my bike shorts back. It looked like I had half a softball under my skin." The problem, he was told, lay in his quadriceps muscles.

"You tore the top one, I can feel that," one of the EMTs told him. "Based on the depth of the swelling, you probably partially tore the one underneath it." At that point the ambulance workers telephoned the race officials, who decided to pull Scott from the competition.

"I probably would have gotten back on," Scott said.

The wisdom of the technicians' decision was borne out several months later. With rest, Scott's muscles had healed on their own—faster than they might have in a non-athlete, he was told. By being in top condition, his body had been inclined to repair itself quicker.

In the intervening months, Scott would meet Leanne and try again at Florida in 2006. He would complete that year's swim in 1 hour, 14 minutes, and the bike ride in less than 7 hours. Twenty-three miles (and nearly six hours) into the run, Scott again felt that something in his body wasn't right—this time in one of his ankles. But with three miles to go, he didn't care.

"I had seen my dad out on the bike course a couple of times," he said. "I knew Leanne was there waiting for me. Those were all big motivators."

Scott decided to walk those last three miles, breaking into a slow jog only as he reached the finish line—which was situated, however improbably, at the top of a parking garage. He had done it, and he did indeed hear Mike Reilly say his name.

But Scott wasn't finished. He did not want this Ironman to be his last. And he was determined to make sure that when Leanne embarked on her first Ironman, he would be there with her—for every stroke, pedal, and step along the way.

CHAPTER 3

Courageous Warrior of Love

Tracy Tucker-Georges stood in the shower stall at her swim club in Northridge, California, the hot water pounding her face. It was a Friday evening in mid-January 2009, and Tracy had just done a quick thirty-six laps, nearly a half-mile. But her mind was elsewhere, having raced ahead ten months—and four hundred miles east—to Tempe, Arizona.

I am signed up to do an Ironman this year, she thought. *What the fuck did I do? Seriously. And I paid for it!*

She began to have an anxiety attack, right there in the locker room shower.

Can I do this? Tracy asked herself.

It was a question she would repeat hours later as she recorded her waterlogged moment of doubt for posterity on her blog, *TracerX.* ("Sorry, no picture attached," she would lament, playfully, in this particular post.) The stream of questions would only continue: *Can I sustain fourteen, fifteen, sixteen hours of a triathlon?*

A few seconds later Tracy had a ready answer. *Yes, of course I can!* she thought. But that moment of bravado gave way to a hedging of her bets. *I think I can. Right?*

Tracy would tell her readers—fewer than a dozen were registered—that she "was not really sure what part of the Ironman was freaking me out." Was it the swim, "with a couple of thousand of my closest friends—who, by the way, will be punching and kicking me?" Or was it the 112-

mile bike ride, "where I get to pee on myself and my sweet Penelope?" Some Ironman cyclists, usually the pros, had in fact been known to relieve themselves right there in the saddle while pedaling their bikes, to save the precious few minutes it might take to stop and head for a bush.

As Tracy's readership knew, Penelope was her nickname for her beloved Trek Madone road bike, a recurring character in her online diary. (Penelope was actually short for "Penelope Marshmallow Creampuff Pitstop," Tracy's homage to a character in the old Wacky Races animated TV series who slathered herself in pink and was pretty much the only girl in a sea of car-racing men.)

Continuing with the snapshot of her psyche, she wondered whether her anxiety at that moment was rooted in her fears of "the 26.2 miles of running/walking/crawling." And yes, she assured her readers, "you are allowed to crawl; it's in the official 'Ironman rules.' Tanks God for that."

Even before turning off that showerhead, Tracy had gained some insight. *I think it is the run/walk/crawl that is causing my high anxiety,* she realized, and then resolved to put those fears aside, however temporarily, and to "take it one day at a time."

"Wish me luck," she instructed her readers, before adding a postscript intended to erase an image of her that might have flickered in their minds as they contemplated this scene.

"I was wearing my swimsuit in the shower," she wrote.

Anyone who has ever signed up for Ironman, with its yearlong lead time, has surely had at least one instance of serious early doubt comparable to Tracy's that day in the shower. With so much time to prepare, reality can set in quickly. While many participants begin to train in earnest six months prior to a race—building to heavy workouts that they might then taper a few weeks before the big day—most have so incorporated working out into their daily lives that they start preparing, mentally and physically, within days of signing up. The frightening ordeal that awaits—and the exact count of the number of days before that cannon will sound—are never far from their minds.

And so it was that Tracy told the handful of people to whom she had granted access to the *TracerX* blog that she had decided she would begin her training for Ironman Arizona on January 1—five weeks after sign-up, and forty-seven weeks before race day. She particularly liked the symbolism of commencing her pursuit of such a big new goal as she rang in the new year, even if she still worried that "I don't know if there are enough days, hrs., mins. for me to train."

Since signing up for Arizona, she had been keeping her workouts fairly loose and sporadic. On December 9, for example, during a week in which it was so cold in Southern California that it snowed, Tracy and her training partner, known to readers of her blog as Vit Tornado, temporarily converted their actual road bikes into indoor stationary models—by locking their wheels upright in so-called trainers in Vit's garage. They then did an hour of simulated climbing as they watched a training DVD called *Hillacious*.

On Christmas Eve day, she ran a few miles on a treadmill and did some upper-body strengthening, followed by a sedentary Christmas Day with her husband and daughters.

Like most people who have registered for an Ironman, Tracy planned to do a handful of tune-up triathlons in the months leading up to it. As she began her training in earnest in January, her first major target was an Ironman 70.3—half the distance of the real thing—in Oceanside, California, in April. It would be the first half-Ironman she'd ever attempted. Her initial significant test on the path toward that interim goal came on February 1, when she entered a half-marathon that began right on Huntington Beach and continued along the ocean, a race known as the Surf City USA. While her race-walking had long ago given way to actual running, Tracy—like her friends and family—had learned to take nothing for granted whenever she competed, mindful of that meniscus tear in her left knee in 2007 and the subsequent surgery. In this case, any concerns would turn out to be misplaced.

"Hello all (all 4 or 5 of you)," she wrote on her blog. "I just wanted to say that the Surf City Half Marathon was a blast. No rain this year. It was the perfect temperature, sunny with beautiful ocean views!"

Her time was 2 hours, 59 minutes, 6 seconds. Her pace: about 13 minutes and 40 seconds a mile. Perhaps the best news was that she had managed to shave six minutes off her time of a year earlier.

Emboldened by that performance, she would soon record a prediction, online, for that 70.3 in April: She would attempt to complete the 1.2-mile swim that day in 40 minutes; the 56-mile bike course in 3 hours, 35 minutes; and the 13.1-mile run in 2 hours, 45 minutes—for a total of about 7 hours. Her target for the run seemed particularly ambitious, considering that it would require her to run 14 minutes faster than she had in Huntington Beach.

"YIKES," she wrote, not for the first or last time, on the blog. "7 hours seems like a long time, but I want to be realistic. So what the heck . . . at least I'm doing the sucker."

Five weeks before Oceanside, though, Tracy suffered something of a setback when she developed a cold that soon turned into bronchitis, forcing her to miss a full four days of training. "I feel like I'm starting from scratch," she wrote on February 28, a Saturday. "It's a bitch getting sick and being old. OK, I am not really that old. But all the same, I have 5 weeks to just keep plugging along."

Five days before Christmas 2008, the Christmas after he'd signed up for Ironman Arizona, Bryan Reece set out for the longest run of his life, both in terms of the distance he hoped to cover and the time it would take. The goal he had set for himself was 23 miles. Though ordinarily a gregarious, social person—in his short time as a member of Life Time Fitness he had quickly become the equivalent of the mayor of the gym—this was a run he would make alone. The course ran from the gate of the community where he lived near San Antonio, past suburban strip malls, and into parched, rocky ranchland dotted with mesquite, cedar, and oak.

In a month, Bryan would mark the two-year anniversary of his life-changing visit to the emergency room—the hospital would be on his running route this day, and he would acknowledge it with a smile and a tip of his mesh running cap. That he had come so far in such a relatively short time was a testament, at least in part, to what someone could accomplish physically by pursuing a series of progressively more ambitious goals.

"I have run progressive long runs of 14, 17 and 20 miles," Bryan wrote on his friends-and-family blog, *Left, Right, Repeat,* in setting the stage for the day's endeavor. "It is really interesting that somewhere about 80 percent of the way into the run, give or take a little, the mental side begins to take control. There is no doubt the joints, legs, feet and hips are hurting by then but the old nugget between the ears begins to rule. At that point I have found you just have to get it done."

And, at least on this particular day, he did get it done—relying on a strategy that had served him well since he first began studying it on the Web site of a running guru named Jeff Galloway. It basically entailed running for four minutes, then recovering with a walk for a minute, and then resuming running. Though some purists might take issue with that approach, Bryan found he could go longer (and ultimately faster) than if he embarked on a steady jog. And just as Ironman swimmers were permitted to lighten the burden of freestyle crawl, the stroke of choice for most, with a less taxing breaststroke, so, too, were runners permitted to walk during the race—as long as they hit the final cutoff point on the run (around mile 17) by 10:15 P.M., and got to that finish line no later than midnight.

"I really felt pretty good (relatively speaking) when I got to 20 miles," Bryan wrote. "Don't get me wrong, I was ready to stop, but I felt pretty good." The last three and a half miles were mostly hills, and "they really hurt," Bryan said. "More than normal." When he reached his Spanish-style home, its reddish roof welcoming him like a lighthouse beacon, he immersed himself for twenty minutes in the swimming pool in his backyard as if it were an ice bath. Afterward he iced his calves and quads and then lay on his home's stone-tile floor, elevating his legs.

"A little stiff getting out of bed this morning but it passed really quickly," he wrote the following day. "Other than my knees being a little creaky and my hips feeling like they have a little sandpaper in them. I am really glad to have run 23. I know I can gut it out for 3 more miles."

Those three more miles, for a total of twenty-six, were something of a magic number to Bryan. On November 22, less than a year from now, he'd need to run a marathon to complete Ironman Arizona, of course. But just as Tracy Tucker had signed up for a 70.3 triathlon in early 2009 as a key test en route to Arizona, Bryan had registered for the Houston Marathon, on January 18, 2009. As the date neared—and Bryan tapered his weekend runs to just seven miles, to permit his body to recover from that twenty-three-mile push—he had to laugh.

A marathon, to be followed less than a year later by an Ironman? As he wrote on his blog around this time, in reference to signing up for Ironman Arizona:

> I am like many of you, I think . . . a year or a year and a half ago I said, no, no, no. I would never consider even a half Ironman. I could MAYBE see an Olympic distance but all that other stuff is for weird crazy people. But I think my whole life has been a big old, 'never say never.' . . .
>
> I couldn't even think of something like this 18 months ago and now I feel I can do it. I couldn't today, don't get me wrong, but building a plan, executing and going for it on race day will be an absolute blast. And really, not very many people can say they have done it and that means something to me.

While he didn't realize it at the time, Bryan's methodical path to Ironman Arizona—with its looming pit stop at the Houston Marathon—had begun in earnest at that triathlon in Corpus Christi back in August 2007, where the grown-ups followed the kids. That "race" was so short in distance and duration that it wasn't even considered a sprint; it was more of a spurt. Bryan had only recently purchased a bike, and he still struggled to swim for more than just a lap, so he took pains to keep his plans for the day top secret. No one other than his wife and daughter were to know.

"If I fail," he said at the time, "I don't want anyone to say, 'Well, That's okay.' It wouldn't be okay."

Everything was going according to plan, his cover secure, until Bryan's boss, Joe Sando, arrived in town a week before the race.

"What are you all doing this weekend?" he asked Bryan when they met in the branch of the financial services firm that Bryan managed.

The seemingly innocuous inquiry had caught Bryan off guard. During the five years they'd worked in the same branch, before Joe promoted Bryan, the two had sat in offices next to each other and "he never once asked me what I was doing on the weekend!" Bryan recalled.

Now, suddenly, he was curious. *Oh, crap!* Bryan thought.

"Well, Debbie and I are going to Corpus," he said, hoping that would be the end of it.

"What are you doing in Corpus?" Bryan's boss persisted.

"We're just going to go down there and get away," he responded. "We'll be back by Saturday afternoon."

At that point Joe let the matter drop. But Bryan felt terrible. *You just lied to him*, Bryan thought. *You've never lied to him before.*

By early Friday afternoon, as Bryan and Debbie arrived in Corpus Christi, he had a more pressing concern: He was actually going to enter his first—and, he thought, probably his last—triathlon. Never mind that the swim portion would entail just four laps across an Olympic-size pool. That was four laps more than he had ever done in front of a crowd. And while he was confident he could handle the few miles on the bike, he loathed running, and wondered if his mantra of "left, right, repeat" would carry him through the mile-and-a-quarter run.

After he had gone to the race site to pick up his race packet—the ubiquitous envelope at every triathlon that contains the timing chip and the Velcro strap to attach it to the ankle—he began preparing his transition area, where he would return between the swim and bike rides, and between the bike and run portions. Anyone watching Bryan then, in what was basically the patch of grass next to his bike, would have seen him at his full, fastidious best: There were rubbing alcohol and cotton balls to dry out his ears; a pile of towels (he would later learn that few triathletes took the time to dry off); various creams and balms to prevent chafing; and an extra water bottle just for rinsing off his feet, should they become grassy or muddy.

That night, he didn't sleep at all. The following morning he was the second person to arrive for the race. After having his entry number written on his shoulder in thick, black permanent marker—like so many triathletes, he would forever associate that marker smell with fear and anticipation—he put himself in position to watch the first competitors slip into the water.

He took little comfort in the fact that none appeared to be more than five years old. The grown-ups would have to wait until the kids were done. As the temperature climbed over ninety, Bryan only grew more anxious.

When he finally got into the pool, Bryan "freaked out" that he couldn't see the bottom. The pool, at least in his section, must have been ten feet deep. Every lap lane at Life Time, by contrast, seemed no more than four feet deep. Somehow Bryan got his four laps in, although when he emerged from the water his heart rate was at about 190—"totally out of control," as he recalled.

Bryan finally began to relax on the short bike ride, soon reverting to his typical talkative self, thanking every volunteer he saw. When he encountered several EMTs idling in front of an ambulance, their eyes trained on the bike course for any mishaps, Bryan called out, "Thrilled that you're here, hope I never need you." It was something Bryan would invariably yell out to each ambulance crew he'd see during every race afterward, almost like a talisman to ward off bad luck.

The bike course had been flat, except for one gently arching bridge, and Bryan figured he'd encounter similarly benign terrain on the run.

"Well," he said later, "they found the only hill in Corpus Christi, Texas, and they used it as the turnaround for the run course."

Bryan started to run up it but then slowed his pace to a walk, having to catch his breath. "I was pretty gassed at that point," he recalled. "But then there was this guy that ran past me. He patted me on the back. He said, 'Come on, you can run a half-mile, can't you?'"

Bryan wasn't too sure, but he agreed to run with the man. When they got within sight of the finish line, he encouraged his new friend to sprint ahead.

"You go," Bryan told him. "I've got it."

And he did. As he crossed the line, Bryan felt a surge of elation unlike anything he could recall.

"It was the sense of accomplishment," he said later, "and where I had come."

As he stood in the finish area sipping Gatorade with Debbie proudly at his side, someone yelled, "They've put the results up." Bryan learned that he had finished third in his age group, forty-five to forty-nine. He even got a medal. Never mind that there were only four competitors his age.

"I didn't finish last," he said. "We were laughing about it. I said I never had to 'podium' again. I've done it."

The following Monday, Bryan picked up the phone to call his boss.

"I need to tell you something," he said. "I lied to you last week when you were here." Bryan then proceeded to tell him just what he had been up to in Corpus Christi.

"That's great," his boss said, to Bryan's immediate relief. "You know, Ray Baker is doing one this weekend."

Ray Baker was Bryan's counterpart in the Plano office, outside Dallas. Bryan immediately called him, and a bond was struck. Over the next eighteen months the two men would speak almost every day, reviewing their training, sharing tips, and consoling each other on setbacks. Though usually separated by three hundred miles, they would arrange to bike or run at the same exact time, and then call or text each other throughout, like two teenagers working after-school jobs at the same time, but in different places.

Bryan, sweating his way up some hill in the San Antonio heat, would invariably answer the phone to hear Ray, his voice strong, say, "I'm at mile 7."

"Damn," Bryan would reply. "I'm only at mile 4."

Ray was five years younger, and faster, but that didn't matter to either man. Bryan would draw immense comfort from the thought that "somebody's out there." And each would shudder at the idea of skipping a training run or ride or swim after having pledged to the other that he would do so.

With Ray's encouragement, Bryan completed his second triathlon, the sprint in San Antonio that had originally caught his eye on the Internet. Then Ray set the bar considerably higher: He suggested that he, Bryan, and a third manager, Mark Elledge, in Fort Worth, do a half-marathon in Austin in February.

To this point, Bryan had run no farther than 3.1 miles—the distance in the San Antonio tri. As his next challenge, he had been considering signing up for an Olympic-distance triathlon, which would have had a 6.2-mile run. Now Ray was suggesting jumping immediately to more than twice that distance. Meanwhile, of course, Bryan hated to run. And yet, he readily agreed.

The men did not run that race in lockstep, but each completed it, feeling that he could not have run another step. Bryan finished in 2 hours, 15 minutes, at a pace of about 10 minutes per mile.

"It was nothing fast, by any stretch of the imagination," Bryan said. "But it was a huge accomplishment."

Bryan did so well that, even before he'd competed in his first Olympic triathlon, he and Ray started to muse about entering a half-Ironman, which would be twice as long as that Olympic. Over the next year— sometimes together, sometimes solo—they would compete in triathlons and runs of various distances and durations, with the exception of two: a marathon and an Ironman.

"Each one of them was always such a step of accomplishment along the way," Bryan said. "The question at the end always was: What's next?"

Ray traveled to Austin in October 2008 to do a half-Ironman with Bryan. After completing it, the two finally acknowledged to each other "where we were heading." At some point prior to that race, Bryan had said to Ray on the phone one day, "I can see how an Ironman would be doable. I can see how people can accomplish it, with all that training." But the men had always agreed an Ironman was "too big" to even contemplate.

Not now. Not after each had gone half that distance.

Ray decided he'd sign up for Ironman Louisville, a new race that would be held in August 2009. Bryan, who liked the idea of having the full summer to train and then to compete in the fall, settled on Arizona.

But first, Ray, Bryan, and Mark decided, they needed to get the monkey of a marathon off their backs. Houston, in January 2009, would fit the bill.

On January 11, a week before the Houston Marathon, Bryan booted up his computer to post a message for Ray, Mark, and the small group of other friends and family who followed him on *Left, Right, Repeat*:

> Next Sunday is my first marathon ever. I know it will be a long day. I did six miles today and was thinking the whole way about going long. It was a nice change of pattern for me. You see, I work for a major financial institution, in the brokerage arm, and things have been really tough for a while. It has been great to have fitness and training as a distraction from the realities of stress of the real world. So for anyone out there

with a lot of stress in their life . . . start training for some event and it will change your outlook.

A week later Bryan rose in his Houston hotel room at 3:30 A.M. and lay in bed until 4:45 or so. The temperature outside was in the mid-sixties, and the humidity was already high. In a few hours, Bryan's daughter, Taylour, inspired mightily by her dad, would begin her own first half-marathon, and Bryan, Ray, and Mark would embark on their first full one.

Fueled by an early-morning bagel with peanut butter, and an apple-and-cinnamon Hammer Gel—an energy goo that tasted to him like apple pie—Bryan began the race. The course started downtown at Minute Maid Park, where the Astros play, and continued north, before turning west, past Rice University. It then traversed through Memorial Park and back downtown. Though he and Mark were together briefly at the outset, they soon separated. During the first few miles, Bryan was unnerved by the congestion and had difficulty finding a rhythm. But his heart rate was low and seemingly under control.

Beginning around mile 3, however, his hips began to tighten. He would later conclude that his problem was not related to this particular race, or to any gaps in pre-race stretching, but to the physical realities of his own body. (As he would put it, "I have too much gluteus maximus.")

Still, halfway through, he felt good. He was running at a pace just under twelve minutes a mile—only a little slower than during that half-marathon in Austin.

"My pre-race goal was just to finish," he said later. "But we all know that is crap. We all try to come up with some estimate. I was hoping for 5:15—but would have been pleased with 5:30."

At about mile 18, Bryan caught up with the group tapped by race volunteers to set a 5:15 pace, a number emblazoned on two four-and-a-half-inch-wide balloons set atop a long, quarter-inch dowel. Bryan would have plenty of time to commit these dimensions to memory; he actually took a turn carrying the pacers' balloons for five minutes, and would come away "feeling like I was carrying a bridge column."

He was thrilled that the pace group was doing "a 5/1 run/walk strategy"—running for five minutes and then walking for one, just as Bryan had learned to do on the Galloway Web site. But then, at around mile 20, the muscle behind his left knee "began to assert itself." As he later wrote, "It had been nagging at me for a few miles but now it was not to be denied. It knotted up like a monkey's fist knot. It hurt if I walked. It hurt it if I ran. It hurt if I stopped for a few seconds to rub it."

Bryan began to dream about the pleasures that awaited him at the finish line, still a long six miles away:

> I thought beer was about the only cure, so the faster I got to beer, the better. So I began to run as much as I could. The grind through Memorial Park was beautiful, with great spectators who were shouting encouragement all the way. At about Mile 23, I cruised into a "Try Our Water" aid station and looked up to see Mark about 20 yards in front of me. So it looked like I would have a Partner in Pain. (At least for a little while.) We continuously did the math to try to make the 5:30 number. Running when we could, walking when we had to.

And then Bryan saw it: To their left were long tables lined with cups of invitingly frothy beer, set out in rows, as if on a ping-pong table at a fraternity party.

There was only one problem: Bryan and Mark were not quite done. They still had a couple of city-length blocks to go. At this point the pair spotted Mark's wife, Patty, along the side of the road. Though there as a spectator, she had hoped to run this last stretch with them. It was the final motivation the men needed. Patty had no trouble keeping up, and eased her pace if they wanted to walk. "Unless there was a camera in sight, in which case we ran for sure," Bryan said.

Here's how Bryan described the final moments of that race:

> I saw Debbie and Taylour right before the finish, and that was cool. Crossing that line with Mark was really a special moment. We have done a lot of this endurance training "together," with him in Fort Worth and me in San Antonio, so it was neat to cross the line together. (Ray "The Rabbit" had finished earlier and was laying on the floor of the convention center, relaxing at this time.)

I really believe "it takes a village" to accomplish something like this . . . Thanks go to my wife for her support and understanding of long runs and painful legs, to my daughter, who never laughed at "the old man" when he said he was going to do a triathlon or marathon—and congratulations to her for finishing her first half marathon during her senior year in college. She is quite an inspiration to me.

His time was just a shade over five and a half hours.

As he prepared to sign off his blog just before ten that night, Bryan couldn't help but turn his thoughts to the future. "I have already been asked, 'Will you do another?'" he wrote. "I don't know about a stand-alone marathon. I know I will do another 26.2—at Ironman Arizona in November."

Of course, for that race, just ten months away, he would have to swim more than two miles and bike another 112 before he could even set foot on the marathon course. For all the good feelings regarding the peak he had just scaled, Bryan wondered, right there at the finish line, how he would possibly have the energy and stamina to run a marathon after all that swimming and biking. It was hard enough doing what he had just accomplished. He also worried, as he did so often, whether he would be able to stay free of injury or accident during the many miles of swimming, biking, and running that lay ahead.

"But that," he concluded, "is for another day."

Leanne Esler and Scott Johnson spent Christmas Day 2008 watching a recording of the previous year's Ironman Hawaii from their DVR. It was one of four Ironman races on their playlist, and the couple watched them over and over as if they were inspirational family movies—which, in a way, they were. Their life had quickly become a series of races and rides, with the days in between filled with training.

Emboldened by his finish at Ironman Florida in 2006, Scott had decided—on the spot—that he wanted to enter Ironman Hawaii in fall 2007. There were several paths for an amateur to get to Kona: finishing high enough in one's age group in another Ironman to earn a qualifying

slot; getting a spot through a highly sought lottery; or being invited by
the race organizers. Scott had gotten just such an invitation, from Ben
Fertic, the president of Ironman, while in New Zealand, and he was finally ready to accept.

During his Hawaiian odyssey, Scott made it out of the choppy Pacific
surf before the 2-hour-20-minute cutoff and began climbing the hills of
the Big Island on his bike. But at around mile 90, he started having what
he described as "nutritional issues" in the humid Hawaiian heat. He was
vomiting, and he was still about twenty miles from the end of the bike
course. And so, mindful that anyone competing that day—let alone
someone who'd had a double organ transplant—could fall critically ill if
he wasn't careful, Scott retired. "Just to make it to the start line was plenty
for me," he said afterward.

Three days later, Scott and Leanne married on a Hawaiian beach as
seventeen friends and family, many from North Carolina and Leanne's
native Canada, looked on. Though the ceremony was planned in advance,
they had met their minister in Hawaii only a week earlier. No one who
knew Scott or Leanne was surprised that Leanne had first gotten to talking to the minister after a 10K running race in which both had participated. Leanne soon learned he was an Ironman triathlete.

In keeping with Scott and Leanne's sensibility, the service was more
spiritual than religious. The minister compared a marriage to the Hawaiian Islands: What you see on the surface sometimes masks what is growing underneath. He then used a banana leaf to pour seawater out of a
bowl and onto their rings. "It was really, really cool," Leanne said. "You
could relate to him." After they returned to North Carolina, there would
be a big party.

But before they left paradise, Leanne had some business to attend to
from the Hawaiian hotel room where she would spend her honeymoon.

Booting up her laptop, she went to the Ironman Web site to sign up for
her first half-Ironman: a 70.3 in Muskoka, Ontario, not far from where
she'd grown up. The race was scheduled for September 2008, the following year. A few weeks after they were back at home, Scott and Leanne
wasted little time getting to work preparing for that half-Ironman; they
entered a half-marathon in Wilmington, their hometown. What better
way to celebrate their new marriage? Unfortunately, the day would prove

a reminder that running, even absent the other two events of a triathlon, can be a risky endeavor.

Just before the midpoint of the race, as Leanne crossed the Cape Fear Bridge, she tumbled to the asphalt surface. Her side and knee shot with pain, and she realized she was bleeding from her lip. Still, she got up and kept going. "As a nurse," Scott said later, "she's the worst patient ever." When she had about a mile to go, a volunteer who spied Leanne from the sidelines intervened. By the looks of her lip, she would surely need stitches, and the volunteers and a police officer insisted on loading Leanne into the back of a squad car. She didn't stay long.

"Do you think I could get out and you could let me finish?" she recalled asking.

"Wipe the blood off your face," the officer said. "And go."

She did, and she finished. But a rough pattern would soon emerge. For all her lean grace, Leanne could be clumsy and prone to accidents. As she strived to improve her swimming, biking, and running, the biggest hurdle was often the pain. And like so many weekend warriors, Leanne felt that resting on the sidelines until fully healed was not a realistic option—exercise was the foundation of her life, and of her life with Scott.

"It's all I talk about," she said. "I eat, sleep, dream it. It's our relationship. We haven't gone on a vacation without a race. It's who I am. It's what I do. It makes me tick."

Sure enough, just three weeks after that ill-fated half-marathon in Wilmington, Leanne and Scott went to South Carolina to participate in a full marathon. Again Leanne finished, but her breathing was so labored that she feared she might pass out. Over the next twenty-four hours she made two trips to the hospital. The doctors did an ultrasound and checked her kidneys, and they thought she might have problems with her gallbladder. "They couldn't find anything," Leanne said. But the pain—in her chest and abdomen—only got worse.

The following day, she saw her own doctor, who determined that she had torn a muscle in her chest wall during that fall on the Cape Fear Bridge. It was a rare injury, and the only prescription was rest. Leanne mentioned to the doctor that she was hoping to do the Boston Marathon the following April, in 2008. Absolutely not, he said. She would have to stop running for a while. Reluctantly, she agreed.

Less than a year later and sufficiently healed, Leanne and Scott arrived at the Canadian half-Ironman in September 2008. They wished they were back in Hawaii: The water temperature in the lake that day was sixty-four degrees. A drenching rain began to fall before the start of the swim and would continue the entire day. "You have a goal of what you do timewise," Leanne recalled. "When you get there, the goal changes, and you're like 'I just want to finish.'" Still, Leanne managed to emerge from the 1.2-mile swim in an admirable forty-three minutes. The bike course proved more of a challenge. It seemed to her to be one continuous climb, which was made even tougher in the rain. She witnessed several accidents, including one rider who lost both his wheels at the same time and slid into the woods.

Somehow, Leanne made it through the nearly sixty-mile ride in about three hours. She then cruised through the half-marathon, her strongest portion of the triathlon, in about two hours. All told, she had completed the day's events in less than six hours, with the only issue being one of hunger: She concluded, afterward, that she probably should have eaten more than a couple of PowerBars. "I'm horrible on nutrition," she said. It was an issue that would be a factor in future races, but for now, Leanne was exultant. She was halfway to an Ironman, the goal she had set for herself as she watched Scott complete that race in Florida.

Later, she and Scott looked at the Ironman calendar for 2009 and de-cided that Arizona was her best bet. One factor that sealed the decision was that the swim portion of Ironman Arizona was in a man-made lake. Though she lived on the Atlantic, Leanne was almost phobic about ocean swimming, which ruled out a race like Ironman Florida. With its lake swim and relatively flat bike ride, Arizona seemed to Leanne and Scott an ideal first Ironman for her. And though the run, deceptively, was among the hilliest of the North American Ironman courses—right up there with Lake Placid, New York, and Madison, Wisconsin—Leanne took confidence in the fact that she was typically strongest on the run. Scott promised he would join her—not just in her training but in the actual race.

On November 23, 2008, the day of the sign-up, Leanne went onto the blog she kept mostly as a record for herself, as well as for like-minded friends, on BeginnerTriathlete.com—the same site where Bryan Reece served as an online mentor—to log the day's activities. She noted that she had ridden her road bike in her garage, immobilized in a so-called trainer, for a half-hour, beginning at 5:15 that morning. She then walked on the treadmill for ten minutes before doing forty-five minutes of weights, including three sets of triceps French curls and shoulder flies. All of this information was transmitted as matter-of-factly as if it were a baseball box score. But in the notes section, Leanne added some color: "Brrr . . . yet again. I had to run to my Jeep to grab my iPod and it was covered in frost!! We don't see that too often! I'm glad I kept my scraper."

As a postscript, she added, "TODAY is the day we sign up for IMAZ!!"

At 2:10 P.M., she went back online with news: "I AM OFFICIALLY SIGNED UP FOR IMAZ!!!!!!" followed by the kind of exclamation that Tracy Tucker-Georges loved to include in her blog: "AGHHHHHHHH-HHHHHHHHHHH ☺"

Leanne began 2009 with a long gaze toward Arizona, but with a tighter focus on the races that would serve as her lead-up. Having missed the Boston Marathon due to injury in 2008, she had requalified and was due to travel with Scott to Massachusetts in April. She was excited by the idea that she would, she hoped, be able to cross Boston off her to-do list, and in the bargain gain confidence and experience that would serve her well in her first Ironman. She and Scott also planned to do a half-Ironman in White Lake, North Carolina, later that spring, at the site of the same race where Scott had memorably embraced his mother at the finish.

But Leanne's thoughts were not just on the physical and mental training that her Ironman pursuit would require. She also wanted to give these pursuits greater meaning—ideally in service to a charity or cause. She could have made the easy choice and simply joined Scott in his effort to raise money for cystic fibrosis. But for all the ways that Scott's triumph over CF had inspired and changed her life, she longed for a way to give back that would be her own. The answer would come from an unexpected place: a phone conversation with a stranger that would affect the course of his life as much as it would hers.

That conversation, on the first Monday in February 2009, began with a call placed by Leanne to a family in Phoenix. She was responding to an ad for a four-bedroom house just a few miles from downtown Tempe that was available for rent the weekend of Ironman Arizona. Leanne and Scott figured they could fill the house with friends and relatives, who might enjoy a vacation in the desert as long as they were willing to root for their hosts over the course of a very long day.

Leanne asked whoever answered the phone that day if she could speak to Ross Murray, who had placed the ad. No, she was told, he was not available. In fact, Leanne could not have called at a worse time. The woman on the phone told her that Ross and his wife, Daradee, had just lost their son, Liam, born twenty-six days earlier, to a cluster of rare heart defects.

Leanne was stunned and felt terrible about having intruded upon such an awful, unthinkable moment, however innocently. She expressed her condolences and quickly said goodbye. Her eyes filling with tears, she decided she would find another house. These people had enough to deal with, to say the least.

A few days later, she was surprised to receive an e-mail from Ross. The rental house, which the family used as an investment for extra income, was hers and Scott's if they wanted it, he said. He also included a Web link—http://www.caringbridge.org/visit/zipmurray—which Leanne saw was a site on which Ross and Daradee told Liam's story. Leanne began to read:

> Months before Liam was born (18 weeks in-utero), after a routine ultrasound, we found out that Liam had a problem with his heart. After several ultra and echo scans we found out Liam had four heart defects . . . Underdeveloped left ventricle, overdeveloped right, his aorta went into his right ventricle (should go into left), his pulmonary arteries weren't getting blood flow and his ventricles and atrium weren't separated. So in essence Liam had two chambers instead of four.

While serious and rare, Liam's heart defects were apparently correctable. After his birth on January 8, Ross and Daradee were told by doctors at the Scott and Laura Eller Congenital Heart Center at St. Joseph's Hospital in Phoenix that he would require three surgeries in three years—the first just a few weeks after he was born. Leanne read as Ross continued Liam's story:

> From the time he was born until his first surgery, 11 days, Daradee and I spent a lot of quality time with our son. We would change him, swaddle him, mock feed him, sing to him and hold him. This is time we will never forget and always cherish. Daradee and I never left the PCT ICU. We spent every night there for about a month. Liam looked and behaved like any normal baby prior to his surgeries.

It was soon after that first surgery that, as Ross wrote, "the complications started." That first intervention had failed to accomplish what the doctors had hoped, and Liam had ended up on life support. Eventually a clot passed from a pulmonary artery, causing a "severe stroke." After he died, Ross wrote:

> Liam physically sacrificed his heart to show all of us a deeper understanding of Love. We named our son Liam because it means Courageous Warrior. We thought it was a perfect name for what he would need to endure. I ended up changing the meaning of his name to Courageous Warrior of Love.

Leanne read that Ross and Daradee had created a foundation—they fused the word *Love* with their son's name, calling it LoveIAM—to raise money for the American Heart Association.

She had found her cause.

To facilitate the charitable aspirations of its athletes, the Ironman organization had partnered with the financial firm Janus to create the Janus Charity Challenge. Those athletes who wished to participate were given a personal, easy-to-set-up Web page to solicit and record donations, chart their progress, and explain why they had chosen the causes they did. Here's how Leanne—a registered nurse who had no children of her own, and no plans to raise a family—put it on the Janus page she created:

> I believe Ross and I crossed paths for a reason and that reason was to continue to share Liam's legacy and to raise awareness and money for those affected by cardiovascular disease and stroke. Originally my Ironman journey was for me, but Liam is my inspiration and this journey is for him as well. He was a little fighter and though he was not quite a month old, little Liam has made a HUGE impact on MANY people's lives . . .
>
> We all know someone who has suffered from heart disease or a stroke. I was lucky that my husband had a second chance in life and I wish Liam had too.

She then listed her "goals for Ironman Arizona." They were:

1. To finish the race for myself and Liam and to become an Ironman
2. To finish the race with a SMILE!!
3. To raise at least $5,000 for the American Heart Association

Leanne let Ross and Daradee know in a follow-up phone call what she planned to do on behalf of Liam's memory.

"That's so cool," Ross said. "That's awesome."

But as he would acknowledge later, "We didn't really appreciate the gesture at the time, because there was so much going on."

Before they said goodbye, Leanne asked if she could tell Ross and Daradee her husband's story. Ross could not believe all that Scott had endured, and how he had triumphed against such odds, not only to live but to finish an Ironman, of all things.

"Suddenly there was this instant connection between us and them," Ross recalled. "It was complete fate, destiny. Eight years ago, Scott was laying in a hospital bed, unable to breathe, just like Liam. Scott really valued and appreciated life. We went through the same thing with Liam—seeing how short life is."

Hearing how exercise had changed Scott's and Leanne's lives, Ross made a vow of his own. A pack-a-day cigarette smoker in his early thirties, with a waistline that bulged with perhaps thirty extra pounds, he made a promise to himself to get into better shape. He had already decided to do so as a tribute to his son, but now he had an added incentive: to honor the kindness of his new friends.

CHAPTER 4

Kids, Don't Try This at Home

The next Reece to set out on a marathon after Bryan's milestone in Houston was his older brother, Bruce. A representative for a mutual fund company from the Dallas–Fort Worth area, Bruce would occasionally run a few miles or so on a weekend over the years, but his suddenly fanatical younger brother had set him on a more rigorous path in the summer of 2008, a few months before the Ironman Arizona sign-up. As the brothers and their families were vacationing for a week on a beach on the Florida Panhandle, an annual outing, Bryan had turned to Bruce at one point and suddenly lobbed a question at him.

"What are you doing on your birthday?" Bryan asked.

"The boys will be in college," Bruce replied. "I'm going to do what I always do: work."

"Well, you can't," Bryan said. "This year your birthday is on a Sunday."

Considering that Bruce's birthday—his fifty-second—was not until November 16, and this was July, he was more than a little taken aback.

"How do you know my birthday is on Sunday?" Bruce asked Bryan, noting that even he didn't know himself.

"I know because it's the inaugural Rock 'n' Roll Marathon in San Antonio," Bryan replied. "I'm going to run the half. Why don't you run it with me?"

Bruce was intrigued—he'd been following Bryan's transformation with more than a little interest—but he wondered how he could possibly get into half-marathon shape in four months.

"I've already mapped out a training schedule for you, and I'll send it to you," Bryan said—a statement that didn't necessarily surprise his older brother. That week, a plan did arrive, drawn from the Web site of Jeff Galloway, whose advice to alternately run and walk a long-distance race had so resonated with Bryan.

On Bruce's birthday, both brothers indeed met their goal of completing a half-marathon together, but Bruce knew that Bryan wouldn't let him stop there. And so, on February 28, 2009, Bruce found himself lining up at the starting line of the Cowtown Marathon in Fort Worth. His goal, this time, was 26.2 miles—twice the distance he'd run in San Antonio. Only this time, he would not have his brother at his side, which gave him more than a little pause.

Bryan had sent his regrets. He needed to be at home, 265 miles away.

Yet Bruce, an inch shorter but blessed with far more hair than his sibling, who was three years his junior, didn't have much opportunity to focus on Bryan's absence. The temperature at the start of the race was hovering in the low thirties, and the wind howled at fifteen to twenty miles an hour, with some gusts topping thirty. At one point the headwind was so strong that Bruce and other competitors felt as if they had come to a dead stop.

Right around mile 3, Bruce noticed a man dressed in running gear dart from the crowd, right onto the course.

That guy is going to get in big trouble, Bruce thought, *and hey, he looks like my brother.*

And then: *Holy crap, I think it is my brother!*

Bruce wondered if he were hallucinating, though it seemed awfully early in his first marathon to be doing so.

He wasn't. The previous evening, Bryan, Debbie, and Taylour had driven to Fort Worth to execute a plan under a cloak of strict secrecy. Debbie and Taylour would position themselves on the sidelines, the better to get Bruce's attention with a cowbell. And then Bryan would dart onto the course to give his brother a lift.

Since this was soon after his marathon in Houston, Bryan didn't feel he should run the entire 26.2 miles here. Instead, he planned to run a mile and a half alongside Bruce, beginning around miles 3, 8, 12, and 21.

After each segment, Debbie and Taylour would meet Bryan nearby with the car, to ferry him to his next destination. From mile 22 on, Bryan planned to accompany Bruce right into the final chute, stopping just before the finish line.

The plan worked like a charm, and Bruce was especially grateful at mile 22, when he began to teeter a bit with dehydration. But some water and a few bites of banana sufficed, and a cool tailwind helped him navigate the final mile and easily cross the finish line. Two years after he turned fifty, Bruce felt Bryan had given him an enormous gift. By forcing himself "out of his Barcalounger" and whipping himself into shape, Bryan had transformed not just his life but his brother's.

"It does not surprise me," Bruce said a short while later, in reference to all his brother had accomplished in those months after that emergency room visit. "I've always wanted to find a shirt for him that refers to that Sammy Hagar song, 'I Can't Drive 55.' Bryan can't, either. When he puts his mind to something, it's all out."

That day, Bruce pledged to himself that he would repay the favor to his brother—not to compete in Ironman Arizona (he considered himself neither a swimmer nor a cyclist) but to at least be there in Tempe to cheer him on.

But Bryan, in his Ironman quest, was hardly content to inspire just one person. Like Leanne Johnson, he wanted his journey to have a greater meaning. It was around this time that he put up a post on his blog letting his friends and training partners know that he had signed up for the Janus Charity Challenge as part of Ironman Arizona. The recipient of any donations he received, as well as any matching funds from Janus, would be the Lance Armstrong Foundation. Bryan wrote:

> One of my employees is going through chemo, my Mom is a survivor and my Dad, father-in-law and mother-in-law all died of cancer. Additionally, I am going to carry a list of names of cancer survivors and victims with me during Ironman Arizona. They will help me get through 140.6. If any of you have names of anyone you would like to add to the list, please email me.

Bryan also provided a link to the Web site that Janus had set up for every athlete who registered for the challenge, so that they could easily make a donation with the push of a button. Bryan had yet to resolve how exactly he would carry whatever names he collected on his body during the Ironman, but he knew he had plenty of time to think that through.

As for Bryan's own conditioning for Ironman, he was admittedly—and deliberately—taking it slow. He had heard so many stories about Ironman aspirants who'd overdone it, gotten injured, or peaked too soon, and he was determined to learn from their mistakes. As Bryan put it, he was "keeping the running especially light, trying to let the hips/glutes loosen up"—the reader may recall his earlier lament about that gluteus maximus—"before I start putting bigger mileage on them again."

Still, like so many triathletes, Bryan worried that he wasn't training enough. A group of friends from his health club were cycling for hours on the weekends in anticipation of a forthcoming race that was not on Bryan's training plan.

"I feel bad," Bryan wrote, "but I don't think they are going to worry about me during my long rides/runs in Sept/Oct."

In fact, they would worry, but not for any reason Bryan had imagined.

Having been sidelined by the bout of bronchitis, Tracy Tucker-Georges was particularly excited to wake up on the first Sunday morning in March with the knowledge that she was going for a bike ride. Her first 70.3, or half-Ironman, was about a month away, and the previous afternoon Tracy had gorged herself in anticipation on equipment at a shop called Helen's in Santa Monica.

"I got new pedals and a seat for Penelope," Tracy wrote in her online journal, before adding, "OK, the seat is really for me." At another shop she picked up a pair of carbon fiber triathlon bike shoes and a set of tires. The sales assistant who sold Tracy the tires offered to put them on her bike. "Being the big girl that I am," she told him, "I need to do it myself."

By the following Saturday a sweltering fever had come on suddenly, and her doctor traced it to an infection in her inner ear. "I had just gotten

over a cold/bronchitis, had a good week or so then started having head-
aches, dizziness and nausea," she wrote, with palpable frustration, on her
blog. She was put on a course of antibiotics and ordered to stay out of the
pool.

"Now the problem with all this is that it has put a little crimp in my
workouts," she wrote. She added:

> I guess I'm writing this because I'm feeling nervous about
> my upcoming 70.3. I feel like my training is not where it needs
> to be. Maybe it's just that I have only 3 weeks left. And I am
> going to assume [she actually wrote *ass-u-me*] that it's normal
> to feel some anxiety.

By midweek she was feeling a different kind of discomfort. With her
head clear again, she climbed onto the brand-new seat she'd bought a few
weeks earlier and headed out for a long ride.

"Well," she wrote that night, "after approximately 90+ miles, it was
quite clear that my saddle and my 'girlie bits' were not getting along." She
soon exchanged that seat for another, before providing an update.

"I rode for just over an hour tonight," Tracy reported, "and so far it
seems to be working wonderfully. The girlie bits were very happy and I
was able to get in the aero position, which I could not do on my long ride
3 days ago."

As it turned out, getting herself into the aero position—in which a
rider hunches low and forward, the better to limit wind resistance—was
much harder for Tracy than she had let on on her blog. In fact, she had
been battling severe back problems since the previous August. At that
time, after completing an event known as the Santa Barbara Long Course
Triathlon, she had been told by a back specialist that she had a sacral
fracture at the base of her spine. She was ordered "not to run while the
fracture healed" and "not to ride out of the saddle." Swimming, mercifully,
was allowed.

She had also learned from that examination that she had something
called severe degenerative disk disease at her L3-4 and L4-5 vertebrae.
"Which translates," she wrote, "to bone-on-bone, no cushion, disc desic-
cation & arthritis!!!" She continued:

I know, I know: hang up the damn running shoes & just ride the flats, right? The problem with that? I DON'T WANT TO DO THAT. I want to keep on training & racing even though it is really kicking my ass! Well, my back, actually, which then radiates down to my butt cheek & hamstring. Especially with the running.

So just walk . . . right? Yes, that is a possibility, especially given that I am not really a runner anyway . . . it just means I will be that much slower during the "running" portion of my triathlon—also known as My Quest Not To Be The Last Person To Cross The Finish Line.

Tracy returned to "Dr. Steve," as he was known to her readers, in late March to have some updated radiographs taken of her lower back and sacrum. "It still looks crappy," Tracy said, paraphrasing. Again she was told that running was not good for her. "Again," she wrote, "I feel like crying & feel like I really picked a bad sport to fall in love with."

She had no intention, however, of standing down. "Remember," she wrote, "that is what this blog is all about. My road to Ironman." And so, with the expertise and experience of a nurse, and the determination of an admittedly "crazy" endurance athlete, she wrote herself the following prescription:

Keep taking my anti-inflammatories, go to physical therapy, ice my ass, take narcotics & alcohol together . . . oops— maybe not that last part, but it sure does help. There's nothing like a Darvocet & a Bloody Mary.***

That triple asterisk directed the reader's eye to a warning seemingly lifted from a cigarette box—one that was intended, it seemed, as much for the writer as her audience:

"Kids, don't try this at home."

Soon after dawn broke on the first Sunday in April, Tracy was among the first athletes to arrive at the first transition area (known universally as

T1) of the Ironman 70.3 in Oceanside, California. She had been up since 3:30 that morning, wondering whether her battered body could possibly withstand the exertion of a 1.2-mile swim in the ocean, followed by a hilly 56 miles on her bike and the 13.1-mile run she was dreading. She would be accompanied that day by her training partner, Vit, who began his mission to keep her relaxed and distracted as soon as Tracy and her husband picked up Vit and his wife, Lola. Vit was outfitted in camouflage shorts and knee-length compression socks, which are intended to fend off cramping in triathletes' legs but looked, to Tracy's eye, better suited to an octogenarian roaming a supermarket aisle in South Florida.

As she eased her bike into the rack in the area where she would ready herself for her swim—and, afterward, make the change from swimmer to cyclist—Tracy felt at peace. But that feeling was short-lived.

"It is one of my biggest pet peeves," she explained. "Some dumb chick shows up late and feels it is her prerogative to fit her bike and her gear into an area that is already filled. She knocks off the helmet on the bike next to her and feels obligated to tell us how all the bikes need to be stacked!"

Tracy desperately wanted to tell her, "Well, kiss off, bitch!"

Things began to look up when Tracy connected with two other training friends, G-Money and H.R. Pufnstuff, both of whom she'd accompanied the previous fall to Ironman Arizona. And then, it was time to swim. The thousand or so women competing that day were wearing white caps. And when her age group, or wave, was called—as luck would have it, Tracy was in Wave 13, all women ages forty-five to forty-nine—she jumped into the ocean and paddled out to a buoy about a hundred yards away. She was more excited, she thought, than nervous, and she knew she had to "just keep swimming." And, she wrote, "that is exactly what I do." As she told it:

> I have a really nice swim. I find a nice clean line without a ton of people to crawl over or hit in the face, etc. I do get kicked in the face once, causing my goggle lens to be dislodged from my eyeball. No biggie—I'm able to get it back on without a problem.

Before she knew it, Tracy had climbed from the water and was back at her bike in T1. With her bike shoes on and clipped into Penelope's pedals, she was off. She had left the transition area so quickly, in fact, that she would have to maneuver to slide her warmers—which looked a bit like paper-towel holders, only more elastic—onto her forearms, followed by gloves, all while on the bike.

During the first ten miles of what would be a fifty-six-mile ride, her legs felt as if they were made of lead. But soon she found her groove, stopping only long enough for a bathroom break at a Porta-Potty at mile 29—a stop she would find especially memorable because of a Marine who had stationed himself outside and who, for reasons unknown to Tracy, kept barking "Ooo-rah!" as if he were guarding a base latrine.

"When I get back on my bike," Tracy said later, "what to my wondering eyes should appear? A rather steep hill that would require a small gear." It would also require some stamina from that balky back—the one that didn't necessarily appreciate her lifting herself out of the saddle, the better to get leverage. But, Tracy wrote later:

> I don't get discouraged. I'm excited to just take the hill as it comes. "Live in the moment," as Vit says. I have fun with that hill. I talk to other people, and watch them go by me, watch them as I go by. Watch one gal hit the curb & almost tip over! (Glad she doesn't).

The remaining twenty-five miles or so were, blissfully, "uneventful," but as soon as she arrived in T2, where she would trade her bike shoes for her running sneakers, Tracy began to experience "some horrible back pain." She'd taken just a few steps onto the run course when, she decided, it was "time for some medication."

Her drug of choice? Darvocet, a prescription narcotic she broke in half with her teeth.

The first quarter-mile or so was sandy beach, but by mile 1 she felt the need to take the other half.

Yup, I'm doping, she thought. And, in light of that sobering doctor's visit just a few weeks earlier, this was not a good omen. She still had twelve miles to go.

The run course was laid out over two loops, which meant that as Vit, H.R., and G-Money were concluding their first lap, each ran into Tracy as she was beginning hers. "I'm happy to see all my boys," she recounted later. "I'm also thrilled to see some great friends on the course out there with big smiles, cheers & kisses." As her spirits climbed, Tracy began to forget about the searing pain in her back. To the extent that she was occasionally distracted, it was only by the blisters she developed on the bottom of each foot, which, she soon realized, "squished with every step."

As she reached the homestretch, Tracy recalled:

> When my two loops are done I get to make the left-hand turn into the final stretch to the finish. Oh, boy, does that feel good. I see my hubby, tons of people cheering for me & coming over to the finish line feeling delirious. H.R. was there to put the medal [the one awarded to every finisher] around my neck.
>
> *What are you doing volunteering?* I think. Even though he's done and finished the race . . .
>
> I'm a bit loopy. Vit is there. G-Money, too. And there are hugs & kisses all around. I'm extremely happy to have my 1st 70.3 under my belt.

Tracy had finished the race in 7 hours, 22 minutes, and 17 seconds. If it took her twice as long to do a full Ironman, that time would translate to just under 15 hours, leaving her a cushion of two hours to meet the 17-hour Ironman cutoff. Moreover, for all her aches and concerns, she had race-walked her way through the half-marathon at Oceanside that day in 2 hours, 56 minutes, and 4 seconds, a personal best.

As good as she felt, though, and as proud as she was, Tracy told each of her "boys" and her husband soon after the race that she did not think she would be able to do Ironman Arizona. Based on her experience this day, she said, Arizona would simply be too hard.

Her friends and family told her not to think about it, and to enjoy the moment. She decided she would.

"It wasn't until dinner—well the cocktail part of dinner—that I was ready again to go do Ironman!!" Tracy wrote in her postrace report a few days later. "Yeah, baby, let's do it, IMAZ November 22, 2009, here I come!!"

If preparing for any triathlon—let alone an Ironman—is akin to juggling a bicycle pump, kickboard, and running shoes in the air at once, then Leanne Johnson's daily life was beginning to take on some of the elements of a circus in early 2009.

While, unlike Tracy Tucker, she had no children underfoot, she was trying to simultaneously prepare for Ironman Arizona and the Boston Marathon. She was also striving to avoid the accidents that always seemed to plague her and tending to the injuries that never seemed to go away completely. And then there was her work, as a trained nurse working full-time for a clinical research company, where she investigated the safety of drugs being considered for government approval.

Something was always going to get short shrift, and for a while it was her swimming, the element of the triathlon with which she felt least comfortable.

She had begun her training that year, on a Sunday in early January, by jumping into the outdoor pool at her health club in Wilmington, North Carolina—the outside temperature was about forty-five, the water about eighty-four—only to climb out and jump in again. "It was overcast and not really all that warm out, but we figured the cool air would make the pool feel warmer," she wrote in her online diary. "It did seem to help." It was the first time she'd been in a pool at all in three months. With Scott crisscrossing the water in the lane next to her, she swam a little over a thousand yards (about forty lengths), most of it front crawl, in just under twenty-five minutes—about 2 minutes, 11 seconds for every hundred yards. While her pace was somewhat leisurely, she could take some comfort that, at that rate, she would be able to complete the swim portion of Ironman Arizona in a little over an hour.

"Today's goal was just to get in the pool," she said. "Mission accomplished."

Still, no Ironman aspirant is ever quite free of anxiety or worry until the goal has been fully met, and this was no exception for Leanne. Her right shoulder—which she had broken a year earlier on yet another fall, this one involving a railroad crossing on a Sunday group ride—was throbbing as she left the pool.

"It felt okay, about a 2 on the pain scale, with 10 being worst," she said. "But I still feel like my shoulder is a tight elastic band. Hopefully the more I swim, the more it will loosen up."

Her second swim of the year was two weeks later, on a Monday night. This time she went further and broke up her freestyle laps into intervals, alternating straight laps with drills involving a pull buoy between her legs and kickboards.

"Felt slow," she said afterward, "but that's to be expected. Goal of the week is to swim 3 times. One down, 2 to go!" Perhaps most significant, she reported no shoulder pain. Leanne was on her way.

But that night's swim would constitute something of a reprieve. On the first Saturday in February, she drove down to her health club pool only to find that the heater was out again, and that swimmers were being redirected to a nearby YMCA. Scott was bowling, so Leanne decided to go to the Y, "to try to get in as much as my shoulder could handle." She swam for nearly an hour, and nearly a mile, once again alternating sprint drills with those that entailed props like buoys and kickboards. While she felt good about her strokes, her shoulder still nagged. "My pain level gets to be about a 3 or 4 when I first start, and then I have a dull ache afterwards," she wrote. "I may try taking Advil before I swim to see if it helps."

The following morning, Leanne and Scott decided to take a bike ride—not with the big group they often joined but the two of them alone. They chose Wrightsville Beach, a narrow spit of sand lined with kitschy oceanfront hotels and wooden beach houses that looked fragile enough to blow over in a hurricane, as they sometimes did. The couple decided they would do three laps around the beach on the sandy pavement, nearly thirty miles in total. It was windy, but the sun was out, and both felt good. But as Leanne pulled into a left-hand turn lane and headed toward a stoplight, she found she couldn't get one of her bike shoes unclipped from its pedal so that she might have a leg on which to balance as she came to rest.

Toppling over, she stopped her fall with her left wrist.

"It's a bit tender but I think it just might be bruised," she wrote afterward. Still, no one would argue with the thought that consumed her afterward: *I'm definitely an accident waiting to happen.*

While her wrist improved over the next few days, she continued to be stymied by issues related to basic coordination. On a Friday in late February, for example, she strapped her road bike into a stationary trainer in her garage, but the entire apparatus kept sliding across the slippery concrete floor as she attempted to ride in place.

A few weeks later she had another scare:

> I decided to ride the trainer in the garage today. It was pouring rain. As I was getting my bike down from the bike rack I noticed a snake. That's snake number two we've had in our garage. Scott had captured the last one (and named it Fluffy) and we released it about a week ago. I am not sure if this is the same one coming back to us or another one. I grabbed a bucket and threw it over the top of the snake but I am not sure if it landed on him or not. Scott's up in Raleigh all week in training for work so it's just going to be me and Fluffy this week. I may not be riding the trainer much!

Meanwhile, Leanne was in the process of switching jobs. After two years, she had decided to end her position at the pharmaceutical firm to return to her first love: full-time nursing. She would be assigned to a hospital not far from her gym, working only three days most weeks, but on shifts that would last upwards of twelve hours, a regimen so exhausting that it would make it difficult to squeeze in a workout on either side. Sometimes it took an entire day just to recover from that pace.

"I am a little nervous about how I am going to get my Ironman training in," Leanne wrote in her online journal. "But lots of nurses do the Ironman so I am sure I will figure it out."

Early on, she found she was having trouble striking that balance. "Another 12 hour shift at the hospital," she wrote on March 19. "I wanted to go swim after work but I got out late and the pool was getting ready to close. A week later, the story was the same: "Grrrrrrrrrrrrrrrrrr . . . no workout today as I had to work at the hospital. I am getting frustrated. These 12 hour shifts do not leave me anytime to workout!"

On a Saturday in late March, a merciful day off, Leanne and her friend Andrea set aside two hours to run from Wrightsville Beach to Mayfaire, a quaint village of specialty shops and restaurants, a round trip of about fifteen miles. Although Leanne notched a formidable average pace of about 8 minutes and 13 seconds a mile, it left her unsatisfied.

"It was colder than I thought it would be and I underdressed," she confided to her journal afterward. But of more concern was that, as she reported, she "tripped on my own footing and landed on my left shoulder again. It's sore today and feels like it may be a bit bruised."

A few days later she awoke to an unexpected rainstorm at seven o'clock on a Saturday morning. She had planned to do a road ride that morning, but with a friend's baby shower scheduled at 10:00 A.M., she couldn't wait for the weather to clear. And so she again climbed on her garage bike trainer and set off on a pedal to nowhere. Her game plan was to ride for an hour, but with fifteen minutes to go, the entire apparatus tripped over, taking Leanne with it.

"I was able to grab a hold of a box in the garage which broke my fall," she said. "I seem to be unsteady on and off the roads on my bike." Leanne decided this was a sign telling her to stop, so she pulled on a pair of running shoes and did a 2.6-mile loop around the neighborhood, ending on a high. "The run felt good off the bike," she said.

Still, she found herself preoccupied, and not just by her bouts of clumsiness, which she knew could prove devastating in the lead-up to Arizona if she couldn't get them under control. There was also this: "Tomorrow is my last 20 miler before Boston," she wrote. "Twenty-three days and counting. I think I am finally getting a bit nervous." Meanwhile, Ironman Arizona and her pledge to Liam's parents were never far from her mind.

"My Run for Liam Janus Charity Challenge donation page shows I have raised $1,150 so far for the American Heart Association," she wrote in late March. "At this point my goal is $5,000 and I would like to be able to raise more. But for now just reaching the $5,000 mark may be more of a struggle than I had anticipated."

"Every dollar counts," she added. "I need to start brainstorming for some more ideas."

The packet welcoming Leanne Johnson to the Boston Marathon arrived with the mail on Saturday, March 28. "I am finally starting to get butterflies!" Leanne wrote in her online journal. Inside the packet was the card that she would hand in to receive her race bib. She learned she would be in the second wave, which starts thirty minutes after the first. That was fine with Leanne—she was just happy to have qualified, and to be running— but she was disappointed that her running partner, Andrea, would be in the first wave. "So we won't be running the race together ☹" she wrote. "She'll finish before me, but I guess that's ok . . . that'll just be one more supporter at the finish line."

The following morning Leanne headed out for a twenty-mile run with three other friends from the Road Runners Club. This would be one of her last big runs before Boston, and the weather was not cooperating. The group was alternately pelted with rain and baked with sun as the coastal air hung heavily with humidity. Over their final ten miles, they crossed three bridges—mercifully, Leanne stayed on her feet—and then ran to Wilmington's downtown colonial waterfront, where the group pretended they were climbing Boston's infamous "Heartbreak Hill."

Her time was three hours even, for a pace of just under nine minutes per mile. At that pace, Leanne would be within striking distance of her goal for Boston: a time of less than four hours.

While that workout, or even a fraction of it, would have constituted a day's effort for most mortals, Leanne was a triathlete. That afternoon she and Scott went to the pool, where they warmed up and then broke up a 1,500-meter swim—about sixty-five lengths of the pool—into three intervals, before cooling down. "Tonight we're going to relax and put our feet up!" Leanne said.

The following Thursday, with eighteen days to go before Boston, Leanne was cross-training again. She once again headed for downtown Wilmington to run its cobblestone hills, this time with Andrea and their friends Misty and Erin. The group ran for about an hour and was done just before 7:00 A.M. But instead of driving home, Leanne headed straight for her health club to catch a "body pump" weight-lifting class and a thirty-minute swim in a pool with water pocked by the day's cool drizzle. Understandably, Leanne wrote, "my warm up felt slow and I felt really stiff." But once she began the heart of her training—seven intervals of 100 meters each—she hit her groove. By mid-morning, though, her shoulders and arms had stiffened.

Little wonder that two days later, Leanne worried she was overdoing things. After a fifty-mile bike ride, much of it heading into the wind, along the course of the White Lake Half Ironman—in preparation for her next milestone after Boston—she wrote:

> I am SORE. I think I may have slightly pulled a groin muscle but I will ice that tonight and hope that it will be fine for tomorrow's 15-mile run. I needed this ride. I am not very confident right now about the half Ironman we have coming up in six weeks b/c I have been so focused on Boston.
>
> Note to self: you shouldn't plan to train for both a marathon and a half Ironman at the same time. You will become the jack of all trades, and master of none.

The following day, just fifteen days before Boston, Leanne concluded that she had in fact pulled that right groin muscle. "But luckily," she said, after completing a fifteen-mile run, "it doesn't really bother me too much when I run. It feels like it just needs some ice and a good massage."

After she logged a thirteen-and-a-half-hour shift at the hospital the following day, Scott made Leanne a dinner of his "famous quesadillas." The couple then settled in to watch Leanne's favorite show, the weight-loss reality series *The Biggest Loser*, but Leanne was so spent, she soon fell asleep on the couch.

Saturday, April 11, was Leanne's thirtieth birthday. "9 days til Boston!" she scrawled across the top of her online journal that morning. "I can't believe it's single digits."

> Today I am officially a member of the 30-something club! They say your 30's are better than your 20's. I find that hard to believe b/c 20's have been incredible. But . . . I am looking forward to it. Already this year is looking to be a great year. I'm turning 30, running the Boston Marathon and attempting to become an Ironman. What more could a girl ask for?
>
> Scott got me an awesome Aero helmet for my birthday. He even decorated it himself with Canadian flags and maple leafs. The best part was he found stickers that looked like each of our cats (Tyrone and Bella) and put them on the back of the

helmet. I opened it up and he wrote, "Look who has your back!" It was so funny. I love it.

To celebrate the occasion, Leanne noted, she and Scott were "heading out for a 50 mile ride today!"

Leanne was up well before dawn broke over Boston on Monday, April 20, a Massachusetts state holiday called Patriots Day. After a shower and a quick breakfast of a bagel slathered with peanut butter, she, Andrea, and their friend Sami were out the door of the apartment they had rented and headed for downtown Boston. There they would board the buses that would take them and thousands of other runners to the race start.

"The atmosphere was very relaxed," she said later. "I didn't feel the usual anticipation or competitiveness like at some races. I think most of us were just taking it all in and excited to be running the Boston Marathon."

While Leanne had decided she'd be satisfied with any time under four hours, she ratcheted up the pressure on herself a bit when the race organizers were passing out so-called pace bracelets, which were emblazoned with various finish times. Leanne chose "3:20"—3 hours, 20 minutes.

"I didn't really think I could do that but I thought at least this way I could use it as a guide, thinking my paces would be a bit slower, and that I could at least run a 3:30."

The garden-variety advice given to runners participating in Boston is to start out conservatively, saving precious energy for the hills of the second half of the course. Leanne, by contrast, would typically run a race by trying to maintain the same pace throughout. She would later acknowledge that she probably ran the first thirteen miles at Boston at too quick a pace—less than 7 minutes and 30 seconds per mile, much quicker than on any of those training runs near the Carolina coast. The early part of the run was mostly flat and even downhill at times.

That all changed about midcourse with the first of several climbs— most famously, Heartbreak Hill, at mile 20, which had occupied so many of Leanne's thoughts during her training. She needn't have worried, she realized, as there were so many spectators screaming so loudly and packed so tightly along the race route that she felt as if they were carrying her up the hill on their shoulders.

Her real struggles came on some of the downhills that followed. "The last mile seemed long," she said. "But I think it was because I was just ready to be done." And then, after 3 hours, 23 minutes, and 19 seconds— run at an average pace of 7 minutes and 46 seconds per mile—Leanne was done.

> As soon as I crossed the finish line I felt exhausted and my legs felt horrible. We had to keep walking through the line as they keep you moving. They give you water, remove your chip, give you your medal, then your warming blanket, then food. I could barely walk but I think it actually helped me in the long run to continue to move.
>
> Andrea found me at the end when we were picking up our race bags. I was SO glad to see her. After the race we found our way out of the runner area to find our significant others. I was EXCITED to see Scott. He gave me a hug which completed my race day perfectly.

Leanne and Scott flew back to North Carolina the following day, a Tuesday, with Leanne due back at the hospital for a twelve-hour shift on Wednesday. She ended up calling in sick that morning. "Just not feeling 100 percent today," she confided to her journal. "My legs are still sore and I just couldn't see myself standing on my feet for 12 hours caring for patients." She was also sniffling and had a sore throat, and feared she'd caught a cold over the weekend.

After unpacking, doing some laundry, buying groceries, and napping, Leanne decided to get on the trainer in the garage for an "easy spin" that she hoped might loosen her quads, the only part of her body that remained sore from Boston. It didn't really help. For all she'd accomplished two days earlier, "I just feel like I have lost my mojo," she said. "Maybe it'll come back soon."

It had better, she reasoned. With Boston in her rearview mirror, the Arizona desert lay just beyond the horizon.

CHAPTER 5

Walking on Air with My Chest Puffed Up

S eth Cannello knew when he registered for Ironman Arizona that a marathon awaited him. But it wasn't just the prospect of a 26.2-mile run that was weighing on his mind. By early May, with Ironman Arizona a little over six months away, he had yet to run even ten miles in a single outing. In fact, at this point in his Ironman training—really pre-training, because he'd not begun to prepare in earnest in and around his Colorado Springs home—he'd run just nine miles, and only once.

"When I was in the Army," he recalled, "I ran three or four times a week, but only two or three miles at a time." Still, he was supremely confident that he would prevail in Arizona, almost through sheer will, though at this point the date seemed so far off on the calendar, he was barely giving it heed. Contrary to the advice in many triathlon training plans, Seth decided he would save his first marathon for Ironman Arizona. As he explained:

> Everyone always asks me why I'm doing an Ironman. They want to know if it's because I have something to prove. The easy answer would be to say that I want to show people that I've recovered from having cancer and that the struggle of going through all the surgeries and chemotherapy is driving me to push myself. Or that turning forty somehow

inspired me to challenge myself. But neither is the case. The
real reason is because I'm a cocky idiot.

It wasn't only the military contractors extolling the race's virtues
while working out in the Air Force fitness center that Seth ran that had
inspired him to make the attempt. Hearing so many members of the gym
return from any number of races had left him wondering, *Why not me?*

He almost felt like Cinderella, left behind to literally sweep the floor
(at times) while others went to the big dance.

> People will often tell me that they are training for an event
> ranging from a long bike ride to a marathon. In my head, I
> always tell myself that I could do whatever event they are
> planning on doing. I'm not sure if that's true or not, but in my
> head, I believed it. There was one exception to that rule. When
> someone told me they were training for an Ironman, I always
> thought there's no freaking way I could ever do an Ironman.
> I'm always encouraging other people to run in events to train
> hard so that they can compete in sports, races, etc., but since
> I left the Army I never have physically pushed myself. I'm
> tired of being a hypocrite. So I picked the one race I thought I
> couldn't finish.

As he toggled between confidence and—as his parting sentence above
makes clear—a few shades of doubt, Seth began to outline the major con-
tours of his training. The first step was to commit himself to doing some
sort of organized race or ride once or twice a month, from May through
November. Another goal was to use every Saturday or Sunday ("within
reason," he said) through September to "ramp up" his distances until he
was doing at least three-fourths of an actual Ironman. During the week
he would continue the loose routine that had so far served him well: a spin
class at lunchtime on Monday, with an occasional swim of forty-five minutes or so after work; a run of about an hour or so on Tuesday, perhaps
with another swim after work; and early-morning runs or bike rides on
Wednesdays and Fridays, while his children were still asleep, because he
was responsible for taking them to school on those days.

Seth began his campaign to kick those efforts up a notch on May 9, a chilly, rainy Saturday, when he drove about an hour from Colorado Springs to Aurora for his first-ever half-marathon, which was being staged at Buckley Air Force Base. With the temperature that morning hovering around forty degrees, Seth's immediate concern was his Raynaud's, the side effect of his chemo that deprived his extremities of blood in the cold. In fact, it had been such a raw spring that he'd not run outside much at all prior to the race. As he lined up that morning at the start, the sky overcast and the jagged Front Range hovering above, Seth recalled feeling that he was "concerned that I wasn't going to do well." On top of that, the wind was occasionally lashing the competitors with gusts of up to twenty miles an hour, and the course was hilly. Nonetheless, he had a goal: a final time of 1 hour and 44 minutes, or about eight minutes per mile. In the end, he not only finished but beat his goal by nearly two minutes overall.

While he was momentarily buoyed by his performance, reality quickly set in. As he put it later:

> I'm finding out that I'm not that fast anymore. I've always played sports, and working in a fitness center has allowed me to stay active, but I'm certainly not your typical Ironman. I really just jumped into this without too much thought or consideration on the amount of time/effort it would take.

One of Seth's other problems was that he had "horrible" knees and had endured several surgeries on them over the years that made it difficult to train hard every day. Like so many who commit to an Ironman far in advance, he worried constantly that he would get injured well before November and not even be able to start the race, let alone finish.

"And once you sign up for the event," he said, "you can't drop out. They won't refund your money."

Of course, entrants *can* drop out, but the idea of losing more than $500 in registration fees alone—only in extraordinary cases did the Ironman organizers refund competitors, the better to ensure that no one signed up on a whim—was a possibility that Seth, his family budget already stretched, did not want to contemplate.

At the least, Seth now knew that he could do a half-marathon. But like so many triathletes, he got the most jitters contemplating the swim. Setting aside the not insignificant question of how he would be able to tolerate the temperature of the lake on race day in Arizona—sixty-four degrees, if he was lucky—he wondered if he could swim as far as 2.4 miles. In the relatively placid confines of the base pool, he could swim a mile in about thirty-five minutes. At that pace, he'd probably have no problem completing the swim portion of Ironman Arizona under the 2-hour-20-minute limit—even factoring in that it was an open-water swim with more than two thousand competitors flapping and flailing at once. Seth's concern was that, when he swam as part of his training, he typically did the breaststroke, as opposed to the front crawl that most triathletes use most of the time. But in Seth's case, his heart rate during the breaststroke—a vigorous but manageable 125 beats per minute—would escalate to 150 beats per minute whenever he switched over to the crawl. His heart pounding, he could usually go only about fifty yards, or one pool length, before having to stop or change strokes.

If the front crawl is akin to running, then the breaststroke is more like a slow jog or walk. In the crawl, a swimmer is propelled by a pulsing flutter kick and by the arms alternately leaving the water, slicing the air and then reentering the water with momentum as they power backward. In the breaststroke, by contrast, one's arms are always fighting the resistance of the water—they never actually come out—as are the legs, which mostly move sideways before whipping inward. The head, meanwhile, comes all the way out of the water to draw breath, like that of a seal, rather than rolling sideways briefly for a gulp of air in the crawl. The breaststroke is, in short, a less efficient and more labor-intensive endeavor.

"Here's my dilemma," Seth explained. "I could train doing the front crawl and *hope* that my abilities increase, or I can keep my heart rate down and save myself for the bike and run by swimming the whole way using the breaststroke." But could he sustain the breaststroke for nearly two and a half miles and finish the swim under the 2-hour-20-minute limit? He had no idea. For now, with Ironman Arizona six months away, he would continue doing what he was doing—avoiding the front crawl and hoping for the best.

If Seth ever lacked for perspective in the midst of such challenges, there was always the example being set by his father, then seventy, a retired military officer himself who lived nearby in Gleneagle. While Seth worried about such seemingly trivial matters as how best to swim or how he could find the time to run, his father was battling inoperable brain cancer, which had been diagnosed the day after Christmas in 2008. As summer 2009 approached, he was completing his second course of gamma radiation and his second round of chemotherapy.

"The first didn't work," Seth recalled. "It really messed him up. They gave him steroids to reduce the swelling in his brain and it changed his personality a lot. It also made him do some strange things. Luckily he doesn't have that problem this time." In fact, his father seemed to be improving.

In years past, as June approached, Seth and his father would be plotting their latest fishing adventure, maybe on some remote lake at high elevation. This time his father had an even grander plan in mind: an August trip to Alaska. Seth thought it unlikely, given the state of his health, but kept August 7-10 open, just in case.

Like Seth, whom he did not know, Tom Bonnette had never quite gotten over the guilt he felt for laying out more than $500 on his Ironman Arizona registration, which he felt he could ill afford on a teacher's salary. In fact, by spring 2009, he still hadn't gotten around to fixing that balky power steering on the family minivan. Though the noise emanating from the steering column annoyed everyone, and sometimes required the strength of an Ironman just to turn around in a parking lot, he had been assured that the car was safe. He would put off the costly repair as long as he could.

Tom, who'd done a number of half-Ironman races around Arizona, including on parts of the course in Tempe where the full Ironman would be staged, was proceeding in his training without any comparable disruption or interruption. He did most of his running and biking in the early morning, a time when he found it easy to wake up—which he thought of not only as a function of working as a teacher for so many years but also a by-product of attention deficit disorder. Though the restlessness that had made him fidget as a student himself was largely a part of his past, he still struggled at times to find a sense of calm and peace; exercising long and hard, especially before work, would often soothe his mind for the day ahead. And, in the balance, he could continue to aim toward the goal he'd set for Ironman Arizona: not just to finish—he was confident he would do that—but to finish in less than twelve hours, a full five hours before the cutoff time that many average Joes would set as their target. As near as he could tell, based on the numbers registered by his digital Polar heart-rate monitor—on which he could record his various performances on land and in water—he was on track.

In fact, the most immediate challenge he faced in mid-May 2009 had nothing to do with the Ironman, at least not directly. After years of night classes, he had to turn in the final paper for his master's in education, electronically, by 12:01 A.M. on Monday, May 18. Not only did Tom feel a tremendous sense of accomplishment as that date drew near, but he was counting on the raise—an $8,000 bump in pay, effective immediately—that would increase his $53,193 annual salary by 15 percent, to more than $61,000. (This figure included a $2,000 raise just for teaching another year.) Only because of the prospect of being a bit more flush had he allowed himself to splurge on Ironman Arizona. Truth be told, he and his wife, Shannon, needed every dollar they could scrounge. The oldest of their three daughters would be heading to college in a couple of years, and there were many years remaining on the mortgage on the family's four-bedroom home. Meanwhile, as the nation grappled with a recession, everything seemed to cost more.

Tom was so excited to finish his master's that he actually pushed the button on his final paper—a 2,500-word summation of all he had learned in the program—the Wednesday before it was due, for, as he explained: "I was determined not to work my last weekend as an online student and go out on a date with my wife Saturday and do something fun with my kids Sunday after church and not feel preoccupied and stressed." This, in and of itself, was no small milestone. Like many of his students, Tom was forever turning in his papers minutes before the deadline.

The day after pushing the button on his final project, Tom said he was "walking on air with my chest puffed up."

But the feeling was fleeting. On Friday, at lunch, he learned that the Phoenix school district was freezing teachers' pay for the upcoming school year. While disappointed, Tom assumed the policy would apply only to the "years of service" annual bump that was part of his raise.

"That is fair in this economic climate," Tom reasoned. "All the districts in the U.S. seem to be freezing 'years of service.'" Moreover, the district, like others around the nation, had had millions of dollars pruned from its budget by the state legislature.

Tom was therefore stunned to learn that the wage freeze would also be applied to those teachers who had met the educational requirements for a "lane change" to a higher pay scale. In other words, while the time and money he'd spent on his master's, and the loans he still owed, had probably made him a better teacher, he would receive no financial reward for his efforts.

"I just thought it was ironic I found out about it during the very LAST week of my LAST class," he later observed, "only two days after I had submitted my LAST paper . . . EARLY!"

Of his $53,000 annual pay, Tom said: "I know certain people might look at this salary and figure I'm having a pity party. However, my wife is also a teacher with five more years' experience and makes less, actually. (Another district.)" He lamented that some people "do not value the impact teachers have on future work forces" and "might think of the art of teaching in the dynamic classrooms of today's society as robotic, glorified babysitting."

But at this point his worries were more pragmatic. Why, he wondered, had he indulged himself by paying the Ironman entry fee so long before his raise was safely in his pocket—not to mention his new bike frame "and all the other relatively minor expenses" involved in the run-up to an Ironman? "From a pure father-provider standpoint, these purchases didn't make much sense," he acknowledged. "However, I justified it by holding out hope that they would be a drop in the bucket compared to my higher teacher salary."

"Plus," he added, "I REALLY needed to do this thing! Scenes from the *Wide World of Sports* coverage of all those past Ironmans were bouncing around in my head for too long! I knew that I would never race on the Big Island of Hawaii, so this was the next best thing for my 'Bucket List.'"

In early May, Bryan Reece's thoughts were also turning to matters of education. On May 9, the same Saturday that Seth ran his first half-marathon in Aurora, Bryan and Debbie were seated with hundreds of other proud parents at the Bell County Expo Center. Their only daughter, Taylour, was graduating from the University of Mary Hardin-Baylor with a degree in sports management. "It was a wonderful day with grandparents and aunts and uncles and cousins," Bryan announced on *Left, Right, Repeat,* interrupting his usual programming of all tri training, all the time.

Still, there was only so much time to celebrate. "I am back to training after a nice Mother's Day with my mom, wife and daughter," he wrote Sunday night. By then he was already thinking about the next potential bump in the road to Ironman—an Olympic-distance swim-bike-run called the Capital of Texas Triathlon (CapTexTri), which was two weeks away. "I have taken it pretty easy so I don't overdo it before Ironman and get burned out," he wrote as he contemplated his upcoming triathlon. "I am just planning to enjoy the day . . . I know I will pay on the run." As a postscript, he added, "IM training plan starts Memorial Day—the same day as CapTexTri."

On the day of the CapTex, staged locally in San Antonio, Bryan noted that the thermometer read eighty-five degrees—which would have been a record high for Memorial Day in many parts of the country but was actually cooler than the day on which the same race had been staged a year earlier. Bryan felt undertrained soon after he began the swim portion of the day—a half-mile set in Lady Bird Lake—and yet, he managed to record a personal record in the water at that distance, with a time of just over a half-hour. And even though the twenty-six-mile bike course had been rerouted to add a few short but steep hills, Bryan took no longer to ride it than he had the year before, finishing it in under an hour and 20 minutes. He did similarly well on the run, finishing fifteen seconds faster overall than he had a year earlier.

"I feel very good right now," he wrote that afternoon in his online journal. "A little sleepy from the 4 A.M. wake-up but OK regardless."

At 9:15 on Friday night, after celebrating the end of a short workweek with a swim in the Life Time Fitness pool, he sat down at the computer in his home office and wrote four words on his blog—an announcement intended more as a challenge for himself than his friends and family.

"This is Week One."

"This is Week One of Ironman Arizona training," he explained. "I can't believe the plan has begun." Bryan had added a widget for the official Ironman countdown clock to his blog—it looked just like the digital read-out at the finish line—and any visitor to the site saw that Ironman Arizona was now only 177 days away. He then explained that, as part of the first week of what he considered his formal training, he would follow his efforts at CapTex on Monday with a fifty-mile bike ride on Saturday, a ride called the Tour de Cure. He had then scheduled another ride on Sunday, this one only twenty-five miles, "since I have some family duties."

Indeed, he and Debbie would be celebrating Taylour's twenty-first birthday. "By the way," Bryan wrote, "SHE GOT A JOB . . . SHE GOT A JOB . . . SHE GOT A JOB . . . she is gainfully employed as of three weeks from now. I am very proud of her and looking forward to watching this next step in her life." Though he didn't share it with his readers, Bryan was particularly pleased that Taylour had been hired as a salesperson in another branch of Life Time Fitness. In searching for a pitch to lure those seeking to get into better shape, she had a story she could tell: the way her father had changed, and quite possibly saved, his life by taking advantage of the chain's athletic offerings at an opportune moment.

The Friday night after her birthday, Bryan jumped into the Life Time pool to swim off the stresses of the week—like Tom, he was feeling the sting of the recession, though from the perspective of a harried investment adviser. He swam not especially long (about thirty minutes), but he swam hard. After drying off quickly and changing into shorts, he sprinted up the stairs to be on time (barely) for a Pilates class. "I really need some core work," he explained, "so this is one way I will get it, and it is mentally much easier for me than weights."

The following morning he was up early and back at the gym for a "hills" spin class—each participant was invited to crank the resistance on the bike as tight as could be tolerated. Bryan, of course, went even further. After class was over, he stayed in the empty studio and continued to ride for thirty minutes before joining the next class. All told, he had ridden 2 hours and 55 minutes. On Sunday he capped his weekend with a seventy-five-minute run, the South Texas air thick and humid but occasionally pierced by welcome breezes.

His veins coursing with adrenaline and endorphins, Bryan was clearly on a high that Sunday night. But he was perhaps most pleased by a gesture that had been made by his spin instructor, DeAdra, who had announced in her classes on Saturday that Bryan would compete in Ironman Arizona and was raising money for the Lance Armstrong Foundation. She had even passed out the business cards he'd had printed that included the Janus Charity Challenge Web site established to record his contributions, as well as the Web address for *Left, Right, Repeat*. DeAdra also passed on Bryan's request for names—letting their fellow spinners know that he was "compiling a list of people currently battling cancer as well as a list of those who have lost the battle" to carry with him on race day. In underscoring the request to those who buttonholed him personally after class, Bryan said: "I would love to have them along for inspiration. I would be honored. Their battle has been a lot more difficult than mine."

A few weeks later, on a Saturday night in late June, Bryan was relishing the afterglow from an eight-mile run followed by an eighty-minute bike ride. Again, though, his thoughts quickly turned to others—this time Marco Garsed, the owner of a local triathlon store. "Heard about Ironman Coeur d'Alene from a friend of mine today," Bryan wrote on his blog. "He had a very good race in very difficult conditions. A lot of rain and wind on the run. There was also chop on the swim and wind on the ride. But Marco persevered and he is once again, an Ironman. Congratulations, Ironman Marco."

"Also," Bryan wrote, "I am celebrating completion of a Half Ironman by a friend from Boston. Marianne just finished 70.3 miles under her own power. What an accomplishment—way to go Marianne. Next year . . . Ironman. You go, girl!

"I stand amazed at what men and women can do when they strike a goal—create a plan—and execute on that plan," he wrote, in concluding his blog post on that June night. "I am really looking forward to Arizona . . . but much work to be done between now and then.

"About 147 days of work," he added.

Right around the time Bryan Reece began his formal training plan for Ironman Arizona, Leanne Johnson did the same—but only after indulging in a bowl of mint chocolate chip ice cream, a rare treat, the night before at the home of her friends Anne Marie and Jeff. As a result, her stomach felt heavy the next morning, a Sunday, when she, Jeff, and a few other friends set off on a ten-mile run. Ultimately she seemed to burn off whatever she'd eaten and was able to sustain a good pace—about 8 minutes a mile—for a run that took 1 hour and 20 minutes. Noting that there were twenty-seven weeks until Ironman Arizona, Leanne took to her online journal to commit herself to the following plan for the remainder of the week:

MONDAY: work (then hopefully 30-60 min swim)
TUESDAY: channel swim [past the breakers, in the ocean waters off Wilmington], 60 min bike, Body Pump
WEDNESDAY: work (then hopefully 30-60 min swim or easy run after work)
THURSDAY: hills or channel swim or both, Body Pump
FRIDAY: OFF
SATURDAY: 2 hr ride

On the list of concerns she had as she prepared for Ironman Arizona, Leanne would have probably ranked her suspicion that her swimming was a liability alongside her struggles to exercise on those twelve-hour-plus workdays (to say nothing of her dangerous propensity for clumsiness). On the Wednesday after Memorial Day, though, she had a bit of a breakthrough. During a forty-two-minute swim with Scott in the channel—usually a source of anxiety, with its unpredictable current and choppy salt water—Leanne thought to herself, *I think I am finally starting to get it.* That night she opened her laptop and recorded her thoughts on her online journal:

> I've been swimming wrong all this time. I had not been pushing the water back on my down stroke and now I can tell how this makes a difference. I find I use my arms/shoulders more and legs less. And . . . I am able to slow my stroke down and get more distance with each stroke.

The following day, Scott presented Leanne with a book titled *Total Immersion: The Revolutionary Way to Swim Better, Faster, and Easier*. Its back cover promised "a thoughtfully choreographed series of skill drills—practiced in the mindful spirit of yoga—that can help anyone swim more enjoyably," as well as "a holistic approach to becoming one with the water and to developing a swimming style that's always comfortable," and "simple but thorough guidance on how to improve fitness and form." Within a week she was a third of the way through the book, and already able to incorporate one piece of advice in particular: that she lengthen her stroke.

The authors, Terry Laughlin and John Delves, explain, for example, that various studies of Olympic swimmers have shown that "the fastest swimmers took the fewest strokes." Thus, the authors write:

> [G]oal one for anyone who wants to swim better and faster is a longer stroke. This can happen in two ways: (1) more push—using your hands and feet to thrust your body farther through the water by making each stroke as powerful as possible; and (2) less drag—shaping your body so it's more friction-free, allowing it to travel farther with the power each of your strokes is already producing.

On June 1, after a busy day at work that lasted until 7:30, Leanne yet again pushed herself to go to the pool. After a three-hundred-meter warm-up and another three hundred meters of crawl, she swam an interval of five hundred meters—about twenty pool lengths—which, for the first time, took her less than ten minutes (9 minutes, 46 seconds, to be exact). "I think I have managed to lengthen my stroke a bit," she said, ecstatic at her progress. "I am still going to stick to working on swim technique for the next month or two and not focus so much on swim endurance. I have plenty of time for that this summer."

Since her ultimate goal was to improve her performance in three sports simultaneously, she sought to tweak her efforts on the bike as well. After a thirty-eight-mile morning ride around the same time—which Leanne and her friend Andrea finished in 2 hours, 15 minutes, at an Ironman-worthy pace of nearly seventeen miles per hour—the two women set out immediately on a one-and-a-half-mile run. (This drill is known in triathlon circles as a "brick," for "bike-run," and it is meant to simulate the transition that takes place between those two stages in an actual race.) "I just wanted to get my legs moving," Leanne explained. "My goal is to run after EVERY bike ride." She concluded: "Great workout today and was done before 10 A.M.! Gotta love it!"

CHAPTER 6

A Bright Pink Mohawk and a Skirt

Leanne hit the send button on the e-mail just after lunch on the last Tuesday in April. In the "To" field she had typed in the names of more than two dozen family members, including some in her native Canada, as well as friends and training partners. In the subject line she had written something intended not only to catch people's attention but to make her tough-guy, tattooed husband, who had survived so much, blush. *It is all for a good cause,* Leanne had thought as she typed, "Who wants to see Scott sporting a bright pink Mohawk and a skirt at the White Lake Half on May 9?"

In the text, Leanne explained that she was in a bit of a jam. "If you recall," she wrote, "I am raising money for the American Heart Association in honor of Liam Murray. Currently, I have raised $1,375." While that was no small accomplishment, the goal Leanne had set for herself was $5,000. Much of the money she had collected so far had come from a fund-raising night at the local branch of the Rita's Italian Ice chain, where Scott and Leanne had donned aprons to climb behind the counter to scoop. The manager had given them a portion of the night's take for Leanne's Ironman charity effort.

While Leanne still had more than six months to go, she felt sure that as she stepped up her training, on top of her already heavy work schedule, she would begin to neglect her charitable efforts and so had come up with a scheme, which she laid out in her e-mail. The upcoming half-Ironman,

White Lake, was a race in North Carolina set in and around the body of water where Scott had done his first triathlon—the one where his mother had met him tearfully at the end. In what sounded a little like a ransom note, Leanne wrote:

> Hi Guys,
>
> Scott has agreed to shave his hair into a Mohawk if $225 is donated to my Janus Charity Challenge Fund. If between now and Friday, May 8, the $225 is raised, Scott will shave his head and sport the Mohawk the ENTIRE race weekend. If a total of $500 is donated Scott will not only shave his hair into a Mohawk but he will also dye the Mohawk pink or orange or a color of his choice. (He doesn't know this yet!) And last but not least, if $750 Scott will also wear a skirt during the run portion of the race.

Although Scott typically wore his blondish-brown hair in a military-style, brushy buzz cut, he'd committed to growing it a bit longer over the next few weeks, if that's what it took to help Leanne's effort in Liam's memory.

It didn't take long for the people in Leanne and Scott's lives to respond to her plea. The following day on her training blog she wrote:

> Yesterday, we received over $400 in donations for my Janus Charity Challenge, so it looks like at this point Scott will be shaving his hair into a Mohawk for the race. He is close to having to dye it pink too! Hee, hee . . . I love it.

Leanne had given her friends and family a deadline for contributions of May 8, the Friday before the White Lake Half, and that Wednesday she sweetened the pot a bit. "Our friend Marty has also volunteered to be a part of this challenge," she wrote on her training blog. As many of her readers knew, Marty mapped out and led the informal bike rides that she and Scott often took along with a big group on weekends. "If $1,500 can be raised by Friday night at 8 pm, he will wear a pink tutu for the run portion of the Half." (Marty had hoped to do the Mohawk as well, but he worried it might have a negative impact on his work, as a senior vice president of a firm that provides continuing education to physicians.)

On Thursday, after her nursing shift, Leanne set out on a short run and then logged on to her computer to announce the results of her charitable challenge.

While earlier in the week she had in hand pledges of $880, she explained that she had nearly doubled that amount in just the past forty-eight hours. Many people, it seemed, wanted to see not only Scott in his getup, but Marty as well.

As a reward to her donors, Leanne then posted a series of photos that showed Scott's shaven head from various angles, which featured a thin lightning bolt Scott had shaped himself with an electric razor. And the hair that was left was unmistakably pink—Leanne assured her readers that she had colored it herself.

After that buildup, the race at White Lake was almost anticlimactic. Yet for all their goofing around in advance, it would prove a serious endeavor for both Leanne and Scott, one that would yield a few lessons for Leanne in particular for the Ironman. After sharing a predawn bagel and two cups of coffee with friends, in a cottage they had all rented, Leanne set off with Scott for the starting line, about two miles away, a distance they would cover by bike. The water temperature was seventy-six degrees, neither too warm nor too cold, and the 1.2-mile swim was marked off in an easy-to-follow rectangle. Though Leanne swam wide of several of the marker buoys, she felt "pretty solid" the entire way. Rounding the last buoy, though, her right calf tightened into a cramp—one that would grip her muscles like a vise for the bike and run.

Why didn't I eat a banana for breakfast? she thought, mindful that a deficiency of potassium can cause cramping. Still, the cramp hadn't affected her time, and she finished the swim in 43 minutes and 1 second. At that pace at Ironman Arizona, she'd be out of the water in an hour and 26 minutes, nearly an hour ahead of the cutoff.

After struggling a bit to get out of her wetsuit, Leanne began to jog barefoot toward the transition area. Though there were hundreds of bikes corralled that day, Leanne found hers easily, because her race number had corresponded to a spot on the end of a row. While the course was flat, a brisk headwind made her feel as if she were on a never-ending hill. She also couldn't quite get comfortable in her seat, which impeded her from getting into the aero position. Part of the reason Leanne was so uncomfortable was that she was wearing triathlon shorts—which are skintight and thin enough to fit under a wetsuit, as well as being suitable for biking and running. The downside is that they are not as padded in the seat as the traditional bike shorts Leanne usually wore. Perhaps most significant, the fifty-six miles was by far the longest distance she'd ridden this year, since she had placed so much emphasis on her marathon training for Boston.

In the race report she filed afterward in her training journal, Leanne answered the prompt "What would you do differently?" by writing, "Get more miles in on the bike prior to racing and practice in the shorts that I am going to race in!" Still, her time on the bike was a formidable 3 hours and 11 minutes. If her bike time at White Lake were roughly doubled to approximate her performance at Ironman Arizona, and added to her projected swim time, she'd be well under the ten-and-a-half-hour cutoff time for the swim and bike portions of a full Ironman.

As Leanne began the thirteen-mile run at White Lake, the temperature had climbed into the nineties, unseasonable for North Carolina in early May. Still, she was relieved to come off the bike, and she quickly found her pace and relaxed in the knowledge that her natural ability on the run exceeded her swimming and biking skills. About three miles into the run, she made a pledge to herself: If she could somehow catch up to Scott—who always bolted ahead of her in the swim and on the bike, which were his strengths—she would then slow her pace so that they might cross the finish line together. That's something they had never done. Not only would it be fun to cross a finish line with her husband, she thought, but it was the probably the least she could do for him. She suspected he had probably gotten more than a few catcalls from the crowd on the sidelines for that pink Mohawk. And his running—which could be a struggle for Scott in the best of times—had surely not been made any easier by that skirt.

Just before the turnaround, at 6.5 miles, Leanne caught up with Scott. The time on her watch told her she had been on the course for fifty minutes. Scott was obviously growing frustrated in the high heat and by now had taken a break from running and decided to walk a bit. Leanne felt fine herself but chose instead to walk the next three miles with her husband. At a certain point, she began to encourage Scott to pick up the pace and extend his walk to a jog. He was resistant and eventually gave his wife an irritated retort: She should run her own race; he would finish when he finished.

And so, at mile 9, she bid Scott goodbye and set off running on her own. She crossed the finish line after 2 hours and 12 minutes on the run course, giving her a total time for the day—including several minutes in each transition area—of 6 hours, 12 minutes, and 7 seconds. Considering how long she had walked, Leanne felt confident that she could have otherwise come in at under six hours. That was another good harbinger for Ironman Arizona, where she'd have seventeen hours, or nearly three times as long, to cover double the distance.

In her postrace report Leanne pronounced herself pleased after "a great training day for me."

> It showed me my weaknesses and was a great race to gauge what I need to work on this summer. Running is definitely my strongest discipline and I am a "middle of the packer" when it comes to swimming and biking. From this I have learned that this year I have to focus on my swim and bike.

On Monday morning, she expressed some concern in her journal that she had been unable to loosen the knot in her right calf, though she had done no exercise over the previous twenty-four hours. Still, she wrote, she had been seeing a sensational physical therapist, though he was decidedly unlicensed.

It was her husband, of course.

But however much they enjoyed training (and post-training) together, Leanne had been reminded that weekend that she and Scott were individuals, at least when it came to participating in the races together.

"I thought it would be fun for Scott and me to run together but it ended up being frustrating for both of us," she told her online journal. "He felt like he was holding me back and I was frustrated because he didn't want to try to run more. It made me realize that we both love racing but for different reasons."

Leanne ended her dispatch with a pledge.

"Moving forward," she wrote, "I will always run my own race."

It was a commitment that, however admirable, would be sorely tested at Ironman Arizona.

On Friday, May 1, a month after her triumphant finish in the 70.3 in Oceanside, Tracy Tucker-Georges selected as her next challenge en route to Ironman Arizona a race in Monterey County, California, called Wildflower. It was a sprint triathlon with a twist—the bike portion would be on a mountain bike, on wooded trails. The last time she'd ridden a mountain bike had been a few months earlier, when, unable to repair the tires on her road bike, she'd gone for a trail ride instead, taking two serious spills in the process. But Wildflower was too tempting to pass up, in part because it allowed Tracy to get in touch with her tomboy side. On the eve of Wildflower, she "decided to take a bunch of testosterone" and "camp like a real man!"

The Wildflower experience, she continued, "included eating dinner at Big Bubba's Bad BBQ, having it rain on us, setting up my own tent, farting and belching. All of which I managed to do very well."

After a restless sleep—"I just have a difficult time sleeping when I am camping"—she set off for the transition area of the race and contemplated the day ahead: a quarter-mile swim, 9.7-mile bike ride, and 2-mile run.

Heck, she told herself, *I am just going to have fun.*

But it didn't take long for her nerves to get jangled; as was often the case, the source of her anxiety was yet another "dumb chick (bitch) that knew everything." Sure enough, the woman, a fellow competitor in the forty-five-to-forty-nine bracket, told Tracy she had somehow placed her bike in the rack incorrectly.

"Bullshit!" Tracy said under her breath, concealing her protest with an exaggerated cough.

The woman made it clear that she had been doing triathlons for a decade and very much intended to be on the podium where the top finishers in each age group would be celebrated. The last thing she wanted was to have her bike get tangled in Tracy's, costing her precious time en route to otherwise certain glory. After warning the woman not to give her "any attitude," Tracy took a deep breath and said, "Just explain to me how you want my bike and your bike to be placed," before adding that she was not competing for a podium spot herself. Tempers calmed, and Tracy headed for the swim, in Lake San Antonio.

Though her legs felt a bit cramped throughout, she dispatched the swim without incident. She then ran up a boat ramp to the bike transition, "boogied through that," jumped on her bike, and took off. Snaking through the nearly ten miles of wooded paths wound up "being a blast," and this time Tracy took no falls from her mountain bike. The run began, improbably, with a sprint up a long flight of wooden steps for which Tracy hadn't been prepared—"I love Vit for these little tips he keeps hidden from me," she wrote later. But before long, the two-mile run was drawing to an end. Tracy was feeling so good that she "met a nice lady" along the way and ran with her across the finish line, providing an end to her day that was very different from its highly charged beginning. Her final time: 1 hour, 23 minutes, and 9 seconds.

Tracy had not only met her goal of having fun; she'd landed on the podium herself, in fourth place in her age group.

And what of the woman with whom she had tangled? Tracy never saw her again, which was probably just as well.

"Let the insecurities begin" was how Tracy opened a post on *TracerX*, her friends-and-family blog, on a Wednesday night a few weeks after Wildflower. Whatever euphoria she'd felt after that race and the 70.3 had long since dissipated. She was thinking about the Ironman again, as she so often did, and wondering where she fit in, considering all those stories of triumph over illness or hardship that invariably seemed to be at the root of every aspiring Ironman's pursuit—at least as the TV coverage told it. As Tracy wrote:

> I am not a Marine battling for my life and my country. Nor
> am I someone battling cancer. I do not have to battle an abu-

sive relationship, or drug or alcohol abuse . . . maybe an addiction to training. BUT, hey—I know I'm not the only one . . .

"I get worried that I am just a 44-year-old, plain suburban mother, married with two teenaged girls, who averages 15 miles per hour on her bike," she wrote. "Seriously, are there not hundreds of thousands of people like me trying to get by in life and train for an Ironman, too? This is where the insecurity lies: that I am a nobody! Average Jane! Who would be inspired by me and my training for an Ironman?"

Who? The answer dawned on Tracy as soon as she asked it: "Perhaps other Average Janes or Joes. Perhaps some of the people I work with who think it's 'insane,' but who have a certain respect for me knowing what I am doing. Or maybe my daughter's friends who think I am 'awesome.'"

As Tracy tapped away on an Apple keyboard, she began soaring:

> Maybe I just need to accept it: I am signed up, gonna do the training and do my best to kick some Ironman ass! And by "kick ass," I mean, get to the finish line with some semblance of a huge smile on my face and try to do the "running man" down the finish-line chute! My daughters get really embarrassed by my dancing when I do it . . . so I thought it would be appropriate. I may just forget it and/or fall on my face . . . We shall see.

For someone who wears her emotions on her bike-shirt sleeve as openly as Tracy, the ordinary ups and downs of life can get exaggerated in training for something as daunting as an Ironman. And so it was that over the next few days, she'd come up a bit short. Near the end of May, for example, she swam about a thousand yards—roughly fifty lengths of the pool at her club—before she talked her coach into letting her quit practice early "to drink beer."

And so they did, together.

Two days later she, Vit, and yet another creatively nicknamed training partner—Pimp Daddy J-Z—set out for a four-hour bike ride, but Tracy quit before two hours because she had a bad headache and was "extremely hungry." After riding back to her car, she discovered she'd locked her keys inside, so she'd have to pedal two more miles home—which she did, rewarding herself with toast and eggs.

"Tomorrow, I rest, finally," she wrote in her journal.

June 6, which fell on a Saturday, had a great deal of meaning for Tracy. As she wrote on her blog, she knew it was the anniversary of D-Day, but it was also "Vit's Day," her beloved lead training partner's fortieth birthday. And perhaps most significant of all, it was the date of the Camp Pendleton Mud Run.

"Not quite the same as invading Normandy," Tracy observed in her report on the race, "but trust me, there was one part that felt like HELL (more on that later.)"

The start of the Mud Run, at least, had certainly been a lot of fun. Tracy and Vit were among nine friends who would be running in the muck—much of it man-made, it was one of several obstacles arrayed along the course—and in solidarity they'd all decided to chip in to create and wear matching T-shirts. On the front was a big yellow smiley face sporting a camouflage bandanna (this was, after all, a military base), its eyes and mouth spattered with mud. The message on the back of the shirt: A RACE ONLY A MUDDER COULD LOVE. Rain was in the forecast—"that, in and of itself, is not a bad thing for a mud run," Tracy said—but she was more worried about the threat of lightning. It turned out to be a false alarm; it never rained, and even the sun showed itself occasionally on a day that was comfortably cool.

Among those in Tracy's group was "Southpaw Mama," otherwise known as Vit's sister Cherie, who had come down from Washington State along with her husband, "B-Meister," just to participate. Otherwise known as Brett, who was in the airline business, B-Meister had decided to show his love of his country by carrying an American flag with him the entire race. On particularly muddy patches, he would pass the flag temporarily to one of the volunteers stationed nearby, who were Marines from the base.

In celebration of this rare occasion, when she actually had female companionship in a race, Tracy, Southpaw Mama, and the three other women in their group decided to stick together, alternately running and walking. They were doing so with careful deliberation because one of the women, nicknamed T2, had sustained a foot injury a few weeks earlier and could not put much weight on her heel. After mile 4 of the 6-mile race, the woman decided she'd had enough and dropped out.

About a half-mile later, Tracy and the women who remained came upon the race's second big mud pit. There the Marines had also stationed a six-foot wall for the competitors to climb over. Tracy hoisted Vit's wife, Lola, and Southpaw Mama over the barrier, then set about clambering onto it herself. Pulling herself to the top, she brought one leg over, then the other. Her plan was to then turn around and lower herself down the other side, gingerly, mindful of her balky back and knees. But her plan went awry when she began to slip and so made the split-second decision to jump.

It was six feet down—plus another foot or so of water and mud. When Tracy landed she "felt and heard a sickening pop." It was a sound, she would later say, that she had heard two other times in her life—when she blew out the anterior cruciate ligaments in her right knee and, a year later, in her left.

This time she knew immediately that she had "done something very wrong" to her knee.

She tried to stand up and take a step backward, but she was unable to. When Lola and Southpaw Mama noticed she was still in the mud pit, they came back and climbed in to help her out. Tracy attempted to compose herself, no easy task considering that she was caked in dirt, and silently told herself she had just "bruised" the bones in her knee. There was a mile and a half left to go in the race, and she was determined to finish it, limping and somehow even jogging a little with her friends.

At one point toward the end, she came upon a small hill. "With the kind, helping hand of a handsome Marine, I made it over," Tracy said later. With Lola and Southpaw Mama at her side, she actually ran through the finish chute.

After posing for a photo with the gang, her smile obviously pained, Tracy found her husband and told him about her injury. He helped her over to the medical tent to get some ice and an Ace wrap.

"Keep in mind that, at that time, I was still in denial about my knee, despite the amount of swelling that was going on," Tracy said later. Indeed, her immediate priorities after getting her knee wrapped were to change clothes and get a beer with the gang. After that, she would take a nap and head out to another restaurant for Vit's birthday celebration.

"Despite the injury," Tracy wrote in her online journal that night, "I will be back next year for the Mud Run. Maybe I will get help going over the wall—I will definitely take it easy next time.

"For now," she added, "I must focus on healing, keeping myself strong and getting back to my training."

In her dispatch she never directly mentioned Ironman Arizona, now less than six months away. But as she struggled to fall asleep that night, it was all she could think about. Had her dream of being crowned an Ironman in the Arizona desert just ended in a giant mud puddle?

That same day, Leanne Johnson was experiencing some pain herself, though in her shoulder. A continent away from Tracy, she was participating in a 5K not far from her home in Wilmington to benefit a local woman who was battling leukemia. With a time of 19 minutes and 5 seconds, Leanne not only set a personal record but was the first woman to cross the finish line. She was proud of herself but was fairly certain that the course was probably a bit less than five kilometers. Still, she had not run a 5K in under twenty minutes since high school, more than a dozen years earlier.

When she began the race, she'd been concerned that her legs felt heavy from working a particularly long week, much of it on her feet. Afterward she felt spry enough to join up with a group of friends for a forty-mile bike ride. Leanne hung toward the back—"I pretty much anchored the entire way, which was fine with me"—but still finished in an impressive 2 hours, 5 minutes. "The more I ride with people who are better than me," she said at the time, "the more I will improve on the bike."

It was only on the following day, after a 1,400-meter swim—about sixty lengths in her health club pool, a much shorter workout than she'd planned—that Leanne acknowledged the throbbing in her right shoulder. "My shoulder is really achy," she wrote in her online journal that night. "It may be from being in the aero position yesterday."

A day later, she worked her shift at the hospital but didn't exercise at all. It was the third anniversary of the day she first met Scott, and that night the two of them ate at Elijah's, down by the harbor, just as they had on their first date and on the two anniversaries of that occasion.

"I think my shoulder appreciated the day of rest," she wrote that night. "I am generally feeling fatigued from this weekend's workouts and standing all day at work on my feet."

Leanne's shoulder was still "really sore" the following Monday, when she suffered through a 1,500-meter workout that included several intervals with foam pull buoys between her legs. By immobilizing her legs, those drills would only put more strain on her shoulder. But she began to realize that the main stress on her upper body might not have been from her training. It was, she thought, a product of her relatively recent return to nursing from her desk job at the drug company.

It was raining when Leanne woke up the following morning, so she shelved her plans for an outdoor bike ride in favor of a spin class at the gym. It was a fun but arduous indoor trek, led by an instructor Leanne hadn't encountered before. Afterward, one of the women who had participated walked out the door and proceeded to faint. Leanne would learn later that the woman had been dieting and had decided not to eat before class. Leanne ran to retrieve a packet of nutritional gel from her gym bag and, with the calm bedside manner of a nurse, gave it to the woman once she came to. An ambulance crew was called as a precaution.

The experience would serve as a reminder to Leanne that spinning on a stationary bike in a climate-controlled room was more of a strain on the body than it appeared. Still, she continued the day's workout with twenty minutes on the treadmill—a regimen so boring that she referred to it as the "dreadmill"—and began to contemplate finishing off a little indoor triathlon with some swimming. Her shoulder was so sore, though, that she thought better of it. Noticing the rain had stopped, she decided to run the 4.5-mile loop around nearby Greenfield Lake, a neighborhood of hardscrabble bungalows.

Leanne chose to hold off swimming for another week, the better to rest her ailing shoulder. She also made an appointment to see an orthopedist. "Heading to see him this morning," she wrote in her journal on June 25, a Thursday. "Not really sure what he'll be able to do to help me. I guess we'll see."

After a series of X-rays, Leanne sat down with the doctor in his office. He immediately cut to the chase: The fracture she had sustained to that same shoulder in 2008, when she fell hard on the railroad tie during a Sunday morning group training ride, had in fact healed nicely. The joint was intact, Leanne was told, and nothing was impinged.

Leanne was immensely relieved, even after the doctor examined her further and told her she might have a tear in her rotator cuff. It was also entirely possible she didn't, he added.

Regardless, his prescription was straightforward: Leanne should get some good physical therapy and learn some exercises that might ease the pain in her shoulder. Only an MRI could determine definitively whether the rotator cuff was torn, he explained. But if Leanne already knew now that she was unlikely to have surgery in response to what that procedure might find, then, the doctor said, she should hold off on any further diagnostics.

She told him she wanted to wait, at least until after Ironman Arizona. And she certainly wasn't dropping out of the race.

In her journal that night, Leanne summarized the doctor's parting words to her:

> He feels I really cannot do any more damage. If things don't go better he said to come back . . . or if, after IMAZ I feel like I cannot stand the pain any longer then he said to come and we'll do the MRI and treat it appropriately. So for now I am going to try PT [physical therapy]. Now the issue is finding time to get it in. I am working M, T, W next week, and then we are heading out of town for a few days.

Three days later, with the doctor's reassurances, however qualified, ringing in her ears, Leanne slid into the pool for her first swim in two weeks. She felt slow at first—"not to mention unmotivated," she acknowledged that night—but noticed a steady improvement as her workout went on. All told, she swam for a half-hour and covered 1,500 meters. "Shoulder seemed OK," she wrote that night. "We'll see how it feels tomorrow."

In fact, her shoulder felt so good that she did not even mention it in the next day's journal entry.

But over the weekend, as she and Scott visited friends in Baltimore, her shoulder began to ache yet again during a swim at a local athletic club.

"Aghhhh!" she wrote in her journal upon her return to North Carolina. "20 weeks til IMAZ!!! Seems far away, but it'll be here soon enough."

CHAPTER 7

Mommy's Recess Time

Less than a month after Tracy heard that pop in her right knee during the Mud Run, another mother from California, also in her forties, set out on a day's journey that would push her past the threshold of anything she'd tried before. It was the Fourth of July, and Laura Arnez was attempting to ride one hundred miles on her bicycle for the first time. She was doing so not in an organized race but on her own, beginning on the paved trail along a canal near her home in Elk Grove, a suburb of Sacramento nearly four hundred miles north of where Tracy lived. Laura had set this goal for herself in preparation for her first Ironman—Ironman Arizona 2009, now just a little over four months away. Laura knew that riding a century was an unavoidable way station on the road to Ironman. Her only companion this day was her trusty iPod. Programmed by one of her daughters—everyone knew Laura was a technophobe—it alternately pumped the songs of Michael Jackson, Beyoncé, and *The Phantom of the Opera* at low volume into her headphones.

Less than seven hours later, Laura returned home, drenched but defiant, her first century ride under her belt. But even she would admit that her accomplishment was nothing compared with the challenge of simply carving that time for herself, and on a holiday Saturday, no less.

At forty-six, Laura felt blessed to be a mother of five children, ages seven to eighteen. The two youngest had been adopted from the Sacramento area, through foster care. The second-youngest one, Mary (now nine), had been brought home by Laura, a social worker, and her husband, Tom, a project manager, just months before Laura ran her first marathon. At the time, Mary was just two weeks old. Little wonder that Laura would occasionally miss a school pickup as the craziness of everyday living in the Arnez house was further complicated by her Ironman quest. Her elementary-school-age kids knew enough to walk the half-mile home with a group of other families if she didn't show up.

"It takes our whole family for me to train hard and, hopefully, finish strong," Laura explained.

In the bustling kitchen of her two-story home—situated in a cul-de-sac, with a basketball hoop and plenty of room for football and Frisbee—Laura had posted a motivational sign some years earlier. By July 2009 it had been partially papered over with bibs from her many running races—and lately from her triathlons, too—as well as with photos of the children. But the message was still readable: IF YOU NEVER HAVE A DREAM, HOW ARE YOU GOING TO HAVE A DREAM COME TRUE?

Laura found her Ironman training to be such an affirmation of the seemingly bottomless capacity of the human spirit—not just to endure, but to love—that she was thinking of adopting a third child, which would bring the total number of children in the family to six.

"I really think I can now," she said. "Before it was like, no way, there's just no way. But this Ironman thing—it's building my confidence." She had come to this conclusion even before participating in the race itself.

Laura's kids—three boys and two girls—liked to refer to her perpetual swimming, biking, and running as "Mommy's Recess Time." A mile-a-minute talker whose mood was almost never down, Laura nonetheless craved the kind of exercise that would get her heart pumping, whether it was running for miles outdoors with one of her many girlfriends or taking back-to-back spin classes at a local gym.

"My personality is mostly up," Laura acknowledged. "Someone asked me, 'Do you feel like you're addicted to working out, almost like you have to do it?' I don't. I truly don't. But my older ones will say, 'Mom's a happy mom when she gets to run. Go run, Mom, run.'"

Laura's own mother, who raised her and her three siblings as a single parent, would marvel at the transformation in her own daughter in

recent years. As a child growing up in Sacramento, Laura wouldn't have
run anywhere. In fact, outside of gym class in school, she didn't do much
at all.

As Laura described her younger self in an e-mail to me:

> I consider myself a "bookworm" who, in her Hispanic cul-
> ture, "ate too many tortillas and refried beans and too much
> chorizo!!" I never competed in sports as a child. I was some-
> what chubby! But I always admired athletes growing up . . .
> especially the runners! I always remember hearing of the
> marathon in my city, and how it would close down major
> streets. I thought to myself, "Those people are AMAZING!!"

Looking at Laura now, it was hard to imagine her as the child she
described. Standing five foot three, she had sculpted calves and biceps
that were reminiscent of Madonna's in the paparazzi photos of her emerg-
ing from a yoga studio. But the comparisons ended there. Laura, who was
deeply tanned and had thick, dark-brown hair well past her shoulders,
weighed just under 110 pounds in the months prior to Ironman Arizona
2009. That was somewhat amazing, considering that she figures she already weighed more than eighty-five pounds by the end of the fourth
grade. Recently, she said, one of her children had seen an old photo of her
and wondered, *Who's that little girl standing by Grandpa?*

"My own kids," Laura said, "didn't even recognize me."

Laura said her diet, laden with traditional foods from her mother's
native Mexico and supplemented with hot dogs and Cheez-Its, would
have been even worse had an older sister not been diagnosed at age ten
with diabetes. "The good news is, we didn't have a lot of sweets in the
house," Laura recalled. The prototypical kid picked last in gym class,
Laura added:

> I just remember reading a lot. I remember reading *Bridge
> to Terabithia* and being all excited about that. I always had a
> book. In high school, I remember going to my Dad's—my par-
> ents were divorced—my Dad had a house with a pool. I re-
> member all day long I would just sit and read Stephen King.

She began to thin out a bit toward the end of high school—not as a result of doing anything physical (she was still sedentary) but because of metabolism. She would only start to think of herself as athletic after she graduated from high school and enrolled at Sacramento State, where she would major in psychology. This was in the early 1980s, a time when aerobics classics at gyms were continuing to gain in popularity. When Laura's mother joined a gym, Laura began to take those classes. "I always loved music," she explained. "I loved just dancing around." She began to eat healthier foods, in smaller portions, and in the bargain felt her self-esteem rise.

"I felt a lot better about who I was," she said. "Just feeling pretty. I never felt that pretty. I never dated much in high school. I had one boyfriend."

Laura met Tom, an electrical engineering major at Sac State, through the Christian youth ministry in which they both volunteered. He would prove an invaluable role model in her desire to get in better shape. "He ran a marathon when he was seventeen, in Napa," Laura said, shaking her head. "It was just him and his buddy. They didn't eat anything during the race. They had crappy running shoes. Tom finished in 2:40. I mean, *Golll-lly!* He's just a natural. He loved running."

The couple married in 1985, and had their third child, Matthew, in 1997. It was around this time that Tom began to encourage Laura to realize that dream she had as a young girl growing up in Sacramento: to become a runner, just like those who would run through the streets near her home that were closed for the marathon. She was in her early thirties at the time and had left her job as a social worker—her specialty was ministering to underprivileged children at risk—to be at home full-time with her own kids. Laura had continued with the aerobics and had been lifting some weights, but now her husband began exhorting her: "Go out there and run," or "Run for thirty minutes, then stop," or, at the least, "Run until you're tired." Laura was ready for these assignments.

"There's a little area around my house," she said. "I would fast-walk, then walk-jog, then run, then think, *How far can I run without stopping?*" Laura eventually signed up for a few 5Ks and 10Ks, with Tom running alongside her. In one of those early 5Ks, Laura placed third in her age group, finishing in about a half hour, a pace of about ten minutes a mile.

"I was super-excited," she said. "I never had a medal. I never got anything when I was a kid."

Tom's response? "That was pretty fast," he told his wife, "but I think I can get you to run faster." And, as it turned out, to run farther, too.

As the new millennium dawned in 2000, a girlfriend of Laura's, Patty Shijo, told her that they should celebrate by doing "something *cra-zy*!" A mother of three, Patty had already run her first marathon. "She was like, 'Run a marathon with me,'" Laura recalled. "I was like, 'Heck, no!'"

Instead Patty offered a counterproposal to Laura: "Just train with me."

Laura agreed, and soon six-mile runs were being extended to eight-mile ones—the longest distance Laura had ever gone. Before long the women were running ten miles. "I was thrilled," Laura said. "I thought that was the biggest thrill in the world." Ten miles soon became twelve miles and, shortly thereafter, twenty miles. And yet Laura still resisted signing up for that marathon, even though her friend had long since done so.

"It was the same old me: no confidence," she explained. "I'm always afraid: What if I try and I fail?"

Tom, as he so often did, stepped in with a pep talk.

"You know what, honey, just do it," he urged her. "If you have to stop at twenty, I'll be there. I'll drive you home. It will be no big deal."

That did the trick, and Laura soon signed up for the California International Marathon in Sacramento. That day, another friend participating in the race, a schoolteacher who was not as fast as Laura, promised to keep her loose. She told Laura to imagine her running just behind her, to encourage her. Laura's goal was just to finish and, she hoped, to average about 9 minutes and 30 seconds a mile. When she crossed the finish line, the clock read 3 hours, 50 minutes: an average of 8 minutes, 45 seconds a mile. She was so fast, in fact, that she came within five minutes of qualifying for what is arguably the most prestigious road race in the United States: the Boston Marathon.

Now Laura had a new goal, one that seemed tantalizingly within reach: to get to Boston. The following year she ran in the Rock 'n' Roll Marathon in San Diego, finishing just two minutes behind her time at the California International the year before—but, once again, coming up short in her bid for Boston. Later that year, she again registered for the

California International, certain that on her hometown course she could shave five minutes off her time of a year earlier. But when she and Tom awoke at 4:00 A.M. on the morning of the marathon and peered outside, they were disheartened by what they saw.

"It was the most horrific day you could imagine," Laura recalled. "The winds must have been going forty miles per hour. It was pouring." Her husband said, Pacific Shoreline—another marathon, in Huntington Beach—is four weeks away. "You're already trained," he said. "Let's go down there."

Laura thought her husband had suggested a fine alternate plan, but she still wound up running the first ten miles in that stormy California International to give a boost to a friend, who was not trying to qualify for Boston or any other race—she just wanted to finish, and did so. Tom's recommendation would be vindicated four weeks later, in January 2002, in Huntington Beach, where Laura finished the race in 3 hours and 43 minutes—two minutes under the cutoff for Boston.

That spring, she and Tom traveled east.

That she finished Boston in just over four hours, as did Tom, seemed almost beside the point. The once chubby little Laura Arnez, now age thirty-nine, had put down her books long enough to compete in, and complete, the Boston Marathon. It was a notion that would have seemed almost unthinkable, at least until the past few years. But when the reverie faded, Laura couldn't help but wonder: What next?

As she continued to run hard, Laura found she was increasingly susceptible to injuries—particularly plantar fasciitis, a tight soreness at the bottom of the foot. A friend recommended she buy a road bike, and after Isaiah, the couple's youngest child, joined the family in 2003, Laura added swimming to her repertoire. "I knew my older daughter was a pretty good swimmer," Laura said. "I thought, *If I'm seventy years old, I can always swim*." Laura took some lessons at her gym, and before long she had an inspiration: *I want to do a tri*. She even struck the weekend-warrior equivalent of a barter arrangement. Some of Laura's girlfriends had said they wanted to run better, and she offered to help them in exchange for their guidance in her swimming. "It would be something new," Laura said. "It was yet another thing I thought I couldn't do."

Up until this point in the story, Laura Arnez's evolution as an athlete had proceeded steadily and relatively uneventfully. But that was about to change. The problem was Laura's swimming. It wasn't a matter of technique (she had developed a relatively strong front crawl after just a few lessons and with the help of tutoring from her friends) but a matter of fear—a fear, specifically, of open water. It was almost a phobia, Laura said, one that her mother recalls her youngest daughter experiencing as far back as she can remember, in the ocean. At one point, Laura had even considered hypnosis as a potential remedy. While no one in the family could recall how Laura's aversion to lakes and oceans had started, its manifestations were on display for everyone to see in the lake where she was to complete the swim portion of her first triathlon, in Sacramento.

Struck by a full-blown panic attack, she paddled over to a kayak, her breathing labored, her heart racing. Laura was worried she might drown.

She'd had the same reaction on two earlier practice swims in the same lake—on those two days, she couldn't even swim—and her symptoms had been eased only slightly by the subsequent purchase of a wetsuit. But here she was in that sprint, wearing the wetsuit and still struggling.

Somehow Laura willed her body to calm down. She let go of the kayak and managed to finish the half-mile swim that day: "I got out of the water, got on the bike, and I was happy. I even passed a bunch of people." The following year she decided she would try to go twice as far, in an Olympic-distance race that began in the same lake and continued over the same surrounding roads. Again she finished—this time without much agitation in the swim portion. No one she knew was surprised that Laura was not content to rest on her laurels. "I'm a marathon girl," she declared.

But when a girlfriend suggested a half-Ironman—which featured a 1.2-mile swim—Laura balked. "You know me," she told her friend. "I could never swim that far."

But the desire to push herself would not abate, so Laura signed up for her first half-Ironman, in Oceanside, five hundred miles south of Sacramento. Only after she registered did it hit her: The community hosting the race had the word *ocean* in it, which meant the swim would be held in the Pacific.

Why did I pick the ocean? Laura asked herself.

Still, her fears would only mount four days before the race, when she began vomiting and her temperature began to rise. A friend attempted to reassure Laura by suggesting, "It's just nerves."

"No, honey," Laura responded. "This is the flu. I can tell. My whole body aches."

She told Tom that she'd made a decision: "I'm not going to do it."

Tom, however, was not inclined to let her off the hook, at least not this early.

"You know, you've registered," he reminded her. "Why don't you go to packet pickup"—typically the day before the race, when bibs and timing chips are distributed—"and spend some time with your girlfriend. You may feel better."

Laura's kids had been planning to go to the race, as had her friend's children. If she took Tom's advice, at least they could all visit together, she reasoned.

Laura's older daughter, Megan, now in high school, had her own proposal and suggested to her mother, "Just do the swim. That will be challenge enough for you. Get in there and get scared and get freaked out and do it."

To everyone's surprise, Laura was amenable. But Tom, as is his wont, upped the ante yet again.

"Bring everything," he suggested, referring to her bicycle and helmet, as well as running shoes and shorts. "Just in case you get out of the water and want to continue."

When dawn broke on the day of the race, the storm whipping the ocean reminded Laura of the one that had sent her packing from the marathon in Sacramento. And yet, still suffering from the flu, she jumped off a dock with several dozen other women when the wave number for their age group was called out.

When the panic set in almost immediately, Laura reached for a nearby kayak, settled herself, swam a bit, grew agitated, and then reached for another kayak. Only later did she learn that the temperature of the choppy water was just fifty-six degrees and that her daughter had watched race organizers pull several men—bigger and, it seemed, fitter than Laura—from the water, chattering with what turned out to be hypothermia. As she waited for her mother on the shore, Megan's concerns grew. But while it took Laura nearly an hour, she somehow finished that swim.

When she stepped out of the ocean, shaking, Laura stripped off her wetsuit and headed straight for the medical tent. Surely, her family thought, her day was over. She had met the goal Megan set for her: She had conquered her fears and completed the swim. But as she sipped the hot soup provided her by volunteers, Laura was seized by another thought— *I can do this*—and, pulling on a shirt, she headed for her bicycle.

"Once I got on my bike, I was fine," she said, later. "And once I was running, well . . ." Her voice trailed off—there was nothing more that needed to be said.

"That was a miracle race," Laura concluded.

On the seven-hour drive back to Sacramento, Laura found herself thinking about all those telecasts she'd watched of Ironman Hawaii, first on ABC and later on NBC. Every year, those telecasts launch countless numbers of Ironman pursuits. "I'd always watched the Hawaii Ironman," Laura recalled. "I'd always watched the stories. I think it was always in the back of my head. After I did that half—and several more halfs—I was like, *I would love to do a full Ironman*. But I just didn't think I could do it."

She added: "It was always, 'I'd love to do it, but . . .'"

For all the time she spent exercising, Laura did not believe that she needed a full Ironman on her résumé to feel complete, and she certainly considered her life to be bigger than sports.

"For me as a person," she explained, "I feel like it's more important to be a good mom and a good friend and a good wife. I want to be a good person, and have a good spirit about me."

She added: "If I was just doing this, and had never adopted, I wouldn't feel good about who I am."

She also felt that, in training for triathlons and competing in them, she was setting a good example for her children.

"My children see, through my actions, that dreams can come true," she said, "if you try hard and accept the challenges." To make sure everyone got the message, Laura put up that sign in her kitchen about needing to have a dream before being able to make a dream come true.

Confident that his wife had her priorities in order, Tom intervened to provide yet another push, this time in the fall of 2008. Megan, their oldest, was going into her junior year of high school. If Laura wanted to do an Ironman while Megan was still living under their roof, Tom reminded her, she would have to sign up this fall, given that the lead time for each race was a year in advance.

"Do it now," Tom told Laura. "If you wait, Megan probably won't be there. She'll be off at college. Get it out of your system."

By this point Tom and Laura had been married nearly a quarter-century. He had known exactly what buttons to push.

"You know what," she told her husband after contemplating the possibility. "I should do this."

The only question that remained was: Which Ironman should she do?

Ironman Florida was certainly out, because the swim was in the Gulf of Mexico. Laura knew that a friend had done the Ironman in Idaho, which used a lake. But her friend had told her that the water there had been "pretty darn cold" and that the lake surface had been windswept.

Another friend had done Ironman Arizona. As in Idaho, Laura was told, the swim was in a lake, though this one had been relatively calm, and the bike and run courses were relatively flat. Because it was held in November, Laura could do open-water practice swims near her home all summer in preparation.

Registering for the race by computer, on November 24, 2008, had seemed like an Ironman in and of itself. Laura tried for more than an hour to get on the Ironman Web site, to no avail. At one point she called her husband and told him she was giving up. She would try again next year.

"Keep trying," he told her. "Keep trying."

She did, and eventually signed on. Like Seth Cannello sitting at his computer around the same time in his home in Colorado Springs, Laura had gotten one of the last available slots before Ironman Arizona would be declared sold out.

Laura felt relieved, particularly at the thought of swimming in that man-made lake in downtown Tempe. From the looks of the course map online, it appeared almost soothing, like a giant bathtub.

CHAPTER 8

A Saw Blade, Hammer, and Chisel

Tracy Tucker-George's suspicion that she had done grave damage to her right knee during her leap into the mud pit would prove correct. During an appointment a few days later, an orthopedic surgeon confirmed her worst fears: She had torn her ACL plunging from that six-foot barrier. She received this diagnosis in mid-June, a little over five months before Ironman Arizona. When she screwed up her courage to ask whether, with immediate surgery and diligent rehabilitation, she might make it to the starting line in Tempe, her doctor shook his head. She would need at least six months to get her knee back to full strength, and even then it would be too soon and risky to put her knee through the strain of a 112-mile bike ride followed by the pounding of a marathon.

It all seemed so unfair. The anxiety she had felt shortly after signing up for Ironman Arizona had, in the ensuing months, slowly given way to hope, excitement, and a near-daily imagining of how it would feel to hear Mike Reilly say her name as she crossed the finish line. Watching her friends complete Ironman Arizona in 2008, Tracy became convinced that she could attain the same goal. And as they swam and rode and ran together over the past few months, her "boys" had encouraged her in that belief. She *would* be an Ironman. In the days after she received the doctor's pronouncement, her spirits plunged "into a major funk."

Her surgery was scheduled for July 6, and over the course of several hours her doctors worked to rebuild her right knee and also removed a staple that had been left behind during surgery on the same knee a decade earlier. (That prior procedure was the result of a burst of pique by Tracy in a karate class; a "kid who was way taller" had punched her in the chest, prompting her to deliver a "beautiful roundhouse kick" to his head. Her right knee, however, had been injured upon landing it.) Extricating that staple had proven no easy task for the surgical team.

"It involved a saw blade, hammer and chisel," she wrote in her online journal. "No, I am NOT kidding!! I have the bruise to prove it." Some evidence of arthritis was also discovered.

"Knee surgery sucks!" she concluded.

A week later Tracy felt strong enough to take to her blog to reassure her friends and family that she was "being a good patient—despite what some of you may think" and to assure them that "every day I am getting better." Her rehab, she knew, would be a protracted one, but she was "in for the long haul." As she lay in bed or on the couch in that house, evocative of a hot-dog stand, she began to reflect on all the cautionary advice she had received from various clinicians over the past few months, whether it was regarding the fragile bones in her back or in both knees. Even before she required surgery on her right knee, her left would grow so swollen following a hard workout that it would be a week before it returned to its normal size. As she recounted such stories to them, each of her doctors seemed to lay the equivalent of a railroad crossing gate between her and the miles of track that would lead to an Ironman. But even as she began the hard work of restoring the strength and range of motion in her surgically repaired right knee, Tracy still found she couldn't shake loose one thought that overrode all others, however irrationally.

"I have no intention of giving up my Ironman quest," she announced. "So I am going to shoot for next year. Knees willing. Ha, ha!"

A few days later she wrote her new goal in the equivalent of wet concrete that would quickly dry and become permanent.

"IMAZ 2010," she told readers of *TracerX*, "here I come. See you there."

The night after Tracy's surgery, rain poured so torrentially on Wilmington, North Carolina, that when Leanne Johnson arose just before seven the following morning, she began to rethink her plans for a long outdoor bike ride. "I decided to keep it safe and ride the trainer today to avoid any crashes on the slippery roads," she told her online journal. With the humidity high, she would nonetheless get a vigorous workout in her garage, riding her bicycle in the trainer for more than an hour. At the heart of her workouts was "a ladder," in which she'd ride for four intervals of thirty seconds each, with each faster than the one before, followed by a gradual tapering. By the end, Leanne was so bathed in sweat that she was convinced she'd dropped several pounds in water weight. But instead of celebrating, she wound up venturing outside after all, for a two-and-a-half-mile cooldown run that took her just over twenty minutes. Her caution had paid off, and she felt terrific.

A few days later, though, she began her journal entry on a much less encouraging note. "KLUTZ!" she typed, her fingers pounding the keys. "That should be my new name."

> We rode 30 miles out to the tackle/bait shop on Highway 20—accident free. Then, while reclipping into my pedals standing still, I went for a tumble in the parking lot. Landed on my bad shoulder, and scraped my elbow, knee and hand. Now I'm feeling a bit achey.

She had signed up for a sprint triathlon in Raleigh the following day and didn't want to back out, at least in part because it was a part of her buildup to Ironman Arizona. "Hope my legs hold up!" she wrote.

The race went fine, and her time—a little over ninety minutes—was fast enough for her to place sixth out of fifty-two in her age group. But, as if on cue, her shoulder began to throb the following day, a Monday morning.

"I think I may have bruised it in my fall on Saturday," she worried.

After a twelve-hour shift at the hospital, she iced her shoulder, and while the pain subsided, it didn't disappear. A mostly sleepless night followed, though Leanne thought it was more a result of the late-evening coffee she had drunk, uncharacteristically, at the hospital as her long day wound down. At about three in the morning, she left her bedroom and headed for the couch, to see if turning on the TV would help. It must have: At some point she dozed off, though her alarm woke her before six.

However groggy she may have been, she roused quickly during a predawn run up and down the hills of the downtown waterfront; she and a friend covered eight miles in 1 hour, 18 minutes, at an average pace of 9 minutes and 45 seconds per mile, and afterward Leanne felt revived. She went directly to the health club and proceeded to swim. To her immense reassurance, her shoulder stayed quiet. As she was drying off, she realized that a one-hour spin class was about to begin, which she took.

Leanne was out the door and back on her bike before six the next morning, for a bike ride in which she, Scott, and a group of others would ride two laps around the full perimeter of Wrightsville Beach. There must have been more than forty of them in total, and they quickly separated into small packs. Leanne, as she so often did, lagged toward the back. Her friend Noelle, a faster rider than Leanne, hung back with her, and soon the two women were joined by another friend, Erin, as they battled a headwind. "My legs felt a bit heavy today," Leanne said afterward, "no doubt from Saturday's 60 miles, Sunday's race and yesterday's hour-long spin class." She was hardly whining, though. "Gotta suck it up," she said. However much she had lagged most of the other riders, Leanne's final time was nonetheless encouraging: She covered the eighteen miles in just under an hour.

It was only when she, Erin, and Noelle dismounted their bikes and plunged into the saltwater channel for a 1,500-meter open-water swim that Leanne began to tighten a bit with anxiety. She wondered which "critters" might be swirling around her, worrying, as usual, that a shark might be circling somewhere nearby—a fear she was able to dispatch by reassuring herself that it was irrational. She was further calmed by the sight of Nicole's pink cap bobbing close in front of her. All told, the women covered the distance in about 25 minutes, or about 1 minute and 40 seconds for every 100 yards. At that pace, she'd do fine in the freshwater lake at Ironman Arizona. Leanne toasted her accomplishment with another cup of cereal, blueberries, and yogurt, the same breakfast she'd eaten before the ride. Though she felt like she was eating constantly and was never fully sated, her five-foot-two-inch frame remained lean. Whatever she was eating was quickly burning off.

In the days and weeks that followed, Leanne continued to check off the milestones on her training plan. Before dawn on July 23, a Thursday on which she was not scheduled to work, she and Erin set out on an 84.5-

mile bike ride, the longest Leanne had ever attempted. Most of it would be on Route 210, the two-lane paved road that snaked out of town toward a bait-and-tackle shop that loomed like a beacon.

"We dodged a couple of dogs, saw a dead snake and that was about it," Leanne said, noting that her legs "felt good" the entire way.

Two days later, on a Saturday, Leanne was back on her bike and set off for another ride that would take her 74.5 miles. But when she and Scott arrived at the parking lot of a local triathlon store, their bikes on the rack of their truck, Leanne realized her front wheel was flat. Scott dutifully changed the inner tube, but nothing else seemed to go right thereafter. He felt from the outset that his rear brake wasn't working properly, and after three miles they stopped so that their friend Jeff could fiddle with it. About two miles later, Scott's rear tire blew. Luckily, he was able to remain upright and steer his bike to the side for his second tire change of the day. "Once we got going, the ride went well," Leanne said later.

If there was a lesson to be learned that day for the Ironman, it was this: While the sun remained cloaked by puffy clouds for much of the day, the relative shade was deceptive; the late-July air was stifling and humid. And though Leanne drank a full bottle of Gatorade and another twelve-ounce bottle of water, she was so parched afterward that she knew she had not consumed enough liquids.

"Not sure how I can make myself drink more," she wrote in her journal that night. "Maybe I need to set the time on my watch?"

Leanne tried to beat the high humidity on Sunday morning by setting out on a ten-mile run in and around her neighborhood before 7:30. She felt drenched not long after she began, but after finishing in 1 hour and 20 minutes, at a pace just over seven and a half minutes per mile, she allowed herself a rare pat on the back:

> I was able to do some good IM mental training. I tried to envision what it would be like during the run, especially the end of the run. The last 20 minutes I picked up the pace and tried to finish strong.
>
> I am sort of in "awe" of myself right now . . . I can't believe my legs are not hating me for the torture I have put them through since Thursday. I guess this is what you call "adapting."

But with an Ironman beckoning, the odometer always seemed to reset to zero on Monday morning. And so it was for Leanne. Whatever "awe" she felt on Sunday would be of little consequence going forward.

"I'm feeling a little bit stressed about trying to fit everything in this week," she wrote in her journal. Her training plan called for her to exercise about nine and a half hours that week. While that was two hours less than she had done the prior one, Leanne was scheduled to work so many shifts in the coming few days that she didn't know when she'd be able to find the time or summon the energy to meet that goal. Her plan included about two hours, ten minutes of swimming, three and a half hours of biking, and nearly four hours of running.

And with that, she powered down her computer and headed off to log a dozen hours of overtime. But first she'd decided to make a pit stop along the way: As a down payment on her pledge to herself, she swam in the health club pool for nearly an hour, covering 2,700 yards, more than half the distance of the swim portion of Ironman Arizona. She then showered and put on her nurse's uniform for the real workday ahead.

That same day Bryan Reece logged onto his computer to dash off a quick blog post for *Left, Right, Repeat,* updating his readers on his latest endeavors. He and Debbie had just returned from their annual vacation on the Gulf Coast of Florida—the same trip on which, a year earlier, his brother's improbable path to a marathon had begun.

"Off the beach and back to work," Bryan wrote.

But Bryan wasn't really thinking about his job as an investment adviser.

"Now the real work begins for Ironman Arizona," he wrote. "I think all year I have been looking at November saying, it is SO far away. Well, folks, the counter today is below 120 days. It's really time to get to work."

Laura Arnez's training for Ironman Arizona began in earnest in California wine country, at a race appropriately called Vineman, a 70.3 in Santa Rosa staged that same July. This would be her fourth time competing in the race and, if the past were any guide, her fourth time completing it.

Still, she was "as nervous as ever about the event." Unlike in years past, she had committed herself to a forthcoming race—Ironman Arizona—that would be double this distance. And it was just four months away.

In that spirit Laura set a target time for herself that was somewhat arbitrary. She decided that if she could finish Vineman in 6 hours, 30 minutes or less, she could "definitely complete the full IM with time to spare." While she acknowledged that "there are no proven formulas to really calculate this all out," her main purpose in establishing a time was to "gain some confidence." She was also seeking to push herself a little beyond her previous best at Vineman: 6 hours, 42 minutes.

Like many triathletes who are uncomfortable in the water, Laura had generally preferred to start in the back of the pack. But today she wanted to begin in the middle—to simulate for herself what it might be like in Arizona, where more than two thousand swimmers would be swirling around her. As in Arizona, the 1.2-mile swim at Vineman was in a body of water—the Russian River—fed by mountain streams, not the salty ocean water that particularly unnerved her. Still, the day's experiment could simulate only so much: Unlike the mass start at Arizona, where every swimmer begins simultaneously, Vineman divided up the participants by gender and then again by age, staggering their starts in so-called waves. Laura's wave probably had two hundred women in it, all in their forties.

Wearing a wetsuit to ward off the chill of the river, Laura had a chance to do a little warm-up swim before her wave was called.

Maybe more open-water swims have prepped me, she thought, realizing that she wasn't feeling her usual attack of nerves. Once the actual swim began, she responded with a slow and steady stroke. These good feelings lasted all of five minutes, until she bumped into another swimmer and lifted up her head. Suddenly her heart rate began to quicken, as did her breathing. Unable to calm herself, she couldn't find a rhythm in her swimming and wondered whether she could continue.

With few other options, Laura closed her eyes for a brief moment and put on a little mental slide show. It featured each of her five children—Megan, Nathan, Matthew, Mary, and Isaiah—in school photos and vacation shots. As this montage flickered, she began to sing a bit to herself inside her head, choosing a piece that her children had recently learned at church, something about God helping you when you need it most. As she opened her eyes beneath her goggles, Laura realized that her initial sense of serenity was returning. Soon the cadence of her front crawl—*right then left then right then left*—was back as well. For the remainder of the swim, she felt not the slightest twinge of fright. As she emerged from the river, she looked at her watch and realized that her swim time was about the same as it had been the previous year. That would probably set her back in her goal to finish twelve minutes faster overall, but she immediately saw the bright side.

The hardest part is over, Laura, she told herself. *Just move forward, strong.*

As she got on her bike, however, she was quickly consumed by another concern: It was already hot, and most of California was still asleep. By the time she began the run, she would surely be baking in the sun. To calm herself, she conceived an internal mantra that might light a fire, literally, under her bike ride: *Beat the heat*, she told herself. The faster she rode, the cooler the temperatures would be at the start of her run. She would be riding fifty-six miles, forty-four fewer than on that first century she'd completed just a few weeks earlier, on the Fourth of July. She felt her bike training kick in. She felt prepared.

About halfway through the bike portion, which featured rolling hills that took the cyclists through wineries in Guerneville and Windsor, Laura singled out a man slightly ahead of her in bright red bike shorts.

Stay with him, she told herself.

Sometimes she would power past him on the climb, only to see him surge past her on the downhill. But she always managed to catch up, as if they were tethered to each other by a long elastic cord. Laura's mental trick sharpened her focus, so much so that she stopped paying attention to the odometer mounted on the gold-and-silver-padded handlebars on her black Cannondale triathlon bike, a model known as the Ironman 800. When she did finally sneak a look at the odometer's digital readout, she was surprised to see that it read "50."

OMG! she thought—Laura was an avid texter, and her mind sometimes seemed like an extension of her smartphone—*I only have six to go, and I feel great!*

Two miles later, though, she watched the man in the red shorts suddenly wobble erratically to the side of the road as his tire went flat. Laura slowed down to see if he needed assistance. They were probably the first words they'd exchanged, though they'd been together, in a sense, for several hours.

"Just ride and run fast for me, okay?" said the man, who was probably in his fifties and whose name she would never learn.

Hopeful that his tire change would be relatively quick—there were so-called SAG wagons (for "support and gear") circling to help riders in just such a predicament—Laura said she would do her best, and off she went. After crossing the bike finish line and dismounting, her bike shoes clicking on the pavement as she walked into the transition area, her feelings were mixed.

"Usually when I get off the bike, I REALLY want to GET OFF the bike," she recalled. "Today it was bittersweet. I felt like I could really keep on riding." Laura hit the button on her bike computer and then, in disbelief, hit it several more times to make sure she had read it correctly. Her time was 3 hours, 16 minutes—"crazy better," as she put it, "than last year or any year."

No way did I do that well and still feel this good, Laura thought to herself. She was thrilled at the thought that her personal record was yet again within reach.

As she began the run, Laura heard someone say that the air temperature was ninety degrees but that the pavement was probably a hundred or more.

Okay, thirteen miles of this? Laura asked herself, but quickly banished that thought with yet another mantra that she began repeating silently: *Drink and eat and you'll be fine. This is what you love to do.*

Running, of course, had been her gateway to becoming physically fit and confident, and it was always her favorite part of any triathlon. "The run is really fun cause no matter how I feel, I always love to put my shoes on," she once remarked. "I feel more in control on the run, and I pass so many people who probably hate the sport the way I hate the water. LOL."

Before long it really did feel as if her feet were burning inside her orange and white Mizuno running shoes, though some relief came in the form of giant misting machines that the race organizers had placed alongside the course.

"For 250 bucks," Laura suddenly said aloud, as if at one of her kids' basketball games, in reference to the race entry fee, "I think the run should have misters the whole course. Who's with me on that?"

Another runner, a man who looked especially spent to Laura, nodded in agreement, and they both laughed as they looped around the winery that signaled the halfway point of the run course. Later, Laura would remember that she had said something to him about the "glass being half full" and that, this being July in California, it could have been even hotter.

"C'mon," she told the man, who was of medium build and appeared to be in his late thirties, "let's get to that finish."

No, he told Laura. He would keep running, but he couldn't match her pace. She should go ahead without him. And, for that matter, he told her he was "way too hot" to think about glasses being half full or half empty, even if they were wineglasses. As was often the case when someone made a fleeting race friend, Laura again didn't catch the man's name or where he was from. While running faster than he was, she felt her pace had only been "so-so"—about ten minutes a mile, which was slow for her. But it turned out to be fast enough.

Laura crossed the finish line at 6 hours, 26 minutes—4 minutes under her goal. "I was sooooo happy that the fatigue and heat didn't even bother me," she said.

After the race, she pushed through the crowd of athletes and spectators to try to find Tom. He'd competed as well, but his starting time was much earlier than hers. When she finally located him—maybe forty-five minutes after she'd finished—they embraced, and he told her there was a guy she had to meet. They'd just been chatting over a few bites of chicken breast sandwiches, and the man had said he was from Phoenix.

In fact, he'd done Ironman Arizona the previous year.

When the couple approached the table where the man was still eating, the man and Laura immediately burst out laughing.

"Hey, it's the girl with the cup half full!" he said. Tom had somehow managed to befriend Laura's impromptu running buddy, whose name was Chad Rose. He reassured Laura that the bike and run courses that day had been "way harder" than those he'd encountered in Ironman Arizona, "based on the heat alone."

"If you can finish this and run and chat and be *that* happy out there today, you will be fine for Arizona," Chad assured Laura.

Wow! Laura thought. *What a major confidence builder!*

Chad told Laura to "friend" him on Facebook, and promised to provide her with reams of advice on the challenge that awaited her.

At some point after she got home, Laura made her way to her bedroom and picked up a single-page typed printout she had recently placed on her dresser.

It was a poem, "Tri-mantra," by Olivier Blanchard, that she had come across online at some point. She kept meaning to frame it and hang it on her bedroom wall, but for now she was just glad to have it close by. She paused for a moment to read it silently to herself—not for the first, or last, time.

> *In my world,*
> *the water is cold,*
> *the wind is hard,*
> *and the road never ends.*
>
> *In my world,*
> *there are no losers.*
> *Only competitors*
> *still on their way,*
> *and spectators*
> *waiting to be inspired.*
>
> *In my world,*
> *victory is not weighed in gold,*
> *but in determination and courage.*
>
> *In my world,*
> *there are no boundaries,*
> *no limits,*
> *there is no end.*
> *Every day is the last day of my life . . .*
> *and the first.*

In my world,
the word "can't" does not exist,
and nothing is impossible.

Laura thought of her performance at Vineman, and of the chance encounter with Chad, and of all she had accomplished thus far on her own Ironman quest. She couldn't help but smile. Forget being half full; her cup now felt like one of those biking water bottles, overflowing after being held under a garden hose.

Her fears—and there remained many—could wait for at least another day.

CHAPTER 9

The Incline

The mosquito bites that traced the stubble in Seth Cannello's beard line and dotted his forehead like chicken pox were still raw and swollen as he guided his family's battered Toyota Camry along the two-lane highway outside Colorado Springs. It was midday on Wednesday, July 22, and though red-rock formations with names like Garden of the Gods and Kissing Camels were ablaze out his passenger-side window, Seth's mind was elsewhere.

He had just returned, spent, from a two-day fishing trip in the Wyoming wilderness with a buddy from work, and little seemed to have gone as planned. Even before the trip began, he had had to accept that his father would not be able to join him, as intended, because of his ongoing treatments for brain cancer. Seth and his friend James had been pelted by those mosquitoes since almost the moment they began to ascend the mountain trail, despite their having slathered themselves with repellent and donned nylon jackets. Although they were relieved to have reached their campsite, at an elevation of about eleven thousand feet, their respite was short-lived. Rain began to fall, and the downpour would continue throughout the night. Tossing in his sleeping bag in his tent, Seth had remained stubbornly awake. Their reward finally came the next day, when they began pulling golden trout—a fish neither had ever caught before—out of a nearby lake. The following day, though, Seth remained groggy from the three-and-a-half-hour hike down, followed by the eight-hour drive home.

But there would be little rest for him, at least not for a few more hours. With Ironman Arizona looming four months to the day from now, Seth had scheduled a workout for himself that appeared in no triathlete's training manual. He had intended it as a way to take advantage of the geographical edge that living and training at elevation in Colorado might provide him come November, when he would be much closer to sea level in Arizona.

His goal today: to ascend, yet again, the Incline, an unrelenting one-mile trail cut straight up a shoulder of Pikes Peak, looming from the parking lot below like a thin, ramrod-straight scar cut into a forest of pine and evergreen. The trail had once been the roadbed of the Mount Manitou Scenic Incline Railway, a cable car that shuttled visitors from an elevation of about 6,600 feet to 8,600 feet, according to the Web site Inclineclub .com, which its devotees had created in tribute. The average grade then, as now, was about 41 percent, but in some spots it tilted upward like a barricade, at nearly 70 percent.

Towering another six thousand feet above the Incline was the summit of Pikes Peak, swaddled in clouds. Though usually snowcapped even as late as summer, its top was bare on this day.

Long after the Manitou railroad was shut down and dismantled, the ties that held its tracks in place remained, sometimes just a few inches apart. Fitness buffs like Seth had been drawn to the dusty strip like a magnet. Since signing up for Ironman Arizona, he had climbed the Incline about a half-dozen times—occasionally with friends, but usually alone. Although most triathletes prepared to swim, bike, and run by swimming, biking, running, and lifting weights, Seth had thus far been almost lackadaisical about, if not indifferent to, his preparation for Ironman Arizona. And he appeared, at times, to be paying the price.

On the winding drive to Pikes Peak he catalogued the various ailments with which he had been coping. A few weeks earlier he'd embarked on a century bike ride, his first, known as the Elephant Rock 100. Because the summer had been unusually cold, he had spent little time riding his bike outdoors, preferring the relative comfort of that unfinished room in his basement. As soon as he began Elephant Rock, in pitch-black darkness (it was 5:15 A.M.) and alone (his preference), Seth feared he'd made a mistake. He didn't feel ready, or in shape—an assessment that didn't change as he struggled to point his old LeMond bike into a strong head-wind and up one hill after another along the course route between Colorado Springs and Castle Rock. Despite taking several breaks, including one pit stop in which the lines for the portable toilets were never-ending, Seth was happy with his final time of just over six hours. Later, though, he would discover he had tweaked a hamstring muscle, an injury so painful he'd reluctantly decided to forgo one of the few other organized events on his training calendar: a race in mid-June, the Xterra Buffalo Creek Off-Road Triathlon, that put participants through a one-mile swim, twenty-mile mountain bike ride, and five-mile run.

Then there was his right hip, which had begun throbbing after Elephant Rock and never seemed to get better, despite his daily doses of Motrin. The pain had become so searing, he admitted, that it was waking him up at two or three in the morning.

During the day, he found he couldn't do much of anything, not even ride the stationary bike or jog on a treadmill at work. He finally went to see an osteopath.

"He did a bunch of different tests on my hip," Seth explained. "He turned my leg and wrenched it back—and I just shot off the table." A series of X-rays were ordered, which showed, mercifully, that none of the bones in Seth's hip was broken. The doctor's diagnosis was tendinitis.

In the few days since, including the fishing trip, the stronger anti-inflammatory drugs the doctor had prescribed seemed to be doing the trick. Seth was feeling better, though he was worried about the precious time he'd lost from his training.

It was with the intent of setting a challenge for himself that he stepped onto the Incline that July day. The first three hundred to four hundred yards of the one-mile trail were deceptive in being relatively flat, allowing for a quick pace. Built more like a runner than a swimmer or cyclist, Seth, at six foot three, had sculpted calves, lean, bony knees, and thighs that climbed to a high waist. He'd dropped fourteen pounds during his initial Ironman training and couldn't afford to lose much more.

After about a quarter-mile, the trail began to turn rapidly upward, at which point the Incline definitely constituted an aerobic workout, but Seth barely broke a sweat. Twenty-five minutes later, after a slow jog without any stops, and with a Rocky Mountain vista stretching before him, he reached the summit.

For all the aches and pains in his hamstring and hip, and for all his concerns that he wasn't training as much or as often as he should, that sort of performance suggested that he was probably far better prepared for Ironman Arizona than he was willing to admit—to himself. Here was a guy who, less than a decade earlier, had been stooped at the waist for an entire month following lymph node surgery, during which a surgical team had bisected his abdomen in an effort to halt the spread of his testicular cancer. He had not only battled himself back to good health; he appeared to be in outstanding condition.

But, he was quick to acknowledge, even if he stayed free of further injuries, he would have no idea until he was well into the race at Arizona whether he'd feel confident he'd done enough to prepare.

"I'm just going, right now, off how I feel," he said, explaining how he was training without adhering to the sort of diligent regimen that others were surely following. "To me, I almost feel like I need to let my body heal. I'm at the age [forty] when I just wouldn't heal otherwise."

At one point earlier in the year, he had discovered the need to build that recovery time into his workouts when he realized he would grow so "tired and sore" that he "wasn't putting forth the effort that I should have." "Even though I was doing the distances, I didn't feel like I was training. I was a zombie. I was just existing."

And so he pulled back, having learned this lesson: "I think you just have to trust your gut. My gut tells me if I keep training the way I am, I'm going to finish my race."

And yet, for all his confidence—a confidence that he himself characterized as bordering on cockiness—Seth knew he had to make some adjustments. He wasn't swimming enough—maybe once a week, when two or three times was probably warranted at this stage. He resolved to get to the pool more—no easy task, because it was on a different military base—but was also intent on continuing to stick with the breaststroke and avoid the more taxing front crawl. He also knew he would have to steadily lengthen his workout times, in all three triathlon sports, over the next few months, to build endurance. And while he recognized that to do so, he would have to follow a more organized plan—he had, in fact, downloaded two different training programs from a Web site—he was determined to defy the so-called experts and reserve the right to set those regimens aside.

"If it says I have to run thirteen miles, and I don't feel like running that day, if my body is broken down, I'm not going to do it," he said, adding: "For someone like me to follow an exact training plan is a little ridiculous. I don't have the time. I have to go pick my kids up. I have to stay late at work if something has happened.

"Sometimes," he explained, "you need a day off, even when it's not scheduled."

Seth also said he was determined to continue to train alone—rejecting, for example, an opportunity to do the Elephant Rock 100 with several friends.

"I'm not going there with anybody," he said of Ironman Arizona. "My plans aren't to run next to somebody there. I kind of feel like that's the way I should train. Maybe I'm wrong."

Unlike Laura Arnez, whose children cheered her on and encouraged her to take that recess time, Seth's wife and three daughters paid little attention to his pursuit.

"My wife thinks there's something wrong with me," he said, laughing. "My kids kind of do, too. I'm either at work or I'm working out."

He added: "I'll come upstairs on the days I have to take them to school, or take them to their grandparents' house, I'll come up from a ride or run, and I'll be completely drenched with sweat. They're always making little comments about how sweaty I am."

Seth was impervious to their good-natured needling, knowing that life would no doubt return to normal by Thanksgiving, the Thursday after Ironman Arizona. What continued to rattle him, though, was the nagging worry about how his Raynaud's syndrome would be affected by the low water temperature of Tempe Town Lake during Ironman Arizona. A few weeks earlier, he'd gone scuba diving with his wife at a lake in Denver, so that they might both become certified.

"The water was freezing," Seth recalled, and, despite wearing a wetsuit, he could barely stay in for more than a few minutes. Though the lake was cold, it was probably several degrees warmer than what he'd encounter in Arizona. And if he required all the time allotted for the swim portion of Ironman Arizona, he'd be immersed in that water for nearly two and a half hours.

Though not ordinarily outspoken, Seth was beginning to think he needed to reach out to the organizers of Ironman Arizona to advocate a bit on his own behalf. "I'm going to have to ask the race director if I can wear gloves"—meaning waterproof gloves—"or not enter the water until just before the race starts."

He had not yet done any research on whether such accommodations were even possible, though he did know that the Ironman organizers were, in general, determined to make few exceptions. Competitors who were missing limbs or were wheelchair-bound, for example, were provided no more time to complete the various stages of the race than others who might be able-bodied. While many triathlons begin with the swimmers running into the water in groups, or waves, those friends of his who'd done Ironman Arizona told him that the swimmers got into the water, up to their chins, and waited there to begin the race en masse—more than two thousand of them taking their first strokes simultaneously.

Seth, his bravado gradually evaporating, was beginning to obsess a bit over the ten minutes or more he might have to spend treading water before the starter's cannon went off.

"I'm afraid," he admitted, "I'll be frozen by then."

Life Time Fitness, a sprawling marble-and-granite structure on the outskirts of San Antonio, could, for the uninitiated who might catch it only in passing from Highway 281, be confused with a megachurch, right down to the two-story, skylight-illuminated entryway. In one of its training rooms, DeAdra Harston pushed the click wheel on her iPod just after 8:30 on a Thursday morning in late August, and the big speakers arrayed around the room began to pulse with the opening organ chords of the 1960s hit "Gimme Some Lovin'." Elevated at the front of the room as if on a small stage, DeAdra sat atop a stationary bike wearing a bike top and shorts, her blond hair bunched haphazardly atop her head. Before her, all but three of the fifty gleaming gray bikes arranged in long rows on the battered blond-wood floor were occupied.

Crouched atop the bike at front row center, like the most attentive kid in a fourth-grade class, was Bryan Reece.

Clad in charcoal black bike shoes, cleated to the pedals, along with a gray LiveStrong bike shirt and black padded bike shorts, he looked like he was ready for a hundred-mile outdoor ride, as did so many others in the class, which was noteworthy only because Bryan had been so adamant after his very first class that he would never dress like this, at least indoors. And yet here he was.

On an oversize screen at the front of the room, DeAdra was playing a video of the 2007 Tour de France, albeit with the commentary turned all the way down, so as not to interrupt the classic rock sound track she'd picked out for the day. The video was intended for motivation, but also as a way for the participants to, if they wished, seek to replicate the cadence of Tour riders like George Hincapie and Fabian Cancellara as they climbed the side of a French mountain.

"Hey, you guys!" DeAdra said through a microphone that was attached to the headset around her ear, as Aerosmith's "Sweet Emotion" came on. "Today is hills. Welcome to class. Let's get those legs fired up."

"Hills again?" one woman groaned to herself, though not so loud that DeAdra could hear.

"Add some load," DeAdra instructed, which, the participants knew, was a sign to turn the small red wheel between their legs from left to right so that the lever on their front wheel would create more resistance, as if they were beginning to climb.

As the riders began to adjust, DeAdra, who had heretofore been barking at them a bit like a drill sergeant, suddenly morphed into Dr. Phil.

"Meg, we missed you," she shouted to a woman in red. Pointing toward another, DeAdra told the class that the woman had begun spinning a few weeks earlier, with the goal of rendering her jeans so baggy she would need new ones.

"She met that goal," DeAdra announced with obvious pride. "She needs to buy new jeans." Several people craned and acknowledged the woman with a smile and a nod.

"Shelby, we're going to get you in shape for volleyball," DeAdra said to a girl in her late teens, seated in the far-left corner in the back, who would soon be back at college. "Ruth," DeAdra said toward the back, as if now taking attendance, "you're starting your new job this week. Next week: front row."

But the encouraging happy talk was a bit deceptive. The entire class was already perspiring profusely, with small puddles starting to form beneath them, as DeAdra interrupted her shout-outs with instructions that they continue to "add load." Occasionally, in a bid to pump their heart rates ever higher, she would coax them out of their seats for thirty seconds or so, only to send them back, to rest, before motioning them up again.

Bryan, meanwhile, was somewhat in his own world, his gaze fixed about fifteen yards in front of him, past the screen to the front wall. Though he sometimes came off the saddle when DeAdra instructed, he also seemed oblivious to many of her commands, sitting while the rest of the class stood. It wasn't that he wasn't pedaling hard—with his cheeks red and his breathing rapid, he was probably getting a workout in the upper end of his target heart rate zone—but periodically he'd close his eyes, a peaceful smile on his lips.

He was, in fact, visualizing himself on the bike course at Ironman Arizona, which he'd studied firsthand as a volunteer a year earlier. Soon he would be in Tempe yet again, though this time as a participant—three months to the day from now, if all went according to plan. He practiced such visualizations "every single day," adding, "If I'm out riding by myself, or running by myself, I'm thinking about it. If I'm doing an eight-mile run, I'll think to myself, *I've got to be able to do more than three of these.* Or if I swim two thousand yards nonstop, I think, *It's going to be two thousand more before I get out of the lake.*"

On many nights, Bryan's sleep was filled with recurring dreams of the race—some of them replays of inspiring scenes of tenacity and endurance he'd witnessed as a spectator. When he'd awaken, his head would be full of ideas of strategies he wanted to pursue on race day, as well as mistakes he didn't want to make.

Bryan had even dreamed about the most embarrassing scene he and Debbie had witnessed at Ironman Arizona 2008. Standing on a bridge over Tempe Town Lake, which offered an unparalleled view of the transition from swim to bike, the couple couldn't help but notice the man who'd begun to remove his swim trunks before moving fully into the white transition tent. Even Debbie stole a glance, at least until the man bent over to apply an anti-chafing roll-on in preparation for the grueling bike ride ahead. ("Okay, that's just too much," she had told her husband, looking away.)

Like the high school student who worried he'd inadvertently show up for the SAT naked, Bryan was determined that, when his time came, "no one will see my butt outside the tent."

After a final simulated hill climb, set to Styx's "Renegade," DeAdra exhorted the spinners before her to extend their arms skyward, fists clenched. It was, she said, their "Rocky" pose, meant to simulate the film boxer's famous climactic run up the steps in Philadelphia. After cooldown exercises, Bryan headed down the stairs to the café, receiving numerous "attaboys," pats on the back, and handshakes. Everyone seemed to know he was trying to become an Ironman, and everyone knew he had been raising money for cancer research as part of that quest. Like a politician, he'd been slipping them the business cards he'd had made up, the ones that said PLEASE CONSIDER MAKING A DONATION BENEFITING THE LANCE ARMSTRONG FOUNDATION IN ASSOCIATION WITH IRONMAN ARIZONA, followed by his Janus charity Web page address, the URL for his blog, and his phone number.

Though DeAdra is typically the one doing the motivating at Life Time Fitness, she admitted that Bryan may well have given her more inspiration than she had provided him. "We are going to help Bryan raise that $5,000," she said. "Everyone is rooting for Bryan, wherever he goes. Everyone wants to talk to Bryan. Everyone asks him, how's your training going?" She was particularly struck by his standard response to well-wishers: "This race is bigger than me, and their struggle"—by which he meant that of the cancer survivors and victims whose names he planned to carry with him on race day—"is bigger than mine." DeAdra had lost her own father to cancer, and it was emotional for her to watch Bryan during each spin class knowing that somewhere on his body, in a place yet to be determined, he'd be carrying her father's name throughout Ironman Arizona.

It wasn't just that Bryan was vocal about taking the focus off himself; he genuinely appeared to live that philosophy. The prior Saturday, DeAdra had joined Bryan and more than a dozen other members of the gym for an organized sixty-mile group bike ride. As the temperature reached record heights, Bryan and DeAdra noticed that two riders were struggling. Both had made an innocent, though costly, mistake: They'd filled the water pouches strapped to their backs, known as CamelBaks, with ice instead of water, thinking that as it melted they'd be able to sip cool refreshment through the tubes that extended to their mouths. They hadn't realized that because the packs were insulated, the ice had remained frozen, and before long they were dehydrated. At a certain point Bryan sprinted to the end of the ride, where he'd left his black Lexus SUV, and drove back to pick up the two parched men, arriving not a moment too soon. One of them would have to be taken to the emergency room to receive fluids intravenously.

The way DeAdra recounted the scene, it was as if she were describing Superman, not an investment adviser who, less than three years earlier, was literally having difficulty pushing himself out of his easy chair without a little light-headedness, a side effect of the blood pressure medicine he'd been prescribed. She still remembered what Bryan had told her, after his very first spin class: He wanted to get in shape so that he might live long enough "to see my daughter grow up, graduate from college, get married, and have babies." Even DeAdra's husband had been inspired by all that Bryan had accomplished. Her husband's weight, she said, had slowly crept up over the years from 190 pounds to 240. But in recent weeks, he'd diligently dropped twenty pounds, telling his wife, "I want to be like Bryan."

"I've dropped a third-grader," Bryan himself said, noting that between the moment in January 2007 when the doctor told him he might soon die and now, he'd lost almost forty pounds, usually hovering now at around 210. Gone, for the most part, were those steaks he used to devour—"I'm staying away from anything with eyes," he explained, with fish being a notable exception—as well as the martinis with which he'd typically wash that beef down. His one regular indulgence now was red wine.

"I'd love to be around two hundred," he said. "I don't know if I'll make it."

In recent months, he'd had all of his suits for work re-cut, and the waists taken in from forty inches to thirty-six or thirty-seven. He'd not needed any medication for his blood pressure or his heart in almost two years.

The nation was then still mired in a recession, one that Bryan had felt acutely in his capacity as a branch manager for a financial services firm. Bryan believed that, without his Ironman training, the anxiety he felt amid the country's dire economic times—and the struggles of his industry in particular—would likely have overwhelmed him.

"Our stock dropped," he said. "You can't imagine the impact on people's personal net worth." And it wasn't just his clients who'd lost a sizable portion of their savings; Bryan had, too.

Bryan had to marvel himself at how his life had changed. *Had I not had the issues with my back, had I not gone to the doctor, had I not started doing this, everything that happened to the market and our firm . . . I don't know that I'd be here today.*

Like DeAdra and DeAdra's husband, Debbie said she was amazed at the transformation in Bryan, whom she'd married nearly two decades earlier.

"When he does something, he jumps in with both feet," she said. "He's so much more relaxed when he gets home now. It's his stress reliever from work. I think he really enjoys the cycling part of it. He enjoys running more than he thought he would. He's always been an outgoing person, but he's even more so now." Like Bryan's brother, Debbie found herself wanting to be more like her husband. During those years he hadn't set foot in a gym, she hadn't, either. So when he joined Life Time Fitness, she did, too. About a year later, on Taylour's twenty-first birthday, she signed herself and her daughter up for a sprint-distance triathlon—a first for both of them. "It was fun," Debbie said. "Would I do another? Probably so. Would I do an Ironman? Let's say this: I have no desire to sit on a bike for 112 miles."

In fact, as she contemplated the challenge that loomed before Bryan at Ironman Arizona, it was the bike ride that scared Debbie the most. "He's already done a marathon," she said. "He could swim that far, the 2.4 miles, if he puts his mind to it. But riding that far—that's the one that concerns me."

Bryan himself was about to step up his training dramatically. For the first few months of 2009, he'd paced himself deliberately, so as not to get injured. That meant he might run once a week for an hour, an hour and a half, or, lately, an hour and forty-five minutes; do one long bike ride a week, of two to three hours, sometimes speeding up and slowing down in intervals like those in his spin class; and each Friday night he might do a long swim, as much to "wash the week away" as to build endurance.

But in just a few days, his calendar told him, he'd be just twelve weeks away from Ironman Arizona. And for the next month and a half, he planned to step up his training to fifteen to twenty hours a week, before gradually tapering those workouts as the big race approached. As a guide, he would use a training plan set forth on the Web site Endurance Nation.com.

"It is two-a-day workouts for me for the foreseeable future," he said. The two to three hours he was riding on a Saturday might now be expanded to six hours, and his run on Sunday expanded to two to three hours. Before long he'd even stage dress rehearsals of all three Ironman events.

Bryan did feel a bit jittery about trying to keep himself free of injury in the few months left before Ironman Arizona. He had lately been haunted by the experience of a colleague who'd been training for a bike race called the Hotter'N Hell Hundred. Just the previous Saturday, the man had set out before dawn on an eighty-mile training ride.

"He had ridden the same course several times," Bryan recalled. "He felt very comfortable and confident, even though it was still dark. He was going down a hill, somewhere around thirty miles an hour, and hit a dead deer in the road."

"He is," Bryan confirmed, "no longer going to be riding the Hotter'N Hell Hundred."

The man had proceeded to slide about fifty feet and had the road rash on his elbows and thighs to prove it. But he was lucky he wasn't hurt far worse, having hit the road with such force that his helmet cracked in four places and was completely skid-marked on one side.

Bryan's takeaway from this story was that, for all the efforts he had made to keep himself from pulling a muscle or blowing out a knee or suffering any other injury, there was only so much he could do to steer himself free of accidents.

"Obviously, the closer to the race you come," he said, "the more careful you are."

CHAPTER 10

This Is Going to Hurt

Leanne Johnson noticed the small cut above the knuckle of the ring finger on her right hand as soon as she awoke on August 9, a Sunday. But she paid it little mind and went for a short run around Greenfield Lake with her friend Andrea. After they returned, though, that abrasion had morphed into a small blood blister, which was sufficiently nerve-racking to the nurse in Leanne that she showed it to her friend. Each wondered aloud to the other whether Leanne might have burned her finger, absentmindedly, on her flatiron. After a quick shower, she showed Scott, and he concurred with their hypothesis: It was probably just a minor burn. And with that, the couple, joined by Andrea, headed for the beach for the afternoon.

It wasn't long after they arrived on the sand that Leanne realized, with some alarm, that the blister was spreading and her finger was beginning to swell, the small cut having grown longer and wider than the nail on Leanne's ring finger. Leanne could now even feel her pulse throbbing beneath the lesion. With her medical training, she wasn't taking any chances. She and Scott bid Andrea goodbye and headed for the twenty-four-hour urgent-care clinic.

The initial diagnosis surprised Leanne: The doctor suspected she'd been bitten by a brown recluse spider. Roughly the size of a quarter and common throughout the South, this arachnid is typically harmless and will bite a human only when provoked, usually because someone has rolled over onto one in bed or put on a garment in which the spider had decided to nest, according to a University of Kentucky Web site on spiders. That said, the wounds from their bites can be painful and can take several weeks to heal.

After the clinicians punctured Leanne's blister and swabbed it, they drew some blood from her arm and found that her white blood cell count was elevated, probably in response to an infection. She immediately began a course of antibiotics, but even after the treatment, the blister grew ever larger.

"I was really getting worried," Leanne confided in her online journal. While her wound did not appear to have spread further overnight, its change in color from purple to red didn't make Leanne feel any better. "I had to call in sick to work," she said, "because no one wants to have a nurse care for them with a swollen, infected-looking finger."

Leanne was heartsick, and even a little embarrassed, to have to miss work because of a spider bite. While she had come to accept that she could be clumsy enough to occasionally topple from her bike, even in the relative comfort of her garage, getting bitten by a spider was not something she had considered as she mapped out various contingencies for the late summer and early fall. But it wasn't just her work that threatened to be upended by her mysterious bite. This was crunch time for Ironman Arizona—the period when, like Bryan Reece, she and Scott planned to load on the laps, miles, and hours of their training.

"Not sure if I will get any workout in today," Leanne lamented to her online journal that Monday. "Everything I have read says to not do any strenuous exercise, as that will spread the spider venom into the bloodstream."

During the day she managed to get in touch with an infectious disease specialist at the hospital where she worked. He felt confident that she had a staph infection caused by "some sort of insect," and that he "couldn't rule out a spider bite." Leanne's anxiety only seemed to increase.

By Monday evening she felt like she was going stir crazy. Setting aside any fears she had of further complications, she decided to go for a hard eighteen-mile bike ride—four loops around the lake—at a brisk average pace of nearly nineteen miles an hour. The blister didn't impede her grabbing her handlebars and, mercifully, there were no signs of any venom spreading further. She ran a bit that night, too, at the Wilmington Athletic

Club. The following morning, she awoke early and drove to the loop at Wrightsville Beach, where she met another friend, Annemarie, a favorite running partner who'd been sidelined since giving birth a month earlier. The pair walked one mile, then ran the last two. "I've missed her," Leanne told her journal that night. "Annemarie did awesome. She'll be back at her fitness level in no time." Leanne then climbed on her bike yet again and did two loops, for a total of eighteen miles, much of it in the face of a strong headwind.

"My legs felt fatigued from biking last night but I thought I may as well get used to it, because they are going to feel fatigued during my IM," Leanne said afterward.

And what of her finger? "It's doing better today," she told her journal, late Tuesday. "The swelling has gone down and the blister/rash has stopped so I think it has stabilized." Still, she felt confident she was "going to have a nasty scar!"

By Saturday the 15th, nearly a week after her bite, Leanne was back on track—so much so that she followed an eleven-mile run (from the YMCA to downtown Wilmington, then around Greenfield Lake and back) with a "90-minute Roast," which involved a half-hour class in which she stretched using various-size kettlebells, iron weights that look like small cannonballs with handles; a thirty-minute spin class; and a thirty-minute run around the Y.

"My arms and legs were soooooooooooo sore when I woke up," she reported to her journal Sunday morning. "I learned that when training for an IM just stick to the plan and don't do anything extra."

If Leanne went a little overboard with running and spinning and lifting that day, her swimming was another matter; her blister—which was still healing—had kept her out of the water for nearly two weeks. This was precious time away from swimming during a crucial period in her training, and it had cost her—a fact she realized on a weekday morning in mid-August, when she and her friend Erin got up early to do an unofficial roughly Olympic-distance triathlon.

They had designed the "course" themselves and were the only entrants.

They decided to begin with a bike ride of twenty-nine miles or so, originating at the community pool in Erin's neighborhood. "My legs were a little heavy at first but the muscle soreness from the weekend was gone and I felt no pain in my right shin/foot," Leanne told her journal, referring to an ill-fated attempt over the weekend to try out a new pair of ASICS Kayano running shoes. She had tried to save a few dollars by ordering the "kids' version, size 5.5," only to learn that they were bigger than the equivalent women's size, and Leanne was left with a sore shin as a result. *Lesson learned*, she thought.

A five-mile run in Erin's neighborhood, known as Covil Farm, followed, and while Leanne felt a bit heavy, she sped up as the run progressed. The women finished off with nearly a mile-long session in the pool, and Leanne's assessment was blunt: "Not a good swim for me." As Leanne recorded that night in her journal: "It has been almost two weeks since I swam due to my finger and I felt like a complete slug in the water. From now on I need to make an effort to get in the pool! Swimming is my weakness and I avoid it. I need to learn to love it."

If there was any consolation, it was that Leanne and Scott returned that night to Rita's Italian Ice, where they again climbed behind the counter to scoop, with the proceeds of all the orders they filled going to Leanne's charitable effort for Ironman Arizona in memory of baby Liam. At the beginning of the evening, she had collected just over $3,000, meaning she still had about $2,000 to raise over the next three months to reach her goal of $5,000. The night's take was $223.

A few days later, on Friday, she made good on her pledge to focus anew on her swimming, putting in more than an hour: a three-hundred-meter warm-up; a 2,450-meter straight swim, which was probably the longest swim without a break she'd ever attempted; and a two-hundred-meter cooldown. While she was exhilarated, her right shoulder, which had not bothered her during her layoff from swimming, began to ache about halfway through her workout, as it had so often in the months prior.

"I need to get swimming more!" Leanne vowed afterward, in what was becoming a familiar refrain.

Among the last big hurdles on her training calendar between now and her Ironman attempt was a 70.3, or half-Ironman, in Augusta, Georgia. When Leanne went to the Web site for the race, she was stunned to learn from the countdown clock that it was just thirty-three days away.

"Yikes," she wrote in her journal, after learning that her swim group, or wave, would be the twelfth to be launched into the water that day. "I feel like I am ready for the bike and run . . . it's just the swim that I am worried about."

Three days later, her anxiety only increased when she thought about the start of the swim at Ironman Arizona. Unlike in a 70.3, where the swimmers might be staggered in groups of seventy-five to a hundred, every swimmer—more than two thousand men and women—starts an Ironman swim simultaneously.

"Reality is starting to set in," she wrote in her journal. "I am scared. I have never started a race with that many people. I think my strategy will be to wait a few minutes and let everyone clear out before I start.

"I doubt," she added, "that a few minutes at the beginning is going to cost me much time in the long run . . . ?"

Her tentative plan for approaching the swim appeared to have relaxed her, even if the question mark she placed at the end of that sentence betrayed her lingering concerns.

Throughout the summer, Seth Cannello could never seem to get any momentum in his Ironman training. He had to sit out the Xterra race in mid-June because of that pulled hamstring and throbbing hip. And when he finally felt pain-free, or somewhere close to that, work or some other distraction seemed to intervene.

"Have officially started my training program" he wrote in an e-mail the last week of July. As he explained his tardiness in commencing, "It has been hard setting aside the time, and I've had to split workouts up in order to complete the time requirements. It has been raining a lot, which has also made it hard. Tonight I was supposed to swim, but the pool was closed due to weather warnings." On a positive note, his hip was feeling much better, and he hoped it would no longer be a problem.

Months earlier, Seth had circled August 1 on his calendar. It marked the date of a half-marathon at the United States Air Force Academy, a significant milestone on his training plan. Seth had, of course, made a conscious decision to designate the 26.2-mile run at Ironman Arizona as the first full marathon he'd undertake, however much he might have benefited from running that distance at least once before his Ironman—especially since it would follow hours of swimming and running. Still, he knew he had to run at least a half-marathon before Arizona, and the timing of the Air Force Academy run, a little over three months prior to his Ironman, seemed appropriate.

What Seth hadn't counted on, though, was the carpeting.

A week prior to the Academy event, he learned that the military had approved the financing for the new rugs he had long ago requested for the Air Force fitness center he managed, for installation on the weekend of August 1–2.

Even if he had been tempted to ask for Saturday off, he knew his request was likely to be turned down. He was the only manager at the fitness center who was scheduled to be in town that weekend and who had "escort privileges," a status he had achieved after receiving special training on how to monitor "guests" working inside a restricted area at the base. The fitness center, however innocuous it seemed, fell within that category. Seth would have to find another half-marathon.

He hoped that, during the installation, he could at least run on a treadmill or ride a bicycle while the workmen put the carpeting down nearby. "But I felt bad," he said afterward, "so I helped them pull old carpet out, move furniture and install the new carpet." He wound up working twelve hours each of those days.

"It was a great workout," he said. "But I missed the run."

When he woke up Monday, though, it was the swim that was on his mind. Whether he chose to do his beloved breaststroke during Ironman Arizona or even experimented with a few intervals of front crawl, he knew that the blood would likely drain from his fingers in just a few minutes without some protection. And so, after work that day, he decided to reach out to the race officials directly, to see if some accommodation might be made for him during the swim. He sent out a note under the subject line "Athlete Inquiry—Ford Ironman Arizona":

> I have Raynaud's Disease, which affects my circulation in
> my extremities. I didn't think it was going to be an issue for
> the IM. However, since I started training in open water, I've

found my condition really hampers my performance. I was
wondering if I can wear gloves and if my entry into the water
could be delayed until the start of the race? Thanks for your
time.

Two days later, Seth got a personal response from Paul Huddle, one of
the race's co-directors. Huddle, a multiple Ironman finisher himself,
wasted no time getting right to the point:

> While I have no problem with you waiting until a minute
> or two to go before the start cannon is fired to keep you out of
> the water until the last minute, gloves are not permitted in the
> swim portion of our Ironman events.
> I'm copying our head referee, Jimmy Riccitello, in case you
> would like to discuss this further with him.
> Train safe and we'll see you in November!

As he read the response on a computer monitor in his windowless
basement, near the stationary bike where he would spend so many predawn hours pedaling to nowhere, Seth was despondent. He couldn't imagine swimming without gloves for even a half-hour, let alone at least ninety
minutes, in that chilly water. While he had overcome many setbacks in his
life, and more recently in his training, he began to seriously wonder
whether he was destined to hear the sound of the cannon that Huddle had
referenced in his e-mail.

Bryan Reece lay in bed longer than he should have on the morning of
Sunday, August 9, and once he did finally get up, he paid for his sluggishness during an eight-mile run. "At least it wasn't a billion degrees when I
finished," he recorded in his online journal afterward. "It was only about
80 million degrees."

> Man, this has been a hot summer in San Antonio. We have
> set a record for continuous days over 100 with no end in sight.

Hopefully we can get some rain soon. I have dust in my front
yard that I used to call grass! The lawn guy still bills me for
mowing it . . . but what is it he is mowing? We can only water
every other week for about a minute and then that's it.

Four weeks later, on the first Saturday in September, he found himself
"lollygagging" again—though this time he was procrastinating to avoid
starting a far more ambitious workout than an eight-mile run. His training
plan called for a "big brick," using the shorthand for a bike ride followed
by a run, just as in an actual triathlon. Today he was scheduled to ride
sixty-three miles, followed immediately by a 2.5-mile run. "This IM plan
is pretty cool, but also intense," he observed.

Wildlife today include a deer running across the road
about 15 yards in front of me and then jumping a barbed wire
fence—this was very, very cool. Second wildlife sighting was
a snake cruising across the road. I hit his tail and then carefully looked at my wheels to be sure he wasn't up in the spokes.
He wasn't, but I saw him too late to totally avoid him.

Then there was all manner of roadkill—deer, possum,
skunk and even a stalking buzzard (big sucker, too) looking
for something to eat. Dr. Seuss had it right, "Oh, the places
you'll go."

Before signing off, Bryan noted in passing that he had taken advantage
of an end-of-summer sale at the Performance Bicycle Web site and gotten
a great deal on a top-of-the-line helmet by Giro. "I hope it is as cool as I
think it will be," he wrote. "There are lots of vents and I hope the air flow
is big enough to keep my melon protected."

He spent the next few days tapering his training, with just light workouts, in preparation for an Olympic-distance triathlon on Labor Day in
Austin, hosted by a local bike shop, Jack & Adam's. "Very organized, nice
expo, cool technical t-shirts, a race hat and water bottle—but no medal"
is how Bryan described the race, which drew more than 2,500 participants. As for his performance that day:

Time was 3:09 . . . pacing in line with IMAZ pacing . . . really tried not to overcook the bike so I had something left for the run . . .

Swim was 35-36 (minutes) . . . was a cruise . . . caught a little draft and hung on it for a while—focused on form a bit, counted strokes, etc . . . really pleased with the "straightness" of my swim.

Worked through T1 [the first transition]—it is so dry here that the little bit of water on your feet and the dirt made for nasty mud in the bike shoes, with rocks and all sorts of other stuff . . .

Rolled out on the bike—focused on pacing and nutrition (these were the absolute needs of the day—practice for Arizona). Rode what I thought was a smart race which was actually pretty fast (for me). Bike was 1:15-1:20

Rocketed through T2 and out on the run—legs felt really good (well done on the bike power consumption) but I had overdone the calories—I took in about a half a bottle too much which is 150 excess calories. Doesn't sound like much but I think with the volume of liquid it filled me pretty full. After a couple of miles the stomach felt better . . .

Had a fun finish with another guy in my age group— I passed him with about ¼ of a mile to go and held him off. I finished ahead by 10 seconds—that was a fun way to end the race. Run was 1:00 to 1:05, with about 6 minutes in two transitions.

I was also very pleased with the lack of recovery time needed. I felt great Monday afternoon and after a day off Tuesday was ready to train again.

The following Sunday he'd committed to participate in the Prairieman, a half-Ironman in Grand Prairie, near Dallas.

"For the record," he observed, "I don't think 70.3 miles under your own power should ever be referred to as HALF of anything." He had been praying for rain all summer, and he finally got his wish—and then some—in the three days of near-continuous downpours leading up to Prairieman. There was no letup during the race itself, which was set in and around Joe Pool Lake in Lynn Creek Park, and it rained the entire time Bryan was on the course, so hard that parts reminded him "of hurricanes, tropical storms and tsunamis. You could actually feel the rain during the swim."

The swim felt LONG—my time was 51 minutes. We started in pretty flat water and about three minutes into the swim I thought a big power boat was going back and forth in front of me. The waves were that big. There were white caps and big waves throughout. I thought they would be a big help after we turned the corner but they were actually quartering you so they were pushing you further out into the lake so you had to swim back in to fight their effect. There was some feel of body surfing which would have been good if it had been in the right direction. Did I mention it was still raining?

T1 was pretty slow—about 4:20 . . . The bike was treacherous with flooded streets and HUGE puddles . . . When someone passed you, you virtually drowned in the spray off their back tires . . . They cut the bike short in the pre-race meeting due to the conditions—they said they didn't want people to try for a PR or for people to take chances on the bike. I saw several people down and almost went down three times myself . . . Once was really close—my back tire was sliding right and left and I really don't know how I saved it. I think it was just luck and instinct.

The bike was 42 miles, according to them . . . just under 44, according to my Garmin. Bike time was 2:26 for a 17.2 average speed, assuming 42 miles. Extrapolating to a 56 mile ride would have been about 3:15.

Did I mention it was still raining? Everything was wet. My cycle shoes were full of water, my socks were soaked. How about this: when you bent your head down on the bike, water had collected in the air vent holes of the helmet, trapped against your scalp, and it just ran out all over you. It was like you dumped a glass of water on your head. T2 was about 3:07.

I had kept my run shoes in a plastic bag so they went on dry. That lasted about 4 seconds. I wanted to try to run a good half marathon . . . I usually fry myself on the bike and then just survive the run. Well, this was a bit different. I ended up running a 2:25 half marathon . . . just 10 minutes off my half-marathon personal best. I felt GREAT . . . Used Galloway's run/walk method as always and was running past people in the last three miles. And yes, it was still raining.

As Bryan walked to his truck afterward, "dreaming of being dry," a passerby asked him and Debbie if it had been his "most miserable day" as a triathlete. After thinking a bit, Bryan told the woman it was "actually a pretty good day." In the process of explaining what he meant, he provided a good rough draft of a triathlete's manifesto:

> Yeah, it was wet. Yeah, it would have been easy to quit or not start. But that is not what we do. We deal with what comes—and we adapt and improvise. We realize transition times are not so important that we can't use Ziplock bags for a moment of "dry-sock feeling." We realize that we are fortunate that not EVERYONE in the world thinks we are crazy for wanting to play in the rain. We also realize how important those around us are, in a new way.

Here, of course, Bryan was referring to Debbie. If any tri spouse had ever been more loyal and dedicated and selfless, Bryan had not met her or him. Debbie had been at Prairieman from 5:30 to 9:00 in the morning, standing "soaked to the bone" as Bryan did his pre-race preparations, swam, and made it through the first transition. Only then did she retreat to her car to try to get some sleep and then read a magazine. She was back out in the rain as Bryan left the park for the run (his bike portion had been so fast that she had missed his coming in), returned to the car for about two more hours, then came back and got soaked all over again to watch him finish. "She was a trooper," Bryan wrote, "and in addition to her Sherpa Deb duties, she had to deal with a lot of wet crap to try to get home." Bryan's overall time that day was 5 hours, 51 minutes. Assuming the bike course had gone the full fifty-six miles, he estimated his time would have been about 6 hours, 36 minutes—"a personal best for me by a long shot."

Less than a week later, he climbed on his bike yet again for an organized sixty-five-mile ride known as the La Vernia Wild West Hammer-Fest. In contrast to his almost biblical experience in Grand Prairie, this day's ride was hot and dry—actually, blissfully uneventful, as Bryan thought while he rode, with none of the slipping and sliding that had characterized his ride at Prairieman.

But about two hundred yards from the finish line, he took a corner hard, skidded on some gravel in the road, and suddenly felt the wheels of his bike sliding out from under him, as if on ice.

This is going to hurt, he thought, almost as if in slow motion, as he felt the pavement draw near.

Pay attention to whether you hit your head.

Bryan was wearing his new helmet—a present Debbie had given him for his fiftieth birthday, which was the following weekend—and he would consider himself extraordinarily lucky that he had not waited to use it. It protected his skull by absorbing much of the impact of his fall, so much so that the outer shell cracked like an egg, just as it had been designed to.

As he lay on the ground, Bryan took a quick inventory. He noted the road rash—a painful form of friction burn in which some of the pavement was often left behind in the wound—on his knee, calf, hip, forearm, and elbow. The pain in one knee was so severe that he also wondered if he might have done some structural damage. And he was alert enough to realize he might well have suffered a concussion.

He then noticed that his Garmin 310XT, a small navigation-and-training computer strapped to his wrist, had shattered and was, in all likelihood, "no longer waterproof." He didn't especially care, but the extent of the damage was yet another reminder of how hard he and his bike had hit the ground.

Somehow he was able to walk his bike across the finish line. An ambulance had been parked nearby, and several EMTs who had seen him take a spill coaxed him inside to examine him.

It took the crew forty-five minutes to clean his wounds, using gauze to meticulously remove the fragments of gravel embedded in his skin.

They also spent a fair amount of time checking his head. Though he appeared to have avoided a concussion, it would be several more hours before they could definitively rule out such an injury. Bryan's main concern, though, continued to be the sharp pain in his kneecap.

After the crew led him gingerly down the back steps of the emergency vehicle, he summoned the courage to call Debbie.

"I just got out of the ambulance," he told her.

"Ambulance?" she asked, with understandable alarm.

As he somehow drove himself home, Bryan's thoughts turned to Ironman Arizona, now just two months and three days away.

I can't believe I may have screwed this up.

CHAPTER 11

His Time to Fight Had Ended

With her children safely delivered to school on a sunny Wednesday morning in late September, Laura Arnez loaded her wetsuit into her family's van and set out alone on the short drive to Lake Natomas. Lined with ancient oak trees and populated by ducks and the occasional squirrel, the lake was more than a mile long and perfectly suited to the goal she had set for the day.

In two months, Laura knew, she would be coaxing her body to swim 2.4 miles in Tempe Town Lake. As of this morning, her longest swim to date was exactly half that distance, a feat she'd accomplished a handful of times before—in the pool where she usually trained, at events like Vineman, and, on a few occasions, here in Natomas. As she drove, she made a concerted effort "not to think of this as my longest swim ever." Instead she played a bit of a game with her mind: Using various landmarks along the shore to gauge her distance—there were no buoys, and no lap lanes, only the measurements calculated by previous swimmers—she'd swim six-tenths of a mile out and then six-tenths of a mile back.

I've done this before, she told herself. *No big deal.*

This time, though, she'd have to repeat that workout in its entirety before she'd consider the day's mission complete.

As she stepped onto the sandy shore and waded in with a few paddles of breaststroke, Laura's first thought was that the water was "getting colder and colder every time." Yes, she had her wetsuit, which stretched from her chin to her cuffs to her ankles, but it hardly seemed to help. Laura began a few strokes of front crawl, and her breathing and heart rate immediately quickened in a rapid panic. Over time she had grown accustomed to this feeling, though, and how to deal with it.

Slow and steady, she told herself as she hit an imaginary clicker to once again initiate that mental slide show featuring her children and husband, this time set to songs like "The Music of the Night," from *The Phantom of the Opera*, which played softly in her head.

Breathing on her right, Laura kept the shoreline in sight and tried to sync her arms to the melody in her mind. Her sense of calm and serenity returned, interrupted only briefly by the thought that she was "in water with no bottom." But that anxious perception, too, would be short-lived.

The first out and back were really nice, she thought to herself after she had made the turn at the halfway point of her first loop and her starting point once again came into view. Once she had completed the first 1.2 miles, Laura paused only to take a two-minute breather. *Let's go again, Laura,* she urged herself.

"That is when I noticed, man, I am getting really cold now," Laura recalled afterward. "My hands were beginning to get numb, my feet, even my arms through my wetsuit." Still, she pushed off and persisted. *Let's go, Laura, let's take care of this and get out!* she told herself, as sternly as if she were a fitness trainer coaching someone else. Now she wasn't daydreaming about her family at all. Her mind was filled with seductive images of steaming-hot cups of coffee and thoughts of how warm and cozy the van would feel "after standing in sunlight."

She could feel her pace quickening as she rounded an imaginary buoy at the halfway point for her final lap that day. By now the water seemed to be growing choppier, and her stomach groaned with hunger. *I can do this!* she whispered. She wasn't sure she'd ever been colder in her life, but she did know this: She wasn't fatigued. Kicking hard, she reached the spot on the lakeshore where she had started, and climbed out. As she reached the van, she realized her hands were "sooooo frozen" that she had difficulty unzipping her wetsuit.

It was only then that she looked at the watch on her left wrist. She'd reset the stopwatch to zero when she began, and now it read 1:45—an hour and forty-five minutes. Laura instantly did the math: that was thirty-five minutes under the cutoff at Ironman Arizona, giving her plenty of wiggle room—should she need it, which she hoped she wouldn't.

She then asked herself: *Could I ride a bike right now?* Even with the numbness in her hands and feet, her answer was immediate. *A resounding yes!*

She had every reason to be confident. As at so many other junctures in her Ironman training, she'd accomplished something that day that she'd never done before—something she'd wondered if she could do at all. But she also knew that, for all of her efforts to simulate her Ironman swim on this relatively placid morning, there would be other variables in play in Tempe Town Lake.

Not least, she thought, were the more than two thousand other pairs of arms and legs that, before long, would be splashing on every side of her.

Leanne Johnson, who had been having similar thoughts, awoke with a start. The clock on her nightstand flashed 5:30 on this Friday morning in September, and her heart immediately sank. She'd wanted to be in the pool at the Wilmington Athletic Club no later than then so that she could get in a swim before work. But she'd forgotten to set her alarm—she'd actually turned it off on Wednesday night, because she was off on Thursday—and had overslept, though perhaps only an Ironman triathlete would consider sleeping until 5:30 oversleeping. Now she'd only have time to shower and head in to the hospital. She doubted she'd be able to swim at the end of the day, either, because her shift ended at 7:15 and the pool closed at 8. This would be her third day in a row without training, but with a fifteen-mile run coming up on Saturday—and her first century ride scheduled for Sunday—she wasn't especially concerned about the temporary layoff.

She and Scott had actually planned to ride the night before, but those plans had quickly gone awry—almost as soon as they left the familiar confines of Greenfield Lake and headed for a neighborhood of bigger, older homes called Glen Meade. Scott's back tire went flat, and he let Leanne repair it. She'd never changed a tire before, and felt proud—at least until the new tube went flat five minutes after Scott began riding on it. He didn't have another spare, and the sky was growing dark, so Leanne rode back to get their truck and then went to fetch him.

The couple's luck didn't improve much that Sunday, when they headed out the door before 7:30, bound for Moores Creek National Battlefield, where Leanne would attempt her first hundred-mile bike ride, the Hot 100. "When we pulled into the parking lot we didn't see any cars or signs of any bikers," Leanne wrote that night. "So we thought maybe there was another entrance to the park. We continued on down the road and found nothing." Scott, who was not much of a morning person in the best of circumstances, "was starting to get a little grumpy," because they were going to be late and miss the usual group with whom they liked to ride.

"Maybe we should just skip it and head to the beach and ride a few loops down there," Scott said, noting that the race was more of a leisurely affair and not timed. But by now Leanne had it firmly in her head that this would be her first century, and so, after some more sleuthing, they finally found the starting point of the ride.

For Leanne, the initial eighty-five miles were relatively effortless, even considering the fifteen miles she'd run the day before. But on the last few miles of this day's ride, she began to feel a sharp pain on the outer part of her right foot. "I think it is the part of my foot that I put pressure on while I ride," she told Scott, adding that she couldn't wait to get her shoe off. She was glad to see the finish.

In her journal that night, she reflected not just on that pain in her foot, which had yet to subside, but on other concerns:

> Can I possibly ride 12 more miles after 100 miles in an IM? And . . . can I run a marathon after that?
>
> I think this century ride put things in perspective for me in regards to IM. It's definitely going to be much, much harder than I ever imagined. In the next 11 weeks I need to get a few more LONG bike rides in . . . I need to run off the bike a bit more and I need to get swimming!
>
> I am definitely going into IMAZ with the goal of "finishing the race." I do not care how long it takes me or what place I

come in. This ride gave me a whole new respect, in regards to what I am trying to accomplish on November 22d.

On Sunday, September 20, the week before Augusta, she made good on her pledge to run more "off the bike," the better to simulate what it would feel like to ride, then run, not just in the 70.3 but also at the Ironman. She returned to the site of the Hot 100 with Scott and a half-dozen other friends for a series of extended drills. The group began with a thirty-mile bike ride, followed by a five-mile run. Leanne then did a second thirty-mile ride, much of it into a headwind this time, followed by a three-mile run. Then it was back on her bike for an eighteen-mile ride—"we were running short of time and everyone was exhausted"—followed by a 1.5-mile cooldown run along the wooded trails of Moores Creek.

"This was my first-ever BRICK like this, and wow, was it challenging," Leanne wrote in her journal. "I am more and more starting to appreciate and understand what IM and IM training is all about. It's mentally challenging as well and I realize how important those 'tired' miles are when training." She also felt she'd had a bit of a breakthrough with her mid-race nutrition. Never particularly focused on eating or drinking while working out, she managed, on this day, to down two bottles of Crystal Light lemonade and a bottle of Gatorade, and to eat a chocolate PowerBar and a pita pocket with peanut butter and jelly. "I will admit, though, I was famished when we were done," she said.

Leanne also had another fleeting thought: *What will I do with my weekends after the IM is over?*

Scott's day had not gone nearly as well as his wife's. His left hip had been bothering him—so much so that he called it quits after the first thirty-mile bike loop. With Augusta looming in just six days, he scheduled a doctor's appointment on Tuesday. Leanne was able to accompany him and was relieved to learn that everything on the X-ray looked fine. Still, the doctor was concerned enough about possible deep-tissue damage that he scheduled an MRI.

That Sunday morning, the 27th, Leanne and Scott awoke at 4:30 in Augusta. Grabbing the breakfast they'd brought with them from home the previous day, they walked over to the hotel where their friends Matt and Sandra were staying, and then headed for the banks of the Savannah

River, where the swim portion of that day's Ironman 70.3 Augusta would soon begin. With her full Ironman less than two months away, Leanne set a goal for herself of finishing this half Ironman in less than six hours.

She got an immediate boost in the swim, courtesy of the current in the river—an advantage, she knew, she wouldn't have in the man-made lake in Arizona—and was stunned to emerge from the river just twenty-nine minutes after she'd entered it. *There's no way I could swim this fast on my own*, she thought to herself as she checked her watch. There was, however, another slight edge that she'd enjoyed at Augusta that would also work in her favor as she sought to race against the clock in Arizona: the "strippers," the volunteers who helped the participants strip off their wetsuits—something they would ordinarily have to do on their own at races of lesser distances.

Leanne found the bike ride, a big one-loop course out in the country, to be challenging but hardly overwhelming. There were some rolling hills, but, she thought to herself, the hills had been harder at the Muskoka 70.3 in Ontario a year earlier. Here in Augusta, she was able to dispatch the fifty-six-mile ride in just under three hours, at a brisk pace of nearly nineteen miles an hour. "I passed a lot of people, and got passed by a lot of people," she noted. On the two-loop, thirteen-mile run through downtown Augusta, she barely broke a sweat, despite temperatures that had climbed to eighty-four degrees. She had hoped to complete the course in two hours and was surprised to cross the finish line twenty minutes faster than that. "I couldn't ask for a better run," Leanne said. "I felt pretty good the entire way."

About the only thing she would have changed was that she would have gotten "those squeezy things" for her shoelaces so she wouldn't have to worry about tying them, as she had had to do several times on the run.

With an overall time of 5 hours, 13 minutes, she'd come in a staggering forty-seven minutes under the six-hour goal she'd set. In fact, of the 119 other women in the thirty-to-thirty-four-year-old age group, only fifteen had finished ahead of her.

"I couldn't be happier," Leanne wrote in her journal when she got home. "I am hoping this race was a result of my IM training. I am both nervous, and looking forward, to seeing how I do at IMAZ."

Despite his aching hip and the doctor's admonition that he rest, Scott not only competed in the Augusta 70.3 but also finished.

"With a smile," Leanne noted.

That same day, Seth Cannello was dealing with news of an entirely different nature. His father, who'd been battling brain cancer, had lately taken a turn for the worse and had only "a few days left." Several weeks earlier, his father had gotten married, in the hospital, to his longtime companion, Wilhelmina, and had since returned to his home in Evergreen, Colorado, not to celebrate his nuptials but to die, peacefully and with dignity. The latest threat he faced was a buildup of fluid between his lungs and pleural cavity, which was making his breathing difficult. Seth had spent the weekend with his dad, and was shocked by his precipitous decline.

> It's very hard seeing my Dad die. He was so strong and healthy just eight months ago. Now he is confined to a bed and can't do anything for himself. He babbles in his sleep about events that happened in the past and will ask questions straight out of his dreams: When are we getting on the bus? How long does it take to clean all those fish? Where are we going to assemble?

Seth was already grieving but was also honest with himself about another emotion he was feeling, however much it might embarrass him to admit it: He was frustrated that the end of his father's life was coinciding with the period in which he had intended to ramp up his preparation for Ironman Arizona.

"I don't think I picked a good year to attempt my first IM," Seth acknowledged, mindful of all the other setbacks he'd experienced. "I would imagine that most first-timers would say something similar, but I really can't imagine a situation that would take me away from training as much as dealing with my Dad's illness."

Still, in the hours they'd spend together that weekend, Seth found that his father relished the opportunity to ask him any number of questions about his forthcoming Ironman, which had proved a welcome distraction.

"He was interested in why I was doing it, what I was doing for workouts, and he was curious about the different aspects of the race," Seth said. "I was really grateful for an unusual topic to discuss."

On Tuesday, the attending nurse told Seth that he needed to go into his father's bedroom to convey a wrenching but essential message: It was time for him to let go. The nurse explained to Seth that, in many instances, terminally ill patients will hang on until they feel satisfied that their loved ones will be okay.

> When I went in to speak with my father, I told him that everyone was going to come into his room individually and tell him they were going to be fine and that he should surrender to his illness, that his time to fight had ended.
>
> Of course, as soon as the words left my mouth, I broke down. It was the hardest thing I've ever done.
>
> I told him that he was the reason I always push myself and that a lot of the accomplishments that I've obtained in my life were due to his guidance and his insistence that winners never quit. But I had to tell my Dad that HIS battle was now over. It was ironic and difficult.
>
> I told him that I really needed his help during my race. I said to him I was going to struggle during my Ironman and that deep down inside I knew that somehow he'd be there for me. When I got tired and felt like quitting, I was going to need him.
>
> He was trying to speak to me but couldn't. I could tell he was fighting to tell me something, but he was unable to. I think he would have told me he was going to be there for me.

Seth's father died the following day. A veteran of the Vietnam war who'd suffered major wounds in combat—including a crippled right arm that had derailed his dream of becoming a pro golfer—Jack Cannello, known to all by his nickname, "Duffy," was buried with military honors in Fort Logan National Cemetery in Denver. "I've never been to Arlington National Cemetery," Seth said afterward, "but I'm sure the scene looks very similar." Joined by his wife and their daughters and dozens of other mourners, he watched as six uniformed soldiers carried his father's casket into a pavilion, where it was covered with an American flag. He then received a twenty-one-gun salute, before taps was played.

Seth said later that he had never felt prouder of having served his country himself—service that none of his friends had pursued. He had enlisted in 1991, just before Operation Desert Storm. (The day he took his entrance exam, the American-led coalition bombed Baghdad.) "Everyone, with the exception of my Dad, didn't think that joining the Army was a good idea," and Seth himself had had his doubts, even after being discharged. But now, as he stared at his father's coffin, he felt a bond and a sense of gratitude. "The Army paid off my student loans, provided me with a job when no one else would and took care of my medical needs when I became ill. I've always been happy that I joined, but I was never *proud* of it until then."

At that moment, he may have been seriously behind in his training for the Ironman, but he knew that this experience would offer a perspective during the race that few of his fellow athletes could match. If his hands felt cold or his legs tired, he promised himself that he would reflect on how his father had coped with serious, life-altering injuries. "He never complained," Seth recalled, adding:

> I was always proud of my Dad for never using his disability as an excuse. When I was younger, my father never spoke to me about Vietnam. In recent years, on our way to our favorite fishing holes, he opened up to me about some of the things he did during the war. He saw some horrible things that would leave lasting marks on anyone.

Reflecting further on his father's death, he confidently made two predictions:

"I honestly think that I am going to feel his presence at the race. And I am going to finish."

CHAPTER 12

Rumors of My Demise
May Have Been Greatly Exaggerated

"That shower was *!#^*$#-ing* ridiculous," Bryan Reece reported to the readers of *Left, Right, Repeat* at 7:30 on Saturday, September 19, describing his efforts to clean himself up, hours after he went down at La Vernia. "OMG that hurt."

Bryan went on to recount how he had finally managed to numb his most painful wounds, in his elbow and hip, and to salve them with some Neosporin and dressings. He had decided he would skip a long run scheduled for the following morning and then see how he felt going forward. He noted that he had now gone eight hours without any symptoms of a concussion and was "feeling pretty good about the head"—which, he added, was the "hardest part" of his body.

Any assessment of how much damage he had done to his Ironman aspirations and training would have to wait. About all Bryan was willing to acknowledge was that his accident "could have very easily been much, much worse."

Bryan made no new postings for almost three weeks—a period of radio silence unprecedented during the Ironman quest of a guy who had always had much to say. On October 8, after having been unable to quell an infection that developed in the wounds on his elbow and hip ("Let me tell you, the road is not a sanitary place"), he returned to his blog with a posting that wryly recalled Mark Twain's famous saying:

"The rumors of my demise may have been greatly exaggerated."

After apologizing for his silence, Bryan provided the best news his friends and family had heard in some time: He had gone for a long run that night, two hours and twenty minutes, and after a full day's work, no less. The only damper on his spirits had come when he'd gone to the Ironman Arizona Web site and seen "the stinking little countdown widget" flashing that there were only forty-four days until the race. "I should go run some more," Bryan wrote. "Follow the plan—follow the plan—follow the plan."

Still, there was no question, at least as of this writing, that Bryan was intending to go to Arizona. "All travel has been arranged for months," he assured his blog followers. "Last equipment purchases (including a new helmet after the crash) are being completed. Only a few weekends remain." If there was a bright spot to all this, it was that Bryan had discovered that Giro, the manufacturer of the helmet he'd given himself for his birthday and that may well have spared him a head injury, offered a replacement program "with a generous discount." Likewise, after describing the training computer that had shattered on impact, he noted:

> I have to say Wow!!! to Garmin. I crushed my 310XT . . . but get this, I emailed Garmin and they said something to the effect of, well, we are sorry but we can't warranty it but we have a $99 repair policy. So, into the box it went and about 7 business days later a box appeared . . . with a BRAND SPANKING NEW 310XT . . . Garmin, I love you.

If Bryan was back, at least as far as those watching from the outside were concerned, he was clearly not yet out of the woods. Two days later, in a post titled "Minor Setback," he reported:

> Had to cut today's ride short due to pain in my left arm. Learned after a visit with the doc that the infection is pretty bad. Got antibiotics and it should be better in a few days.

The next day he wrote again to say that he had noticed some "nasty @&^$!" growing in the wound on his left arm. It was also painful—so much so that, just a short way into another bike ride, he'd noticed his arm was swelling and turned back yet again. "Deb looked at it and we both agreed that we needed to seek medical attention," Bryan said. The "minor" infection was now judged to be more serious, either staph or strep, or even MRSA, a bacterial infection that can be highly resistant to antibiotics and, in some instances, can be fatal. Bryan was immediately put on a ten-day course of multiple medications. While his most recent pain eased a bit, his wound was still full of fluid.

For the foreseeable future, cycling was out, because he could not rest his left arm on his aero bar, the cradles that look like deer antlers protruding from the handlebars of triathletes' cycles, the better to enable riders to crouch low and to enable the wind to whoosh over their backs. Swimming, needless to say, was definitely out of the question.

But Bryan was hardly one to be defeated. "It seems I will be running a lot this week," he said, adding optimistically, "Oh well, I need that the most anyway."

Another long week passed without an utterance by Bryan on his blog, until just after seven on Saturday, October 17, when he sent out a bulletin that read, in part:

> The medical seems to all be cleared up, finally. I have a few more days of pills to go and will diligently take the entire course. I do NOT want that stuff back . . . ever. But it is gone.

That countdown widget that had been at forty-four days had by now dropped to thirty-five, and not helping matters, he said, was the fact that he had spent the entire week in business meetings in Connecticut, with little time to train.

Bryan added that he was looking forward to a long ride on Sunday, and that his bike would then go into the shop "for a tune and some new rubber," to leave sufficient time to break it in before Arizona.

"Most everything else is ready to roll," he wrote. "The anxiety begins to build."

Before he would begin to taper his Ironman training—the better to allow his sore muscles to recover and heal sufficiently for the big day—he scheduled a weekend-long "Ironman rehearsal" for himself. On the night of Friday, October 23, he planned a "long swim rehearsal" in the Life Time Fitness pool. It was the longest continuous swim he'd ever attempted, and when it was over he had covered "somewhere between 3,100 and 3,400 yards," which, at worst, was just shy of what he'd be attempting in Tempe Town Lake. He accomplished this in just 1 hour and 15 minutes, which left him ebullient, considering how much time he'd lost to his infection. Per his training calendar, he'd only have two more long swims before Arizona.

Bryan woke up the following morning later than he'd hoped, but he forged ahead with part two of his rehearsal: an eighty-five-mile bike ride on the roads he knew best, many of them two-lane, gradually rising and falling straightaways that might well have been in Arizona, but for the parched crops and plowed-under fields that served as scenery. Again he was encouraged: His ride had taken him 5 hours, 35 minutes, at an average pace of 15.2 miles an hour. If he could approximate that pace in Arizona, where he'd have to ride only twenty-seven miles farther, he knew he'd be leaving himself plenty of time for the marathon run—arguably more than six hours, based on the swim the prior day.

He also felt good about the nutrition and fluids he'd consumed on his long bike ride. He'd downed two and a half bottles of a concoction called Infinit. Each bottle was intended to last two hours and, somewhat like Gatorade, to replace salts and electrolytes and sustain energy. All told, Bryan estimated, those bottles had infused him with 1,400 calories. He also ate an Uncrustable—a prefabricated peanut-butter-and-jelly sandwich intended for elementary-school lunch boxes—which had added another 210 calories. Still, even with the hundred ounces or so of water that he figured he'd drunk, he still felt dehydrated when he finished the bike ride. "I think I was slack on water intake," he observed. "I think I should have consumed about 36 ounces more water." Determining how to tweak what he ate and drank in Arizona—a far more crucial concern in an Ironman than, say, a stand-alone marathon—was among the reasons he'd done his rehearsal.

After his bike ride, Bryan ran approximately 4.5 miles in fifty minutes, for a pace of just under 11.5 minutes a mile. That was a little faster than he expected he'd run in Arizona, but he felt fine.

Afterward he couldn't help but pause for a moment to take stock of what he had achieved over the past few weeks and months, like a performer perfecting his own one-man show in anticipation of a Broadway opening.

"Consider," he wrote, that his performance over the weekend had followed "a corporate merger, new job at the firm, bike crash a month ago, staph infection for the last three weeks (new prescription on Friday before swim) and travel taking me out of town (and out of my sleep cycle).

"I cannot believe it," he said. "Thanks to all of you for being along for the trip."

He then signed off, as he did every post, with "See you at the finish line."

Despite the financial setback of not getting that bump in his teacher's salary, and the lingering guilt he felt, Tom Bonnette had forged ahead with his Ironman quest. At times he'd been fairly debilitated by severe pain in his right big toe, for, as a result of training for hours at a time in bike shoes that were likely too tight, he'd developed something called capsulitis, or an inflammation of the ligaments at the bottom of his foot. The condition had progressed into Morton's neuroma, a thickening of the nerves between the toes, which forced him to scale back his riding and running substantially in September and October and to endure several cortisone shots. He also lamented the need to buy new cycling shoes with a wider toe box, at a cost of more than $100—an amount, he knew, that he could ill afford to spend. Throughout it all, his wife and three daughters remained exceptionally supportive of his effort, certain that the family would find a way, somehow, to offset those expenses.

Like Bryan and Scott and Leanne, Tom was fortunate to have access to a larger training group, from which he would periodically seek advice. Based in Phoenix, it was called First Wave Tri, and its members followed the training calendars for Ironman set forth in a book called *Be Iron Fit*, by Don Fink. Though he took comfort in knowing that others were out there suffering in workouts as he was, Tom chose to do all his training on his own. His nature was a solitary one, and he reasoned that the only consistent partner he'd have on race day would, in the end, be himself.

However valuable the guidance he received from *Be Iron Fit*, Tom had long worried that he wasn't doing enough to train. Though Fink might advise running immediately after a forty-five-minute bike ride on, say, a weekday, on Saturdays the regimen might involve just a long ride, and on

Sundays only a long run. At some point in late September, Tom ran into some other aspiring first-time Ironmen from First Wave Tri and expressed his concern that he should be doing more—particularly if he were to meet his goal of finishing the Ironman in under twelve hours, a whopping five hours shy of the cutoff time.

The other guys from First Wave Tri told Tom he was right to be concerned. While he'd been following the Intermediate calendar in Fink's book, they'd been doing the Advanced. "I thought we were all doing the same thing," Tom said, shaking his head in disbelief. Based on their own experiences, they advised him to, literally, get with the program—the Advanced program—and start stacking up the bricks, the long bike rides followed by runs, on weekends as well as weekdays. Tom vowed to do so, even if he was still hobbled by foot problems.

On Saturday, October 24, the day Bryan Reece embarked on the bike-run portion of his weekend-long race rehearsal, Tom did a version of the same. For the first time, he rode 104 miles, finishing in six hours. He followed this epic bike ride with a run lasting about thirty minutes.

"Felt absolutely great," he said. "I just broke through. This gave me a lot of confidence."

A week later, he had what he considered to be another breakthrough when he ran eighteen miles in three hours—a brisk pace of ten minutes a mile—without raising his heart rate above 85 percent of his maximum effort.

He was certainly within striking range of his goal: If, at Ironman Arizona, he rode his bike at the same pace as he had on his 104-mile ride, he could probably finish in about six and a half hours; likewise, he was running at a pace to finish the Ironman marathon at about four and a half hours.

To finish the entire race in twelve hours, he would need to finish the swim in about an hour, with little time to spare for transitions. At this point, that target seemed highly ambitious, considering that he had never strung all these distances together in a single day. He felt, though, that he could compensate for any lag in the swim by going just a bit faster on the bike and run. After all, he had the advantage of the Ironman being staged, in effect, on his home turf—much of it on miles of pavement that were as familiar as the corridors of the local high school where he taught.

By early October, three weeks after his father's death, Seth Cannello was questioning whether he had the stamina to make it through all three events in the Ironman. His plan had been to hit his training hard in August and September, but, as he acknowledged ruefully, in an e-mail, "with my Dad's situation, that was put on the back burner."

And then, for the first time since he could remember, he managed to put together a rigorous week of swimming, biking, and running. "I feel like I'm making some progress and improving my conditioning," he observed. "I don't always do everything on my training plan, but I'm getting closer. I spoke with a guy from work who is training for the same race, and he said nobody ever completes what they put down on paper." He added, "Little pieces of info like that make me have a lot more confidence."

Of the various aches and pains that had interrupted his training even before his father's condition had turned grave, Seth said: "My hip is still bothering me, but the pain is manageable. My knees have really been holding up nicely, and I can't complain about the pain or other injuries . . . I've been very lucky so far."

Two days later, he left work at the fitness center to take a run along the base perimeter. It had been a gloriously sunny day, and he marveled that snow had already fallen that early in October. It had come a few weeks earlier than usual, but he figured it was to be expected, given the extended rains and unseasonably low temperatures that had characterized the summer and early fall—all of which had forced him to cut back on his training. Acknowledging that his job at the fitness center afforded him a few perks, he said, "Glad I can exercise indoors."

His gradually improving mood would take a hit, though, about ten days later when he was laid low by a painful sinus infection. "It's making me weak," he admitted, "but I'm still trying to train." Ten days after that, with less than a month to go before race day, he took stock:

> I can't believe the race is going to be here so soon. This has been the fastest year of my life. I always have something to do. I feel like I haven't had any downtime in months.
>
> Today is another cold and snowy day. I really don't like to

run on a treadmill or ride indoors but I don't have much of a choice. The other day I was swimming and looked out the windows located at the end of my lane. Snow was blowing sideways; the scene was pretty neat, until I had to walk to my car after my workout. I was so hot I fogged up the windows instantly.

Seth's wife, Robin, who had never been especially supportive of his Ironman pursuit, now had to deal with his "bragging about how big his legs were getting." Within his family, and among his friends, he had always been known for having very thin legs that appeared to have been transplanted onto his body from a very tall, genetically altered chicken.

As far as the rest of his physique was concerned:

> I've lost what little upper body muscle I had and now weigh 160 pounds. My weight fluctuates from 155 to 170 on what seems like a daily basis. That's pretty light considering I'm 6'3".
>
> Both my Achilles Tendons are getting extremely tight. Other muscles, tendons and joints are doing well. I'm sore a lot, but that's nothing new.
>
> Mentally, I'm worried I'm not training hard enough but I'm not sure if I could take too much more physical stress.

When Bryan Reece wrote, "The anxiety begins to build," he could well have been channeling the journal of Leanne Johnson, 1,400 miles from San Antonio in coastal North Carolina.

By October 3, a week after what she considered her triumphant finish at the Augusta 70.3, Leanne was again awash in self-doubt. While her running times had been strong, she worried that she wasn't getting in the mileage she felt she'd need to meet the challenge of an Ironman. Less than a month from now, she'd pledged to do the marathon portion of a local, Ironman-distance relay race called the Beach to Battleship, or B2B. "To date, my longest run has been 15 miles," Leanne confided to her journal. She wasted little time taking some steps to alleviate her concerns.

That morning, a Saturday, she met her friend Andrea and three others at the beach, well before sunrise, for a long run. They had mapped out a fourteen-mile route that would include the trails behind the University of North Carolina, Wilmington, so that the group would have "a lot of 'surface diversity.'" Andrea and Leanne would run four additional miles at the end. "I felt tired by the end of the run and was looking forward to my Garmin saying, '18,'" she wrote, adding:

> I think the next few weeks I need to start getting mentally prepared for the B2B marathon and IMAZ. I know I can do it . . . but then I keep reminding myself that 140.6 miles is a LONG way.
>
> I need to get a few more good long runs/rides in to feel confident.

The first opportunity came the following day as Leanne and Scott set ⟨...⟩ozen others for a nearly eighty-mile ride down Highway ⟨...⟩ught a headwind most of the forty miles out, and Leanne ⟨...⟩d of the ride that she felt "absolutely HORRIBLE today," ⟨...⟩ting that she'd not taken off more time to recover from ⟨...⟩urting, as she told her journal:

> ⟨...⟩ehind my left knee flared up today. I think it ⟨...⟩pulled muscle. I'm not sure if it originated from my calf or my hamstring. I pulled it two weekends ago doing a crazy brick workout and it's been bothering me since. I've got ice on it and I think I will make an appt to get a massage later this week if I can find time.

The last twenty miles were a particular struggle:

> I felt like I had nothing in the tank and I couldn't even keep up with the group. I think I made some poor nutritional choices as well. It was chilly out so my thirst mechanism wasn't kicking in. I drank only ¾ of a bottle of Gatorade and ½ bottle of Crystal Light lemonade. I KNOW I didn't drink enough.

She did feel that she'd eaten sufficiently, though. From her bike seat she'd dined on a pita pocket with peanut butter and jelly, a granola bar, a package of Sports Beans (think jelly beans, only more nutritional), and a few "Power Bar Coke-flavored chewy things." Leanne realized that she'd learned valuable lessons, and not a moment too soon, about drinking sufficiently during a race, and leaving herself enough time to recover after big races or workouts.

Soon, though, the questioning voices in her head had returned. "Anxiety is starting to kick in a little," she wrote in her journal on Wednesday as she prepared to squeeze in a seven-mile run, beginning just after 7:15 A.M., followed by a forty-five-minute swim, all before starting a shift at the hospital. "I am getting nervous just thinking about IMAZ. Can I really do this? Am I doing enough?" One thought that did make her smile that day, though, was the idea that there would be life after Ironman Arizona. The night before, she and Scott had booked a post-Christmas trip to the Dominican Republic. "We are going to be there over New Year's," Leanne wrote. "7 days ALL inclusive!!"

She found no peace that Sunday, a day on which she and Scott had pledged to do at least a century ride with a group of friends. Leanne, failing to heed the warnings she'd received from her body after Augusta, was attempting to do this "century plus" after logging thirty miles—on hills, no less—on her bike the previous day. This time it wasn't her legs that were suffering, but what she described as her "riding parts":

> I have been contemplating all year about getting a better seat b/c I have been experiencing "seat issues" but usually we do our long ride and then I have time to recover. Today's ride was bad from the start. I wasn't able to get in the aero position at all and then once I realized I wasn't going to get in the distance I wanted today, I started to have a "mental" meltdown. I started to feel panicked about not getting this century ride in.

Scott had been exhausted himself from helping set up and oversee a triathlon earlier in the weekend, and realized he "didn't have it in him" either, so the couple decided to call it a day after sixty miles—an ambitious day, indeed, for most recreational cyclists, but not necessarily for two who'd be pushing themselves nearly twice that biking distance in an Iron-man the following month.

On October 17, the day after she and Scott celebrated the second anniversary of their wedding in Kona—"I wish I was there now," Leanne lamented—she, Scott, and a group of friends again headed out on High-way 210, determined to complete a century ride, no matter how long it took. The signs did not look auspicious: The temperature was 43 degrees as they began to ride, just after 8:00 A.M., and they faced a headwind for nearly all fifty miles out, similar to the one that had dogged their efforts earlier in the month. Leanne never felt she had had a chance to warm up, and yet again she experienced "the usual numbness in the saddle areas."

After seventy miles, the group took a long break. Scott and their friend Misty were intent on pulling over at a small bait shop called Land's Ferry, which served "greasy hamburgers and sandwiches," Leanne reported. Though her husband indulged, she ate nothing, explaining, "There was no way I could stomach something like that in the middle of a century ride." Those who did, though, seemed to quickly burn off what they'd consumed. The group finished in just over six hours, an average pace of a little over sixteen miles an hour.

If that ride felt like the peak of the roller coaster, then Leanne hit the trough, literally, the following Friday. After working five days in a row—normal for the rest of the world, she knew, but not necessarily for a nurse posting twelve-hour shifts—she was fatigued as she set out at 1:00 P.M. for two 4.5-mile loops on her bike around Greenfield Lake. As she tried to unclip from her pedal, her bike shoe got caught and she fell, her knee absorbing the brunt of it. She was sure there would be a bruise the following day. While she managed to get into the pool at the Wilmington Athletic Club and complete a nearly four-thousand-meter continuous swim in just over an hour, she was not satisfied. "Swimming mojo seems to have a disappeared," she said.

Her philanthropic efforts had also stalled. "To date I have raised $3,813.80," she wrote on October 21. "My goal was $5,000. I still have time to raise that . . . but I am definitely out of fundraising ideas."

It was around this time, in late October, that Leanne began a ten-week shift in the oral-and-maxillofacial-surgery clinic affiliated with the hospital, where patients who had suffered acute injuries to the face from car accidents or assaults were treated. Her rotation would continue through Ironman Arizona and for another month afterward, and on many days she'd find herself working from 8:00 A.M. to noon in the clinic, then driving over to the main hospital at Cape Fear for a regular nursing shift until 7 at night.

Never before had her concerns about the potential impact of her work on her workouts seemed more founded than they did now.

The timing, she knew, could not have been worse.

CHAPTER 13

The Yorkie and the Sugar Cookie

On the first Sunday in November—a week to the day after he completed his Ironman rehearsal, and two weeks before the actual event—Bryan Reece awoke not to his alarm but to a twinge in his lower back. Suddenly, and with no warning sounded the previous evening, the muscles in his back now felt aflame. He had planned to ride and run a bit that morning, and he forged ahead—"slowly and gingerly," as he put it. But as he cooled down from the morning's workout, the pain only grew worse. The irony was readily evident to him: It was his balky back that had sent him to the emergency room nearly three years earlier, which set him on the path toward an Ironman; now, it appeared, it seemed intent on driving him off that very same road.

"Doing the ice and Ibuprofen thing to try to get past this," Bryan wrote that night on *Left, Right, Repeat*. "Whatever it might be—go away!"

By Thursday his spirits had only fallen further. "Well, it seems I have moved from one nagging injury to another this whole year," he said. "My back has hurt all week."

Still, he admitted that he sensed some improvement, adding, "I am hoping it will be a comfortable night of sleep and a healthy-feeling back in the morning." He noted that he had scheduled his final race rehearsal for the coming weekend.

In the end, that rehearsal, which was on Sunday, had to be cut short—though its curtailment was not due to Bryan's back, which was, in fact, improving. The skies over San Antonio had crackled with severe thunderstorms that morning, and Bryan, mindful of how long it had taken him to heal from that bike accident earlier in the fall, was taking no chances.

"I really wanted to get the work in," he said, "but the slippery streets and crazy drivers did not warrant the risk."

And so, likening himself to a farmer who had harvested the last of his crop, he took a moment to call time-out and reflect.

"Well, as they say, 'The hay is in the barn,'" he wrote that night on *Left, Right, Repeat*. "The work is done. All that can be accomplished for Ironman Arizona has been banked. For the next two weeks it is take care of myself, don't do stupid stuff, don't get hurt and try to stay healthy."

He then grew a bit philosophical as he attempted to wipe clean the slate on which he had been scribbling over the previous twelve months:

> I have a plan for execution at Arizona. I will work through the day and get the job done. The missed workouts, the missed family time, the missed sleep—I will just have to let all that go, as I work toward getting through 140.6 miles.
>
> I am not expecting to set any age group records, but it will be a PR [personal record] for me, as it is my first. I want to enjoy the day as much as possible and finish. (I keep telling myself there are no time goals for this one except to finish in less than 17 hours.)
>
> From work issues, to stock market issues, to a corporate merger, to consolidation of offices, to new positions and work responsibilities, to bike crashes, to staph infections to messed up backs—the road to Ironman is paved with life.

Bryan ended his dispatch on a decidedly spiritual note. "Please send good vibes my way," he wrote to his family, closest friends, and training partners, "and may God smile upon me November 22 as we work our way through the day."

The following evening he added a coda. He had visited the Ironman Arizona Web site and discovered that the athletes' bib numbers had been posted. There was no apparent pecking order to whom had been assigned which. An Ironman event was nothing if not democratic; everyone, pros and Joes alike, would share the same course.

"I am bib 122," Bryan announced on his blog, adding that anyone who wished to track his progress that day could do so by entering his bib, or last name, into the designated box on the Ironman site. Whenever the computer chip that would be attached with a Velcro strap to his ankle passed various checkpoints—the exit from the swim; the end of each of three laps on the bike; various points on the marathon—the time would be automatically transmitted to a Web page.

"I am 12 days from the start," he said, before offering a closing observation borrowed from none other than the Grateful Dead:

"What a long strange trip it's been."

It was at around this time that Leanne Johnson heard a voice that finally seemed to bring her some peace, however fleeting. She, Scott, and several friends had driven two hours north to Raleigh, North Carolina, for the annual banquet of the North Carolina Triathlon Series. After a twelve-mile trail run there with their friend Nick—featuring more hills than flats, which Leanne found refreshing—she settled in after the dinner to listen to the guest speaker. Dave Scott, a six-time Ironman world champion, began his talk by showing a brief, ESPN-worthy video of highlights culled from his heyday—"way back in the 80's," as Leanne would write in her journal that night. She went on to observe:

> It's amazing how the race has evolved. Our equipment is so high tech now compared to back then, yet they were still able to pull off amazing performances. Dave was very motivational . . . and he had some great insight on the Ironman and pushing your way through it.

As she listened to him speak, Leanne had a flickering moment of self-awareness: "The fear and doubt of the unknown that I am feeling about this race is normal . . . and it was reassuring to hear it!"

She slept well that night, but by the following Thursday, two days before Halloween, Dave Scott's voice had grown distant. After a twelve-hour workday, she plunged into the saltwater channel off Cape Fear for a group swim that was expected to go for about two thousand yards, or eighty lengths in a typical pool. But the channel, of course, was far less cozy than a swimming pool, and Leanne had never especially enjoyed open-water saltwater swimming.

"I started out OK, but then once I got going and everyone started passing me, I started to panic," she wrote in her journal that night.

> My fear in the channel is starting to consume me and I just need to get over it. I used to think it was the fear of the unknown, but now I think it's a little of that and a lot of frustration of not being able to keep up and the fear of being left behind.
>
> I keep telling myself I am a bad swimmer, which if you tell yourself that enough, then it often becomes the truth. For some reason, once I start to panic I lose all concentration and my form gets horrible.

About halfway through the swim, she decided she had to stop, yelling to Scott, who had been lingering just ahead of her, to tell him that she was done.

Once on shore, though, Leanne began to have a change of heart. "I suddenly felt like a failure and decided I needed to do this swim," she wrote. By this point, though, the rest of the group was far ahead, and nightfall was looming. "We knew we wouldn't be able to get the full distance in before it got dark, but we still could manage to do a bit more," Leanne recalled afterward, adding:

> Scott hung back with me, and I felt much more comfortable. I think, for me, swimming in a large group is not ideal. I get so frustrated because I can't keep up. In the past, I've never had to worry about that.
>
> On the bike, I can hold on in large groups. And running is my strength so that is never a problem. I definitely know that in the offseason I need to work on the swim.

Reading those words back to herself, Leanne found little comfort. Whatever she might accomplish in the off-season on her swimming would be of no help to her on November 22, when she embarked on the biggest group swim of her life. On that day, the dozen swimmers who were with her in the channel today would multiply exponentially. Still, she ended the day's dispatch on a defiant note.

"I cannot let this swimming fear get the best of me," she wrote. "IMAZ is not a race . . . I know I can do it . . . and I will!"

Leanne found herself in a better frame of mind on Sunday, November 1, as she and Scott set out to do their last one-hundred-mile ride before Arizona. The initial plan was to warm up a bit with a few loops around the small island of Wrightsville Beach, then to head out of town for fifty miles of two-lane highway, as they so often did, before returning. But as they reached the beach, Leanne said, joking, "We could just do a bunch of laps down here and do the entire thing on the island."

> Scott thought the idea was brilliant. The sun was shining and the island was quiet when we started. Our ride was not stressful b/c there was hardly any traffic and we were close to our truck in case bad weather snuck up on us.
> The first seven loops were fine but eventually it got boring. Very boring.

By loop 10, the couple's legs were tired, but if there was one thing that kept them going, Leanne said, it was that they saw "so many familiar faces." The problem was, they kept seeing *and seeing* those same faces, which, in turn, kept staring back at them.

"I'm sure they all thought we were nuts riding our 100 miles at the beach," she said.

"However," she concluded, "we are done with our LAST LONG ride. We did three century rides for IMAZ. I hope it's enough."

Before pushing the button on that journal entry, Leanne gave it a headline: "Mental training? Or just plain mental?"

While she may have been done with her long riding, she still had a few more swims she wanted to get in before Arizona. She found an opportunity that Monday. After working an 8:00 A.M.–to–noon shift at the oral-and-maxillofacial clinic, she had three hours off before she was to begin another four-hour shift, this one in another department. The channel was certainly out, and since the Wilmington Athletic Club had no indoor pool, she would be swimming outdoors—with the air temperature a crisp fifty degrees. She had hoped to get in another two thousand yards—broken into segments 50, 100, 150, and 250 yards each—but when she got to the gym she began to waiver, and called Scott to tell him as much.

"What happened to the girl who last fall used to swim when it was forty degrees out?" he asked her. Leanne pondered his question, then began wondering the same thing.

When did I become such a wimp?

And so, changing into her suit, she jumped in the pool and got to work. While she didn't do as much as she'd planned—she stopped at about two hundred yards, or eight lengths, shy of her goal—she concluded that "some is better than none." Despite her repetitive ride at the beach the previous day, her legs felt strong, and about the only pain she was experiencing was in her right shoulder. It had continued to flare up all summer and spring, as her doctor had predicted, and was especially sore from all the riding she'd done in the aero position, which entailed leaning on those bars jutting forward from the bike. But Leanne was confident that her shoulder would hold up through Arizona.

Now she turned her focus to one last big run—that marathon she'd be undertaking as part of the Beach to Battleship relay, which was on Saturday. On a sunny day on which the temperature never climbed above fifty-six, she waited as her friend Alex did the swimming portion of the relay (out and back for about 2.4 miles in the Intracoastal Waterway in about forty-five minutes, a blistering pace aided mightily by a strong current), followed by their friend Jeff, who clocked in on the bike (112 miles) just shy of the six-hour mark for the day. Then it was Leanne's turn to run.

Her initial plan had been to take it easy (maybe a four-hour marathon—a struggle for most people, but relatively simple for her), but once she got to the relay and got caught up in the spirit of the day, she decided she would not hold back, and just "go with what felt good." Her first thirteen miles, she concluded, had been "way too quick"—about an hour and thirty-six minutes—and she forced herself to slow down on the second half. At mile 19, though, she suddenly found herself feeling as if she had hit the proverbial runner's wall. Her right knee and hip began to ache, and she reached in the pouch around her waist to see if she could rally herself with some nutrition. She ate half of something called a Hammer Bar, as well as a packet of gel, and immediately felt better.

By mile 21 she had her legs again and decided to keep an even pace of 8 minutes and 30 seconds per mile the rest of the way. As she came down the finish chute, the many friends she had in the hometown crowd erupted, jumping and cheering and yelling her name.

"I honestly felt like a superstar!" Leanne wrote in her journal that night.

The team finished collectively at just over ten hours, which was good enough for a spot in the top five. Leanne herself completed her marathon in 3 hours, 25 minutes—well under the four-hour target she'd set for herself. The experience, though, left her with mixed feelings.

"Running the marathon, I realized just how hard IMAZ is going to be," she wrote. "I know I am going to experience pain." But, ever the optimist, she added, "I also know how great it is going to feel to finish . . . Two weeks to go!"

Leanne and Scott spent the following day, a Sunday, packing up their gear for Ironman Arizona and readying their bikes. On Tuesday, November 10, after an early-morning swim at the gym, Leanne drove all of their gear to a bike shop in Raleigh. By now the Ironman organizers had dispatched Ryder rental trucks across the country to make stops at dozens of bike shops like Inside-Out Sports in Raleigh. For a fee they would then pick up the contestants' gear—and, most important, their bicycles, which could remain whole rather than having to be disassembled for shipment by plane or FedEx. Everything would be waiting at the race site when the participants arrived in Tempe toward the end of the month. As she said goodbye to their stuff, Leanne felt as if "the adventure to Arizona" had officially begun.

That Thursday, ten days before Ironman Arizona, she began her "taper," a pre-race period in which she would exercise only enough to stay loose. She did so not a moment too soon. Her quads and calves ached from the previous Saturday's marathon—so much so that she worried that having exerted herself so late in her training may have been a mistake. On the other hand, even at this late date, she still agonized, telling her journal, "I feel like I am not doing enough"—despite the fact that the whole point of tapering, of course, was to do as little as possible.

"At this point," Leanne acknowledged, "the long stuff is behind me and just staying healthy until the big day is what is most important."

She even got a bit of comic relief that Friday. On the third straight day of rain in Wilmington, she scrubbed her plans to swim at the pool and instead logged on to her computer to get the latest local news. She had to laugh when she read the headline atop the Web site of WECT TV 6, the local NBC station:

"Great White Shark Spotted Off the Coast of Wrightsville Beach."

The area where it had been spotted was not far from where Leanne had been swimming with her group not two weeks before.

"Now," Leanne wrote in her journal, "I can justify my 'fear of the channel.'"

The skies cleared, and she finally got in a thirty-minute swim at the athletic club on Saturday morning, after she and Scott had spent an hour on two of the club's spinning bikes. Scott had not been in the mood to swim, so he sat in a hot tub, reading the newspaper and relaxing. If he had any concerns about Ironman Arizona, they were not evident to his wife. This, after all, would be his fifth Ironman.

After lunch, Scott napped while Leanne started to pack. She would be working twelve hours on Sunday the 15th, followed by twelve-hour shifts on Monday, Tuesday, and Wednesday. The couple were then scheduled to fly to Arizona on Wednesday, after Leanne's shift.

On November 2, as Bryan Reece was nursing his aching back and Scott and Leanne were recovering from their twelve-loop odyssey around Wrightsville Beach, Laura Arnez was preparing to embark on one of the last challenges she had set for herself prior to Ironman Arizona. While drawing confidence from her first century bike ride, on July 4, she knew she would have to push her body (and her bike) beyond the one-hundred-mile mark in Arizona. She had therefore set a goal for herself of riding 108 miles—alone, just as she imagined she would in Tempe.

"I wanted to prove I was really ready to ride, then feel like I could run after," Laura explained. While everyone around her, including her husband and ubiquitous girlfriends, was telling her she would "rock the race, no prob," Laura found her head filled with what-ifs. She had read enough stories about "the healthiest, fittest individuals who had to drop out of an Ironman for one reason or another." Convinced that she could be one of them, she had decided to latch on to the phrase "The journey is the reward." And so, she told herself, this 108-mile training ride "would be the reward, IM or no IM."

On a beautiful fall day in California—sunny with gentle winds—Laura set out on the trail near her home just after 9:00 A.M. Typically she would start much earlier, maybe at 7, but she anticipated that she'd be out of the water in Tempe and just climbing on her bike at about 9. As she had on so many other rides, she began this one by playing a little music from her iPod, softly. But she quickly turned it off, not out of any concerns about being distracted but because she wanted to think about other aspects of her life, including her five children and husband.

> My thoughts drifted to my kids . . . How they were doing. What each of them was going through in life. How could I really be present for them as a Mom.
>
> Some say IM training may take away from family. I found, through long rides like these, that I was really able to think about my family, pray for them, and then BE THERE for them when I was in their presence. Then I would take nothing for granted.

Laura had always felt that it was "a privilege" to be able to train as she did, "not a burden or chore." When she returned from long rides like this one, she always felt like she was "a better person, inside and out." Anyone who knew her for even a short while would conclude that her reserves of energy were seemingly bottomless. Her rapid-fire speech alone would seem to burn as many calories as most mortals would in a workout on an elliptical machine at the gym. As Laura herself recognized,

> Fortunately, God gave me some type of energy gene that I could ride for 7 hours on a bike and come home, cook dinner, take the kids to the park and still have energy for my husband—lol!
>
> I guess in that way I am blessed, and my girlfriends always

tease that I'm taking some illegal substance—lol! I have tons
of energy as is, and when I work out I just get more energy.

She would describe the long ride on which she embarked that day as
"fulfilling" and decidedly "not draining." Yes, even she would have to
concede that she did start getting a little impatient at the eighty-five-mile
mark, until she realized that the next time she hit that milestone on her
bike, it would be in the midst of Ironman Arizona—*God willing*. When
she finally reached her car, and the odometer on her bike read 108 miles,
Laura climbed off her bike and walked for two miles.

Yeah, she told herself, *I could run if I really wanted to.*

The day, she concluded, had been an enormous "confidence booster."
Now the only major obstacle that lay between her and Ironman Arizona
was one last open-water swim, which she'd scheduled for that Thursday,
November 5, at Rancho Seco Lake. Rancho Seco would be warmer, Laura
reasoned, than Lake Natomas, because it was significantly smaller. It also
had buoys marking a well-defined swim lane.

While she was "feeling optimistic about her swim energy and endurance," still, she acknowledged, "it was the panic I needed to always
confront."

When Laura, sheathed yet again in her wetsuit, as she would be in
Tempe, waded into Rancho Seco on November 5, "the temperature literally took my breath away." She guessed it was in the low sixties.

"It was so hard to breathe I almost gave up after five minutes. I kept at
it, though, found some sense of rhythm and went back and forth along
the buoys, looking at my watch every three or four minutes or so."

After a half-hour, shaking and growing depressed, she found she
could take it no longer. While getting out of the water, she caught a
glimpse of her lips in the driver's side mirror of her car and saw that they
had turned purple.

With that, she began to cry.

Whatever serenity Laura had summoned on those almost spiritual long bike rides had suddenly and strikingly evaporated. As she described the moment later, her language was uncharacteristically blunt
and stark:

It was pure hell for me. I knew the nerves would be there race day. But after all that training, to get in cold water and freeze up like this? I felt like an actor who practiced his lines over and over, getting on stage only to have severe stage fright. One last swim, and it sucked.

When Tom came home from work, Laura told him about her letdown in the lake, and she cried again. "You tried," he told her. "You at least went out and tried."

As the evening wore on, she finally found herself able to put the morning behind her. She thought, once again, about all the successes she had notched in her training—not just on the bike and run, but in the swim, too. She reminded herself how far she had come, about how a sedentary, out-of-shape teenager who once watched the marathoners run through her hometown was now not only a marathoner herself but poised to become an Ironman. She had achieved so much. Finally, she thought of the man she'd met along the run at Vineman—the one who'd met her husband afterward, and who had told Laura, "If you can do this race, you can definitely finish Arizona."

His words continued to resonate, because, of course, he *had* done Arizona.

"I kept that thought in my head the rest of the day," Laura recalled, "and fell asleep dreaming of swimming strong."

The roundabout on Interstate 17 at Happy Valley Road, near Glendale, Arizona, was crowded just before 2:00 P.M. on Saturday, November 14, forcing the woman driving the black GMC Yukon to bring it to a momentary but complete stop, the better to allow the bottleneck ahead of her to clear.

Tom Bonnette, who was approaching from behind on his bicycle, had taken note of the Yukon, but he hadn't seen it come to a halt. He would later acknowledge that he had allowed himself to look down, maybe for just a second or two; that brief moment of inattention would prove costly. Before he could realize what was happening, his bike collided with the back of the car, which was in the bike lane, and as he fell, his shoulder and fist hit hard against her tailgate—so hard, in fact, that his hand would leave a dent next to her license plate.

As Tom crumpled onto the pavement, much of his own weight and that of the bike were absorbed by his left hip. *Why now?* Tom thought to himself as he lay momentarily on the ground.

Ironman Arizona was just eight days away.

Several other motorists pulled their cars up onto the curb and ran to Tom's aid. "Don't get up, don't get up," they all seemed to say. Nonetheless, he kept trying in vain to right himself. He would later say that his most immediate concern was not for his own injuries but for his carbon-fiber Valdora bike frame. It appeared to have been "completely decapitated," its handlebars separated from the fork and the entire contraption "just hanging together by the cables."

How much is this going to cost? he wondered.

Tom could tell from the expressions of those gathered around him that he probably appeared as banged up as his bike. He felt stiff all over, and his left hip was, at the very least, badly bruised. Fortunately, he thought, he didn't seem to have sustained any road rash.

As he began to compose himself, Tom assured everyone that he didn't need an ambulance. But he did, obviously, need a way to get home. A woman who'd gotten out of a Ford Escape attempted to take charge of the situation.

"I can see from your ring that you're married," the woman said to Tom. "Why don't you use my phone and call your wife?"

With a shaky hand, Tom punched in his home number, and heard it ring and ring. As a general rule, no one in the Bonnette household answered the phone if the number on the caller ID was unfamiliar, as this one surely would have been. After what seemed like an eternity, the answering machine picked up. This being a Saturday afternoon, Tom knew someone would be home, hear his voice, and click on. But just as he was about to leave his message, the phone lost reception and the line went dead.

"That's okay," the woman said to Tom, "I'll take you home," and she began folding down the backseat of her Escape to make room for Tom's mangled bike. Tom was so disoriented that he kept his helmet on for the entire ride.

His body felt tight all over when he arrived home, but because he wasn't in noticeable pain, he would later conclude that adrenaline had kicked in. Still, he was taking no chances. That night he commandeered the bathtub in one of his family's three bathrooms and filled it with Epsom salts and the hottest water he felt he could tolerate. He walked gingerly down the hall to a second bathroom and filled its tub with ice-cold water, then spent the next few hours shuttling from one tub to another, figuring that the combination of hot and cold would serve to keep him loose.

He knew that all this tub hopping must have looked fairly ridiculous to his wife and three daughters, however much they admired and supported the Ironman challenge he had undertaken. At one point his daughter Paige wanted to take a shower, and the only one available was in one of the bathrooms Tom had taken over. "Are you going to be done with one of those bathrooms soon?" she asked him plaintively.

Tom was so encouraged by how good he felt the following morning that he decided to go ahead with some of his final Ironman workouts. While his wife and daughters went shopping, he headed out for a 1,500-meter swim at the YMCA near his home. It went well, so much so that he decided to do the one-hour run that his training program called for.

He continued to feel good on Monday, and again on Tuesday, and was finally able to declare that his accident, however awful it may have appeared, had not taken him off course for his Ironman, now less than a week away.

His bike was another story; it required $400 worth of repairs. He had no choice but to pay for them, with the race so close. But in light of the raise he'd yet to receive, the bill hurt almost more than hitting that SUV's tailgate.

That night Tom and his wife, Shannon, relaxed by watching *The Biggest Loser*, the weight-loss reality show on NBC that was Leanne and Scott's favorite, too. Hovering in the den, as always, was the family's dog, a pint-size Yorkshire terrier named Oliver.

At virtually the same moment, Tom and Oliver both noticed a sugar cookie that one of the girls had inadvertently left on the coffee table. Leaving out food like that was strictly forbidden, for if Oliver, with his notoriously fragile digestive system, consumed too much sugar, he was sure to get sick.

As Oliver jumped onto the coffee table and clenched his teeth around the cookie, Tom lunged from the couch to pull it from the dog's mouth and suddenly felt his left glute—the same one he'd bruised in the accident— pull taut.

The pain was instantaneous—and sharp.

For all his many months of training, Tom was dumbfounded.

"You think, you're in pretty good shape, you can just jump off the sofa," Tom reflected afterward. "You assume you can handle anything. But I had just had a pretty traumatic accident three days earlier."

The left part of his backside now felt even tighter than it had after the accident. Whatever flexibility he had recovered during those marathon bathing sessions had seemingly been lost in an instant.

If he still felt like this five days from now, Tom was confident that he could nevertheless compete in the Ironman—there was no way he was going to miss it. But he knew that a five-pound Yorkie with a trick stomach and a yen for sweets had probably done more to imperil his dream of a twelve-hour Ironman finish than a half-ton SUV.

His goal, now, would just be to complete the race.

CHAPTER 14

Half of My Peers Are Dead, Half of the Others Are in Assisted Living, and Look What Fun I Have

Seth Cannello prepared for the 785-mile drive from Colorado Springs to Tempe by removing the back row of his wife's ten-year-old silver Voyager minivan and loading it with the materials he'd need for a most unusual road trip. There was his bicycle and full-length wetsuit, of course, as well as a couple of fishing rods. Seth had decided to take off the entire week before Ironman Arizona and planned to make a couple of stops along the way. On Monday, November 16, six days before the race, he set off on the first leg of his journey, a six-hour drive to Albuquerque. He was alone—the better to collect his thoughts and prepare his mind, he reasoned—and would be joined on Saturday in Tempe by his wife, Robin, who planned to fly in. She would then watch the race (an Ironman effort in and of itself, she thought) and accompany him on Monday on the drive home.

Seth's right hip, which had been bothering him all summer and fall and which he'd been treating with anti-inflammatories, tightened up and began to throb on the drive to New Mexico. Once he'd arrived, a short run in the late-afternoon chill didn't seem to help much. He would try his best to put the pain, a result of tendinitis, out of his head. The following day he drove four hours to his next destination, the small town of Show Low, in the White Mountains of Arizona, the site of an Apache reservation. He thought that a couple of nights spent at altitude (Show Low was more than six thousand feet above sea level) would help his performance in Tempe (at an elevation of about 1,100 feet).

Being alone in the mountains also suited his desire to focus his mind for Sunday, and to reflect on his extraordinary year: the pain of losing his father just a few weeks earlier, and the fits and starts of his Ironman training. Moreover, Seth rarely took a vacation that didn't involve the pursuit of a species of fish he'd not caught before—in this case, an Apache trout, found only in the White Mountains.

That he did not meet this particular goal—Seth managed only to pull a few rainbow trout from Silver Creek—did not dampen his mood. He managed to swim for about thirty-five minutes at a local rec center, and left Show Low both excited and a little anxious about the enormous challenge that lay just beyond the horizon.

He was still battling the sinus infection that had begun weeks earlier, which he'd initially treated with a mild antibiotic that had done little good. His doctor had then prescribed a stronger antibiotic, which he was still taking, but his nose was still so congested and the pressure so intense that it made it difficult for him to wear his swim goggles, which seemed to press in all the wrong places. His left hamstring, knee, and hip were also bothering him.

Like so many Ironmen aspirants, he continued to agonize that he'd not trained enough and had never seemed to build up any momentum. Something always came up. "If I'm not working out I'm thinking I should be," he said. "And when I am working out, I feel like I'm not working out hard enough." While he'd done plenty of swimming, biking, and running over the past six months, he'd never done any distance swimming in open water, and he'd not run anything close to a marathon distance. He was banking on the fact that his determination—the same resolve that he'd drawn on to beat back several bouts with cancer—and his heightened level of fitness would carry the day.

Still, nothing worried him more than the prospect of swimming in Tempe Town Lake for at least ninety minutes on Sunday—or, he hoped, far less time than that—without the benefit of the insulated, waterproof gloves he'd stowed, optimistically, in his gear bag. His nervousness on this score had only been heightened a few weeks earlier, when he decided to swim in the Air Force base pool after the heat had been off for two days during a power failure. He lasted just half an hour before he felt he could take the cold no longer; the water temperature was seventy-five degrees, at least ten degrees warmer than Tempe Town Lake would likely be on Sunday.

Although Seth had yet to receive permission from the Ironman organization to use those gloves, he planned to make his case again, this time in person. He had brought along a sheaf of doctor's notes, including testimonials from his general physician and from his oncologist, documenting his Raynaud's syndrome and requesting a waiver on Ironman's no-glove policy.

"My whole plan is not to race, just to finish," he finally said, yet another echo of countless Ironman competitors. "My mentality is usually to try to go as fast as I can. Someone passes me, I then try to pass them. That is going to be a hard part of this race—resisting the temptation to do that."

He was referring, specifically, to the bike and run portions of the race. But he knew that any thoughts of passing other participants would be moot if he could not figure out a way to endure that ice bath of a swim.

Bryan Reece arrived in Tempe on Thursday, also with a bad sinus infection, and one of the first stops he and Debbie made after getting off the plane from San Antonio was at a local CVS for an over-the-counter decongestant. That afternoon he headed for Tempe Beach Park, which had been transformed temporarily into a small, white-topped tent city of sporting gear shops and stands crammed with Ironman-logo T-shirts and mugs. He was there to retrieve his bike, which had been ferried from his local shop by one of the Ironman-dispatched trucks, and to pick up his race packet, which would include the all-important timing chip and the black Velcro strap that would attach it to his ankle.

Standing behind several dozen others who were clad, like him, in T-shirts, running shoes, shorts, and zippered nylon tops, Bryan began coughing, but he was more worried about his back than the sinus problem. The pain with which he'd awakened after a long bike ride three weeks earlier had not subsided. At first he thought it was muscle-related; now he assumed it was a disk problem. As a result, he'd not worked out much since, having done only one 2.5-hour bike ride.

"The only thing that really worries me is my back giving out on me," he admitted, his running shoes digging absentmindedly at the same matted grass near where he'd stood to sign up for the race a year earlier. "Otherwise I'm going to work through the day."

"I know I've done each of the distances," he added, now affecting the patter of an NFL quarterback a few days before Super Bowl Sunday. "I know I can put them together. At this point it's just about managing the day and not overextending myself too early."

"I had all these fantasies about what times I could do," he acknowledged. "But when my back started bothering me I got inside my head and said, 'Forget all that.' The only time that matters is 17." He'd taken a photo at the finish line the previous year when the neon yellow race clock had struck exactly 17:00:00, and he had placed it prominently on his *Left, Right, Repeat* blog so as not to take his eye off the ball.

"Anything less than that is all good," Bryan said, adding that if he required the full seventeen hours, "they still call you an Ironman."

That Bryan was about to engage in an experience so intense that he would place his well-being—and even his life—in jeopardy became clear as he signed off on the single-spaced, light blue two-page "release and waiver" that the Ironman organization required of each of the more than 2,500 competitors registered for Ironman Arizona 2009. He scanned the legal boilerplate quickly, including the sentence "I hereby acknowledge and assume all of the risks of participating in this event," and scribbled his signature. On a separate yellow sheet, he responded "penicillin" when asked if he had any allergies to medication, and proudly wrote "207" for his weight, more than thirty pounds less than when his Ironman journey had begun.

"This is the easy part, I'm afraid," he told one of the race volunteers who was checking him in. The woman—who, after discovering that Bryan was from San Antonio, related that her daughter was a nurse at nearby Fort Hood—then used a black marker to emboss an official red swim cap with his number, 122, before handing him the bibs with that number that he'd pin to his shirt for the bike and run portions. She also gave him two white plastic "special needs bags," which she instructed him to fill with food, clothing, and other items he might require midway through the bike and run courses.

An Ironman was nothing if not a well-oiled machine. If Bryan placed those bags in the designated locations near the swim start prior to the race on Sunday, they would be transported, as if magically, to drop-off points along the bike course and the run so he could retrieve their contents. He had already been thinking long and hard about what he might place in that bag: a favorite nutritional drink for the bike ride, for example; a long-sleeved shirt for the run, as the temperature dropped; and a few items that might infuse him with the inspirational pick-me-up he suspected he would desperately need. Still, the volunteer at the check-in cautioned him: "Don't put anything in your special needs bag you ever want to see again."

Sufficiently warned, Bryan emerged from the white tent, an official registrant in Ironman Arizona 2009.

Laura Arnez picked up her packet about an hour after Bryan and, like him, was struck by the friendliness of the volunteer who did the honors. But as the man placed a blue amusement-park-style band on her right wrist—an accessory that would gain her admission to the athletes' dinner Friday night, as well as the race itself—Laura was struck by the words on the white baseball cap he was wearing: FINISHER IRONMAN ARIZONA 2006.

The man appeared to be in his mid-seventies, and he confirmed that he indeed was. He told her that his name was Dan Dickey, that he was from Phoenix, and that when he completed Ironman Arizona in 2006, he was seventy-two years old.

As amazing as that sounded, it was only part of the story. Dan told Laura that, with three miles left on the run, he had feared he could not continue. As he staggered into a first-aid station, a volunteer there had given him Advil to soothe the pain in his aching legs—and then implored him not to give up. She'd then nudged him onto the course and proceeded to jog backwards in front of him—"like a puppy," as Dan characterized it—for those last three miles, until just before he crossed the finish line, at 16 hours and 55 minutes.

"It was the neatest thing I ever did," Dan said proudly, adding that he still remembered the woman's name: Judy Kamela, of the Phoenix Triathlon Club.

"I wanted to do it again," he said. "I just got too old."

As he spoke, Laura had tears in her eyes.

Laura's concerns, like Seth's, were still centered on the crowded swim—and when she was given her number, 2699, she'd remarked, with more than a little trepidation: "Does that mean there's at least 2,699 other people in the race?" In fact, with cancellations and a few gaps in the numbering of bibs, the race registration was likely to be closer to 2,500, she was told. But that figure had not given her much comfort.

With the experience of her aborted open-water swim a few weeks earlier—the one that had left her in tears—still raw in her memory, she had driven straight from the Phoenix airport on Thursday to Tempe Town Lake so that she could touch the water.

Laura, it's not that bad, she told herself as she submerged her hands. *It's not that bad.*

She knew that in order to avoid automatic disqualification, she would have to finish the swim no more than 2 hours and 20 minutes after it began at 7:00 A.M. on Sunday. But even accounting for time lost to a few panic attacks, which she considered inevitable, she was willing to make a prediction—at least for her performance in the swim portion of the race:

"I should do it in two hours, or a little under two hours," she asserted. "My goal would be to get on the bike at 9."

If she achieved that time, and managed a quick transition, she would have eight and a half hours to complete the 112-mile bike course. To finish the bike ride by the deadline set by the race organizers—a hard-and-fast 5:30 P.M., with stragglers even a few seconds late facing disqualification—she would need to cover an average of just under fourteen miles an hour, which seemed reasonable, given her training rides along the canal near her Sacramento home.

That, in turn, would leave her six and a half hours for the marathon—the part of the race she considered her strongest by far. With six and a half hours left on the clock, she could almost walk the course and make the midnight deadline.

But, in beginning to contemplate the run, Laura knew she was getting ahead of herself.

"My real goal," she reminded herself, "is just to get out of the water, and get off the bike, before those cutoff times."

The following morning she donned her wetsuit and participated in a practice swim in Tempe Town Lake.

"Swim was freezing but able 2 get going and last 40min!" she texted me. "Teeth still chattered 45min after! I'm so lame!"

In the same message, she shared something she'd meant to emphasize the day before.

"Didn't tell u but am Christian and am relying on GOD 2 do miracle! Parting water would be great!"

At around 4 P.M. that Friday, she attended a meeting of Iron Prayer, a gathering of three dozen or so Ironman competitors on a bluff in the park overlooking the appropriately named Priest Drive bridge.

Like Laura, each had come seeking a little spiritual sustenance delivered from a Christian perspective, including from a group that called itself the ICTN, for International Christian Triathlon Network. Many of the athletes in the congregation that afternoon had just picked up their bicycles and stood with them propped at their sides, en route to deliver them to the bike transition area; a number of them used their tri bars to hold the scriptural readings and hymn lyrics distributed by the Iron Prayer organizers.

The first speaker, Chris Anderson—originally from the Black Hills of South Dakota and now "a servant leader" of the Fellowship of Christian Athletes Endurance team in Minneapolis—was introduced as a triathlete since 2003 and a "one-time Ironman finisher."

"First and foremost," the gathering was told, "Chris loves Jesus, and the FCA Endurance team."

Chris, who appeared to be in late twenties and was wearing a bright yellow cotton bike cap, said he just wanted "to share, really briefly, a couple of lessons I learned in my sole—we'll see, only God knows—Ironman." In particular, he said he would explain "three things I've learned that I pray will bless you."

The first was an admonition that the competitors, when offered sunscreen by volunteers at the transition point between the swim and the bike, should be sure to apply it liberally to the six-inch-wide space on their backs where there would surely be a gap between their waistbands and their bike jerseys, which would inevitably ride up.

"I can honestly say the worst part of my Ironman was the sunburn I had right here," he said, twisting his torso to point at the affected area, now safely cloaked by a jersey as bright and yellow as his cap. "Every time I moved, along my belt line, it hurt. I still have a scar. Trust me. I won't show you."

Lesson number two, as Chris told it, was:

> When you get done with the race, and I don't know whose great idea this was, they have pizza. I don't know if it was the state I was in, or if it really was the best pizza ever created. But it was good.
>
> I do remember that the second piece of pizza I ate, absolutely, was sausage. That was a huge mistake. I made it back to the hotel room just in time to puke everything up—all my fluids, all my fuel, from the race. All I could do is lay in my hotel room and quiver like a pile of goo for hours.

Again, there were knowing nods in response to his cautionary tale.

Chris then told the crowd lesson number three: that when he competed in his Ironman, he considered it a "God-ordained race." He sustained no injuries, he said, and experienced no mechanical problems. But when he awoke the next morning and saw the finisher's medal on the hotel dresser, he realized "nothing was different." As he told it:

> I don't know what I expected. But after setting out this major goal and having this amazing race, I thought something would feel a little different.
>
> I'm here to tell you I was OK with that. I understood there was a huge difference between a goal and a purpose.
>
> If you make Ironman your purpose, you will either be significantly disappointed or you are going to chase this thing forever, trying to be fulfilled by something the world can't offer.

Chris then added:

> If you know Jesus, and this sport has started to take His place, you're flirting with idolatry, which is sort of a slippery slope. I urge you, I plead with you, for that twenty-four hours, when you enter the water, know where you're at. Know why you're racing, and that it's for His purposes.

As Chris spoke, Laura nodded and said "Uh-huh" in affirmation several times under her breath. Chris then read a verse from Matthew 6—"Store for yourself treasures in heaven, where moth and rust do not destroy, and thieves do not break into steel"—which prompted Laura to whisper an interpretation in my ear.

For Laura, the biblical imprecation meant, "If I'm not a good person, but I finish the race, it's incomplete. Whether you finish or not, it's the journey."

Laura found the next speaker even easier to relate to. Sierra Snyder, from Pasadena, California, spoke of her second Ironman, at Kona in October. Sierra, who was 32, said she had gone into the race hoping to break eleven hours—and wound up finishing in 10 hours, 20 minutes, which ranked her near the top ten among amateurs that year.

It wasn't her account of her time in which Laura recognized herself, but rather Sierra's describing herself as being "in a complete panic" at the start of the swim. How did she rebound from a panic attack in the water to finish so decisively?

"I said, 'Lord, this can't be how you want me to finish my day,'" she told the gathering. "I was praying, and a complete sense of peace washed over me."

Sierra's final advice to the would-be Ironmen was somewhat counterintuitive: Even in the midst of an event that required them to think of nothing but themselves for the better part of a day, they should try their best to think of others.

This advice was identical to that imparted to Laura by a girlfriend at the gym, only a few days earlier: "We're going to pray that you're so calm that you can say 'How are you doing?' to others around you."

As a "live worship band"—two guitar players, a bassist, a drummer, and two female singers—played an original, closing song with the refrain "My savior's always there for me," Laura left the ceremony, thinking about Sierra Snyder and her triumph that day in Hawaii.

I can't believe she *had a panic attack*, Laura thought.

A few hours later, as the giant speakers outside the Tempe Center for the Arts blared a much more secular tune—The Who's "Baba O'Riley"—Laura filed into the open-air pavilion next to the lake along with hundreds of other competitors, as well as their friends and families. Because most of the competitors would be getting to bed early Saturday night in anticipation of waking up before dawn Sunday morning, the opening dinner of Ironman Arizona was held on Friday evening.

The most inspiring performance that evening may have been put in behind the scenes by Mike Reilly, the ubiquitous announcer and master of ceremonies, who typically carried himself like a slightly shorter version of the irreverent comedian Bill Murray in his days on *Saturday Night Live*. Though his condition was never disclosed to the competitors, Reilly had been on his back at home for a week with the current strain of swine flu, a debilitating virus that had stricken people around the world that fall and prompted more than a little panic on airplanes and at salad bars, where the illness could be spread easily.

More than a few of the first-time Ironman aspirants in the crowd—and there were more than a thousand of them—had no doubt dreamed of hearing Reilly recite their names as they crossed the finish line. None would have any idea how weak and stiff he'd felt as he prepared to make the drive to Tempe from his San Diego home. Anyone who knew how sick he was—a fact he'd concealed from his colleagues at Ironman, lest they grow concerned—would have surely told him to stay home. But Reilly found himself thinking that these athletes would face much bigger hurdles than he did on Sunday, and so he had rallied.

Reilly was right where they expected he'd be, presiding over the evening's festivities and good-naturedly ribbing any number of the evening's participants—including the mayor of Tempe, Hugh Hallman ("One day he might even do this race")—and sharing the stage with, among others,

"Chef Robert" of the Food Network program *Dinner: Impossible,* who'd earlier cooked dinner in front of his show's camera's for several hundred Ironman VIPs. Chef Robert had became so swept up in the moment that he vowed to do an Ironman himself the following year, a pledge that was met with skeptical glances from Reilly, among others. (The chef had acknowledged: "I'm fat, I don't swim, I don't know how to bike, right?")

If those who had seen Reilly perform in other Ironman settings—at hundreds of similar dinners, and in epic performances on the microphone from dawn to midnight on race days—had noticed anything different about him, it was that his chiseled, perpetually sunburned face now seemed to be adorned with a thin mustache. This he did acknowledge to the crowd, saying it was a "Mo-stache," in celebration of the month of "Movember." Like countless other men around the country, he and Paul Huddle and Roch Frey, the race directors of Ironman Arizona, had grown mustaches in support of a monthlong national campaign to raise awareness of men's cancers, including testicular and prostate cancers.

"Trust me, on the last day of the month, I'm shaving it off," Reilly assured the crowd from the stage, which was decorated with faux cactuses, among other desert motifs. "I can't tell you what my wife won't do."

This line provoked audible groans from the audience, and not for the last time, prompting Reilly to attempt a recovery. "I haven't been kissed all month," he said.

Scattered throughout the audience, laughing at Reilly's bad jokes and nibbling on an intentionally simple meal of grilled chicken and noodles, were Seth Cannello, who knew firsthand about the cancers of which Reilly spoke; Bryan Reece, who had dedicated his race to dozens of cancer victims, like his father, and to dozens more cancer survivors, all of whose names he'd be carrying with him on his body; and Scott Johnson, who'd cheated another disease, cystic fibrosis, and seemingly certain death, only to triumph in Ironman.

Had any of them—or Leanne Johnson, Laura Arnez, or Tom Bonnette, who were also there—introduced themselves to the other first-time competitors around them, they'd have found stories that were every bit as inspiring.

One man, from the West, was a recovering drug addict and alcoholic who in recent years had lost his two sons, his job, and his wife, only to begin to reassemble a sense of himself through triathlon.

Another first-timer, Tammy Sue Roberts, was a realtor from Calabasas, California, whose daughter had died. Soon after, the woman herself had been left with a paralyzed vocal cord, and difficulty maintaining her balance, after otherwise successful surgery to remove a brain tumor. As she explained her reasons for doing an Ironman: "I have spent the last several years overcoming devastating events that are not going to get the best of me."

Another contestant, whose mother had been diagnosed with Alzheimer's at forty-nine and died "at a very young fifty-five," said he knew he risked getting the disease at a similar age and that his genetic predisposition was out of his control. "What I *can* control is exercising both physically and mentally," he said, adding, "I cannot wait until I hear those words, 'Travis Holmgren, *you* are an Ironman.'"

Had these and similar testimonials been offered from the stage, the audience would have been kept there until early morning.

Still, those who did speak as part of the formal program provided plenty of uplifting moments.

Mayor Hallman, for example, explained to the audience that the bicycle course—a three-loop affair that traveled 18.5 miles out of town, then 18.5 miles back—passed through the Salt River Pima-Maricopa Indian Community, "the folks whose ancestors settled this valley in 400 A.D." It was also a community that had been "plagued by diabetes."

Two years earlier, the mayor recounted, the first member of the local Indian community had finished Ironman Arizona. On Sunday, eight others from the community—which numbered only nine thousand—would attempt a similar feat.

"They are taking your inspiration and turning the community's problems around from a health perspective," he told the crowd. "You have inspired that community to become healthier."

After the mayor spoke, Reilly gave the equivalent of an annual State of Ironman Arizona address—an attempt to put that year's field of athletes in some statistical context. As proof that the Ironman bug often hits hardest in middle age, Reilly revealed that the biggest demographic competing on Sunday was men between the ages of forty and forty-four—

more than five hundred of them, or roughly one in every five participants. The second-largest group, men thirty-five to thirty-nine, was nearly as large. Similarly, nearly three hundred participants were women between the ages of thirty-five and forty-four.

After citing the number of states and countries represented—fifty and thirty-seven, respectively—Reilly announced that the 1,140 first-timers represented an increase of nearly three hundred over the previous year, and comprised more than 40 percent of the field in this year's race. He then asked them all to stand, and they did, to thunderous applause.

"The best of luck to all of you," he said. "We call you Iron Virgins."

The rest of Reilly's monologue was comfortingly familiar to anyone who'd heard it before, and as much fun as a prime-time reality show to those who hadn't. Once again he did his "Biggest Loser" bit, in which he attempted to figure out which athlete had lost the most weight in preparation for Ironman Arizona. (The winner, who had cast off 110 pounds, was awarded a year's supply of Erin Baker's Breakfast Cookies. "Because you're our biggest loser, we have for you—food!" Reilly announced.)

He also did his oldest/youngest routine, and, as had been the case the previous year, Ed Wolfgram, the psychiatrist from St. Louis, ascended the podium to claim the crown as the oldest competitor at Ironman Arizona 2009, now a year older at seventy-seven.

"Ed, you've got two youngsters here doing their first Ironman," Reilly said, putting one arm around an eighteen-year-old man from Alaska, and the other around an eighteen-year-old woman from California. "What kind of advice would you give them?"

"Well," said Wolfgram, a ten-time finisher of Ironman Kona, "I think it's important to plan for a lifetime of this sort of thing. It's one of the best things you can do. At my age, seventy-seven, half of my peers are dead," he said, to big laughs from the audience. "Half of the others are in assisted living. And look what fun I have."

But no one, arguably, moved the field of participants and well-wishers that night as much as Rudy Garcia-Tolson.

Rudy, age twenty-one, was being honored at the dinner by Ford, the principal sponsor of Ironman Arizona, with its "Everyday Hero" award. An introductory video shown on the podium's big-screen television told Rudy's almost unbelievable story: At age five he'd helped his parents make the harrowing decision to agree to allow surgeons to amputate both his legs above the knee. Neither limb had developed correctly since birth, and "numerous attempts to repair" them had failed, according to the voice-over on the video.

But once fitted with prosthetics, Rudy had been determined to do all the things that other boys his age did. He surfed, he skateboarded, and, before long, he was entering triathlons. A month earlier, he'd even attempted the toughest triathlon of them all—Ironman Kona—missing the bike cutoff by only eight minutes.

"I'm a very competitive person," Rudy said in the video of his performance in Kona. "It was, on one side, very embarrassing. Deep down inside I knew that, with a different situation, preparation, I would have nailed it. I just felt really disappointed in myself. I could have done a lot better."

And with that, Rudy appeared on the stage alongside Reilly, perched on seemingly bionic metallic legs. At Ironman Arizona, he vowed, he would finish the task he had started in Hawaii.

"I want to show the little kids out there who are in the same situation as me that the sky's the limit," Rudy said.

Reilly, who prides himself on giving the needle to all comers, regardless of their station in life, couldn't resist a little skepticism. "Dude, I had you onstage in Hawaii," he told Rudy, a barbed reference to Rudy's failure to complete that particular mission, which drew silence from the audience.

"Nervous laugh," Reilly said, realizing he had misjudged how profoundly affected the crowd was. "You know I had to give him a hard time."

Reilly quickly recovered, though, conducting a moving interview with Rudy in which Reilly observed with awe that the young man had to pedal his bike "without a lot of the muscles that everybody else has."

Reilly also prodded Rudy to reveal his swim time in Ironman Kona.

"It was a 1:05," Rudy said.

"First-timers are going, 'Oh my God, I can't do that,'" Reilly responded, and then said, "When you're running, you're running twenty-six miles. Take us through the logistics of how you feel."

"I get off the bike," Rudy said. "Hopefully I won't feel too bad. I'll have a sandwich and maybe some Cheetos before I get on the run."

That got perhaps the biggest laugh of the night from the crowd of participants, many of whom had planned out their nutrition on the Ironman course as if it were a NASA mission.

"All the first-timers," Reilly said, "are out there going: *Cheetos? I've got to go out to the store and maybe get some Cheetos before I get on the run.*"

After Rudy, in further response to Reilly's question, explained that his "stumps are going to get a little sore, a little swelled," Reilly then grew as serious as he had all evening.

"Rudy, we really want to be able to call you an Ironman," he said. "You've been a true inspiration from this tall"—and here Reilly moved one hand just above the podium floor—"in everything you've done."

Rudy responded by saying, "I'll be giving you guys a lot of motivations. Give me motivations back. It's going to be a long day. We'll get to that finish line. Stay positive. Good luck."

Few of the eyes in the audience were dry, including the eyes of Bryan Reece, who sat close to the stage, near the video monitor. He hoped he might have the opportunity on Sunday to thank Rudy, in person, for the gift of perspective that the young man had given him at precisely the moment he needed to hear it.

About a half-hour after the dinner ended, the race directors invited the participants in Ironman Arizona to leave their seats and gather around the stage for a presentation intended to be as bare-bones and clinical as the dinner had been uplifting and soaring. This was the athletes' meeting, where the organizers would walk everyone through the particulars of the race—for the first and last time.

Much of what they said was intended to put some reasonable fear into the athletes, to ensure that they followed all rules to the letter, lest someone get hurt or worse.

"If you don't cross that mat in the morning, you are out of the race," Paul Huddle said, in reference to the oversize pad that would activate the electronic timing devices on their ankles as they passed under the archway en route to the swim start. "If your chip is in the bag, you're out of the race. It's that simple."

There were plenty of other admonitions:

"Tell your friends and family they will not be allowed in the transition," Huddle warned, in reference to the area where the swim, the bike, and then the run would start. "So you'll have to do the tearful goodbye outside transition."

"Go in and put down your stuff," he continued, now sounding more like a sleepaway camp director, as the bus was about to leave. "Then you can come out and cry some more."

He also told them that they would hear two cannons: The first, at 6:50, was for the three dozen or so professional triathletes competing that day. The overwhelming remainder of competitors—the so-called age-groupers—would start at the signal of the second cannon, at 7:00 A.M.

The evening's program then proceeded to step-by-step explanations of the swim, bike, and run events.

The swim director, Tim Johnson, reiterated that the water temperature was likely to be "a kind of chilly" sixty-three degrees and that wetsuits, for anyone who may have thought otherwise, "are the order of the day."

"If you plan on using hoodies," which were made of the same material as wetsuits but covered a swimmer's ears and neck, Johnson said, "or extra swim caps, I suggest you get in tomorrow during the practice swims and try it out. I often see people over-accessorized on race morning, trying to experiment with new things."

He also spent several minutes discussing a seemingly simple task: how to ascend the metal stairs that had been installed for the swimmers to climb out of the water and onto the shore. (To get in, they were told, each person would have to jump off a dock.)

He then turned to the matter of safety in the water. "If you do need help," he said, "I encourage you to swim away from the other swimmers, raise your hands up, get the attention of one of the kayakers or lifeguards, and we'll get help to you."

After urging the competitors to "be careful out there" and to "look out for each other," Johnson turned the program over to Roch Frey, the race director who oversaw the bike course.

Frey explained that one of the most dangerous points in the entire race day was the first several hundred yards of the bike course—between the transition area and Rio Salado Parkway.

"That's a no-pass zone," he warned. "Please, it's really narrow, and it's kind of congested."

The same held true for the final few hundred yards of the bike ride.

Later, Jimmy Riccitello, the race's head referee, would offer several tips to the participants to help them avoid receiving penalty cards while on their bicycles; these functioned a bit like they might in a World Cup soccer match.

The athletes were reminded to ride to the right and pass on the left, to keep seven meters between themselves and the rider in front of them, to execute a pass within twenty seconds, and to refrain from "repassing" someone who had passed them until the rider who'd passed had pulled ahead by at least seven meters.

Staying too close to the back wheel of a fellow rider for too long would be considered drafting—a maneuver that provided an unfair advantage, because it decreased wind resistance on the rider behind—and would result in a red card from an official who might see it from his or her spot on the back of a patrolling motorcycle. Passing someone on the right would result in a yellow card.

Those flashed with a card, Riccitello told the crowd, were required to stop at the bright yellow "penalty box" tents, near the bike course turn-around point in downtown Tempe. (Those flashed, if they did not stop, would be disqualified, the athletes were informed, as would anyone who received three penalties.)

Once inside the tent, red-card recipients would be handed a stopwatch and instructed to give it back to the official after four minutes, thus adding that amount to their final time. Recipients of the less serious yellow card would merely need to give their bib number to the official, costing them about forty-five seconds.

After explaining to the participants that the thirty-seven-mile bike course would have four aid stations positioned evenly along the way— each would be stocked with orange Gatorade Endurance, bottled water, PowerBars, PowerBar Energy Gels, and bananas, as well as five orange Porta-Potties—the race officials explained the bike cut-offs.

Any cyclist who remained on the bike course after 5:30 P.M. would be disqualified, but there were also two other cutoffs: All cyclists had to begin the third and final bike loop no later than 3:00 P.M.; likewise, anyone who had not reached the halfway point of that third loop, the turnaround at the furthest point, by 4:15 P.M. would also be disqualified.

It was nothing personal, the race organizers explained. Rules were rules, and the cutoff times were established based on the likelihood that someone taking that long to complete the bike ride would be unable to then finish the marathon by midnight.

Also, the competitors were told, there was a "hard cut-off" on the run course as well: Anyone who had not started its third and final loop by 10:15, an hour and forty-five minutes before the end of the race, would be disqualified.

The director of the run course, Mac Cavassar, also had a word to say about aid stations. There would be one about every mile on the run, and he urged the competitors to walk through each one, whether for some much-needed Gatorade (the flavor here was lemon-lime) or, after 4:00 P.M., to sip cups of chicken broth, intended to ward off the night's chill and restore lost salt.

Here, too, each aid station would have Porta-Potties on each end.

"The course is pretty flat, pretty open," Cavassar said. "Which means we can see your bare buns for a long ways. Public nudity, using the side of the road, using someone's private property—please refrain from doing that. We've had some other races where we've had some problems with that."

After a few other miscellaneous rules—no, iPods were not allowed; yes, a jog bra was considered acceptable as a shirt—the meeting was adjourned.

While most of the more than one thousand first-timers had been in attendance and paid careful attention, two were noticeably absent at the meeting's end.

Laura Arnez had left the site as soon as the dinner was over to go to the airport to pick up her husband and children. While she knew the meeting was important, she had also been worried all day about the reliability of the minivan she'd rented, which had already conked out on her once, the result of a battery that needed a charge.

And while Seth Cannello had listened to most of the race officials' presentation, he decided he was too tired to fight the crowd at the stage immediately afterward—when the race officials said they would hear final requests from anyone with so-called special needs.

Seth knew that his desire to wear his swim gloves fit squarely in that category, but he felt that this was the wrong forum in which to mount his appeal. It was just too hectic, with the gaggle of athletes assembled at the base of the stage looking like traders at a commodities exchange, yelling orders.

He would, he assumed, have all day Saturday to attempt to buttonhole an official to plead his case.

CHAPTER 15

My Kayak Angel

Bryan Reece jolted awake at 2:00 A.M. on the morning of Ironman Arizona, with no prompt necessary from an alarm clock. As Debbie slept soundly next to him in the queen-size bed in their room at the SpringHill Suites hotel, Bryan began padding around in the dark for a bowl and a spoon. At a round table just a few feet from the bed, he ate some Cheerios, a peanut-butter-and-jelly sandwich, and half a banana, all while sipping from a sports drink. These, he knew, would be crucial calories that would pay a dividend at the race start, now just five hours away. Calmed by the thought that his digestive system was already beginning its own Ironman, Bryan went back to bed and actually managed to doze off for another two hours.

When the alarm on the digital clock at his bedside buzzed him and Debbie awake at 4:15, he headed straight for the shower and then, after drying off, grabbed a marker. On his left arm, he wrote BELIEVE, with a picture of a little stick figure of a man in a box. The figure was Bryan, and he intended it to remind him to "race my race, no one else's." On his right arm, he wrote EXECUTE, a reminder to carry out his plan for the day and an evocation of one of the mantras of Endurance Nation, the online training group in which Bryan participated.

It was game time.

From the very beginning of his improbable path to an Ironman, Bryan had put his innate organizational skills to good use, and this day represented nothing if not a culmination of the Type A side of his personality.

By the time he had climbed into bed at eight the previous evening, he had long since put final touches on the seemingly endless "Ironman Morning To-Do Lists" that he had begun drafting several weeks earlier at home. His plan was to not have to think at all—from the moment he opened his eyes, through the short car ride to the parking garage at the race site, to the point at which he slithered into his wetsuit.

The list he had prepared for that morning at the hotel had entries that would sound downright salacious in any other context, including "Band-Aids on the nipples" and "Bodyglide your crotch." Each was intended to protect his skin from the inevitable chafing in a day of exercise likely to last from dawn well past dusk. When he arrived at Tempe Beach Park before 5:30, he pulled out another list that instructed him to "put air in your tires" and "fill the Aero bottle with water." He felt as prepared as anyone could, considering the gauntlet through which he was about to put his body.

The final item on the list: "Go find a quiet place to sit down."

And so, after pulling on his full-length black rubber wetsuit—as far as the eye could see, hundreds of men and women were dressed exactly the same—Bryan walked barefoot along the matted desert grass and asphalt of the park and found a spot along the rock wall overlooking Tempe Town Lake.

Just after 6 A.M., the park was illuminated by temporary towers bearing bright white spotlights that revealed the more than 2,500 bicycles in long racks in the transition area. This space—bigger than a football field—would be home base to the participants throughout the day. It housed the oversize white tents, one for men, the other for women, where they would change from their swimsuits into their bikewear, and then again into their running gear. Twenty orange Porta-Potties had been placed there exclusively for the use of the athletes. At the far right corner was the giant inflatable white archway through which they would pass en route to jumping into the water for the swim. The entire transition area was cordoned off from the rest of the world by retractable belt dividers, the kind typically found on movie lines or in banks. Many of the spectators on the other side of that barrier, who were beginning to gather on the Mill Avenue Bridge, just to the right of the park—under which the swimmers would wade just before the cannon blast—wore jackets, scarves, and knit hats to keep warm in the fifty-degree weather.

Piercing the cold air at that early hour was the familiar and even sooth-ing voice of Mike Reilly, whose bulletins, projected over giant speakers arrayed for several hundred yards, would alternately provide athletes and spectators with crucial instructions, play-by-plays, and, of course, good-natured banter over the next eighteen hours.

"If you haven't gotten your body marking, get there," Reilly told the participants, speaking from a small podium near the edge of the lake. "That's the volunteers in the lime green shirts."

If there is an overriding smell to an Ironman competition (at least be-fore it begins), it is the sweet, chemically perfumed aroma of hundreds of uncapped black magic markers, their ink waterproof. Those people in the green shirts—a regiment in an army of nearly three thousand volunteers who'd be working the race that day—dutifully scribbled on the bodies of each athlete, who stood in line as anxiously as if they were getting flu shots at the office. Peeling their wetsuits down partially, each had his race num-ber written large on his right and left shoulders. Each contestant's age was then embossed on his left calf. This precaution was taken in the name of safety: If, in the event of trouble, someone had to be pulled from the water and was unable to speak, a lifeguard or EMT could quickly determine not only who he was but how old he was—which might not be immediately evident under thick swim goggles and a swim cap (red for men, white for women).

"I've got an athlete here who forgot his biking shorts, if you can believe it," Reilly was now announcing, with a little bit of disdain but no evident surprise. "If anyone has an extra pair, small or medium, come near the speaker. We're looking for a pair of bike shorts, so this athlete can race with some shorts on!"

A moment later, he issued another alert.

"We've got a long line for the Porta-Potties," he announced, now sounding less like Bill Murray the lounge singer, as he had the previous evening, and more like Bill Murray the head boys' counselor in the sum-mer camp comedy *Meatballs*. "Just make sure you don't take the Sunday paper in there."

"It's 6:04," he added. "It's time to get your clothes bags done and drop them off. It's time to be moving out of transition."

By 6:20 Bryan Reece had returned from his perch overlooking the lake and was now standing under a light post, his bare feet planted on a rare swatch of concrete. By now, unbeknownst to anyone but his wife, he had taken that list of cancer survivors and victims—it contained dozens of names, typed by him in the smallest font he could find, and then laminated—and placed it between the two swim caps he was wearing. With his orange-colored goggles resting tight against his upper forehead, he stood sipping from a water bottle and helping zip up the backs of the wetsuits of his fellow competitors, as if they were all bridesmaids in the same wedding.

"Finisher—that's my word," one man said to Bryan.

"That's all I care about," Bryan agreed.

Asked what was going through his head at that moment, Bryan was at an uncharacteristic loss.

"The feeling is . . ." he began, and then his voice trailed off. "I just don't know how to say it."

And with that he was off, taking the dozen or so steps to the white archway and then funneling through it with the others, in a scene that was reminiscent of cattle being herded through the narrow gateway to a corral. As he did so, a fellow competitor he'd met the night before recognized him and yelled, "Hey, Bryan, go fast!"

Bryan smiled and headed for the dock. As he did so, he noticed two men carrying a younger man in the same direction. It was Rudy, without his prosthetic legs, which, Bryan presumed, were stowed near the exit of the swim.

Bryan and everyone else who witnessed this scene began to applaud.

Laura Arnez, her black wetsuit distinguished from those of most of her competitors by the dark brown swatches on each shoulder, was determined to ease her anxiety before the start of the swim that morning by finding some way to help others—just as the speakers at Iron Prayer and her friend from the gym had suggested.

She saw her opportunity at around 6:30, when she caught sight of two young women becoming visibly frantic in their attempt to pump front bike tires that had gone somewhat limp overnight. Laura took it upon herself to get hold of a pump, then chatted amiably with the pair. After a few nibbles from an oatmeal-flavored Clif Bar and a few sips of Gatorade, she set about putting on her swim caps.

She had been so worried about the feeling of the cold water on her scalp that she decided to do something she'd never done in any of her training—she would wear *three* tight-fitting caps.

First she pulled on an orange one that belonged to her husband, followed by a hood-style cap that would cover not just her ears but her neck and the sides of her face. Finally came the white Ironman cap on which her number, 2699, had been hand-marked.

"It was a little bit insane," Laura would acknowledge afterward.

Indeed, it was the very thing that Tim Johnson, the director of the swim, had warned the athletes not to do during that post-dinner meeting Friday night—namely, experiment with new equipment, particularly something as potentially cumbersome as a hoodie, on race day. But Laura, who had been en route to retrieve her family at the airport, had not heard his advice.

By 6:56, nearly every participant was in the lake, wading toward Mill Avenue Bridge. Laura, though, had remained on the side of the dock, wanting to be one of the last competitors into the water. But she now worried that she would be late for the swim start.

She made it to the water, however, and after jumping in—one of the last competitors to do so—she took a few paddles of breaststroke. The second cannon blast sounded at precisely 7:00 A.M., and Ironman Arizona 2009 began.

Only a few feet ahead of Laura when the cannon went off, Leanne Johnson counted to five in her head and then began taking her first strokes of front crawl. A few friends had advised her to start at the back of the pack, the better to avoid being jostled by all those arms and legs now moving and splashing with the rhythm of a flock of birds.

Leanne was aware of how jittery she was. She still considered the swim her weakness, and the portion of her training on which she most wished she'd spent more time. Compounding her anxiety was the fact that she'd arrived in Tempe with uncharacteristic discomfort in her lower back. Exactly a week earlier, in the midst of a twelve-day blitz in which she would work all but one day, she had let her mind drift as she and a fellow nurse attempted to help a man who weighed well over two hundred pounds try to sit up in his hospital bed.

"I got lazy," she explained afterward, and didn't properly brace her back and legs. The pain had been there ever since—exacerbated, it seemed, by the deep-tissue massage she had scheduled the following day, the first massage she'd gotten in more than seven years.

But whatever discomfort or jitters she was feeling were alleviated by thoughts of all the love and support that had enveloped her and Scott in the days since they'd arrived in Arizona. Her older brother and sister-in-law had flown in from London, Ontario, as had several of their friends from Ontario. And Ross and Daradee Murray, the couple from whom they'd rented the house outside Tempe—the parents of Liam—were there, too. Leanne was pleased, in the end, with all the money she and Scott had raised in Liam's memory—$7,000—but no feeling compared to the emotional moment when she finally met the Murrays in person for the first time.

Ross, who was thirty-five and stocky, like Scott, proudly told her he'd quit smoking for good and recently done an "Urbanathlon"—a twelve-mile race that involved bikes with monster tires, hurdles, and monkey bars. He now thought he might want to follow the lead of Leanne and Scott and do a 70.3, a half-Ironman distance. That was surely good news—but nothing like that shared by Daradee, who wore a pendant with Liam's birthstone around her neck: She was pregnant, and due to have a baby girl in April.

At least early on, as she made her way along a course set out like a rectangle, Leanne's strategy of hanging toward the back of the pack was paying dividends. She was neither punched nor hit nor pushed under the water, all of which Scott and other experienced Ironman triathletes had prepared her to expect.

As she followed the line of red buoys—which stretched for nearly a mile down the lake and looked like giant three-dimensional raviolis—

Leanne struggled, as so many participants did, with sighting. Those who followed the buoy line were headed straight into the sun, and when Leanne picked up her head, it could be tough to see. But she endured, and just shy of forty-five minutes after she had begun the swim, she found herself, gloriously, within sight of another bridge—this one called Rural Road—and making the turn around the far buoys to begin her return. This is where she felt kicked for the first time, as everyone seemed to try to get to the same spot at the same time, hugging the buoys so as not to take too many unnecessary strokes out of the way.

"I tried to protect my head and stomach so I wouldn't get punched," Leanne recalled afterward. Though she'd been keeping up a good, steady pace of front crawl, she switched briefly to the sidestroke, which gave her an uninterrupted field of vision. Once she was safely heading back toward shore, she returned to a crawl. She knew she was zigzagging a bit—sometimes veering far to the left of the pack, at others to the far right—but she also had a sense that the worst part of the swim, and perhaps even the worst part of her day, might actually be over.

She was on her way, she felt sure, to becoming an Ironman.

Bobbing in the water, about eight minutes behind Leanne, was Seth Cannello.

He, by contrast, had not gotten off to a good start at all. His day had begun at three in the morning in his hotel room, after only two hours of sleep, with some sips of water and a few bites of a nutrition bar. As Robin began rousing herself, he sprinted to the bathroom and vomited. He hadn't felt nervous, but he threw up several more times before finally reaching the staging area. He knew he shouldn't start an Ironman on an empty stomach, so he tried again to ingest something—this time some Gatorade, an apple, and part of a bagel—and the combination seemed to do the trick.

At the least, for the first time in months, his mind was at ease regarding the thought of his hands and the cold water. On Saturday morning he'd wandered back and forth along the lakeshore—with his doctors' letters secure in a leather binder under his arm—until, as if he had willed it to be so, he ran directly into Tim Johnson, whom he recognized as the director of the swim. At that moment a woman was pleading with Johnson to allow her to use not just gloves but also booties—which the Ironman organization did permit, but only when the water temperature was under fifty-eight degrees, a moot point in Ironman Arizona. Moreover, as near as Seth could tell, she had no documentation to support her request, and it was summarily denied.

Sufficiently intimidated, Seth approached Johnson, a somewhat stern native of England, and opened his binder. After a quick glance at his paperwork, Johnson had issued his ruling: Seth's evidence of his Raynaud's syndrome met the criteria for using his black neoprene gloves, and he would also be permitted to hang back on the rock ledge to the right of the dock as the swimmers jumped in the water, so that he might put off his exposure to the cold until the very last moment. While he could have also used booties, because his Raynaud's affected his feet as well, he chose not to push the matter. It was his hands that really worried him.

Once he was in the water, the temperature seemed less of an issue than the near-continuous pounding his spindly six-three frame seemed to be taking. He felt as if he were at sea with a bunch of bumper cars. Indeed, he was pushed under so many times by passing swimmers struggling to find space that he began inadvertently gulping mouthfuls of lake water.

Nearly everyone around him was doing the front crawl, but Seth stuck to his guns with the breaststroke. With his head almost continuously above the water, he was able to see in front of him, but there never seemed to be anywhere clear in which to swim.

"I couldn't find an alleyway anywhere between people," he recalled afterward. "And I knew there were people behind me. I was maybe fifty yards from the start and I thought, *I can't believe I'm having this much trouble.* I even chuckled to myself. I thought, *This is really going to be something if I can get through here.*"

"The swim was completely miserable for me," he added. "There were a couple of times I really didn't think I was going to make it."

One of those times came about a quarter-mile into the course. Seth's goggles were taking on water, badly, and when he began to tug on one of the thin straps that attached them to his head, the strap snapped off completely. The strap that remained, meanwhile, seemed to be hanging by a thread. Seth did his best to suction the goggles to his face and maintain his visibility, while periodically lifting the goggles from his eyes to drain the accumulating water.

After somehow reaching the far buoy and beginning the journey back toward shore, he felt himself finally able to get a rhythm going. But his confidence soon began to ebb. He'd been in the water for nearly an hour and was gradually becoming aware of how cold his body had become, and he began to shake.

Periodically he would stop and just float, then forge on. His hands felt protected, as did his body, but his core temperature was dropping nonetheless. And his feet—he could tell they were blanching.

He had to get out of the water.

When, just before the national anthem and the start of the swim, Mike Reilly had asked those in the water, "Who is going to become an Ironman?" no hand shot higher than that of Bryan Reece.

And then the cannon fired, and he was swimming.

"Everyone talks about the washing machine effect, and I must have missed it," he would say later. "I seemed to be in a great spot, a bubble of water around me, and I just swam and swam and swam."

Bryan did take a kick to the left ear at one point, and at another he found one of his wrists wedged between someone's ankles. As they began to scissor, Bryan feared those legs might actually snap his wrist. "I got it out of there quickly," he said.

Otherwise, Bryan felt such a sense of peace that his thoughts began to wander.

There is our firm's office in Tempe, he thought as he stroked past a gleaming glass building along the lakeshore. *I wonder if Bruce and Debbie*—who he knew would be watching the race from a small boat—*are cold? There is the Arizona State University Sun Devil Stadium. This part of the swim feels uphill. I wonder how many strokes I have taken? Wow, the sun is bright.*

And then, as he felt he was approaching the halfway point:

Did they move the bridge? Oh, here it is, and look—there's the turn buoy. Check the time. Forty minutes. A little fast for me.

Bryan actually eased up a bit on his strokes on the return, and found that portion of the swim blissfully uneventful. He actually felt warm. And before long he was crossing back under the Mill Avenue Bridge and was within sight of the crowds—and the metal stairs that Tim Johnson had mentioned on Friday night.

He also heard Mike Reilly's booming voice calling out the competitors' names and hometowns—"Madison. Madison, Mississippi, that is. Toms River, New Jersey. Mystic, Connecticut"—as they crawled, in some instances, back onto dry land.

Bryan and his fellow competitors' final strokes were accompanied by classic rock blaring from the loudspeakers. Many of the selections, like "In a Big Country" and Bon Jovi's "Livin' on a Prayer," had been deliberately chosen by race organizers for the lift they might give the athletes.

Dizzy and shivering, Seth Cannello put one knee on one of the metal steps leading out of the water, pulled himself upright, and immediately felt a man in a white baseball cap and sunglasses brace him on his right side so that he would not topple over. He gingerly navigated the final steps and made his way to the long cushioned mat that the race organizers had placed over the pavement on the lakeside. Soon, a woman in a red T-shirt—emblazoned on the upper right with a white cross that made clear she was a first-aid worker—came up to Seth and asked him, "How you doin'?"

All he could do was nod.

As the two volunteers began to peel him out of his wetsuit, he managed to sneak a look at his watch. It was almost 8:40, and he'd been out of the water for several minutes. That meant he'd managed to cover the swim course in less than 1 hour and 40 minutes—1 hour, 35 minutes, and 12 seconds, he would later learn. That was almost forty-five minutes under the swim cut-off.

The portion of Ironman Arizona that Seth, like so many competitors, had dreaded most was over. Still, as the two volunteers—now joined by two others—wrapped a trembling Seth in a blanket and eased him to the pavement, it wasn't at all clear that he could continue.

By this point Leanne Johnson, too, had emerged from the water, at 1 hour, 26 minutes, and 30 seconds. Scott, veteran Ironman that he was, had come out nearly twelve minutes earlier. Bryan Reece would reach shore at 1 hour, 38 minutes, just three minutes after Seth.

As Seth sat for several minutes on the ground near the swim exit, Bryan had, unknowingly, walked briskly past him and headed for the transition tent, where he would change into a bike shirt and shorts illustrated with the logo of Lance Armstrong's LiveStrong Foundation, as well as arm warmers that he planned to shed along the course as the temperature (his, and that of the air) climbed. Bryan took his time getting dressed—fourteen minutes—but the truth was, as he explained, "my hands were cold, and it took a while before I could operate my fingers to dress."

When Seth was finally brought to his feet, he was steered not to the right, to the transition tent, but to the left and inside the medical tent, where a volunteer sat him down and gave him a cup of steaming broth. He was surrounded by several other swimmers also trying desperately to get warm.

Anyone who saw how pale and clammy he looked, or met his haunted, vacant stare, would have come to an inevitable conclusion: Seth Cannello was surely, and obviously, done for the day.

As 9:00 A.M. came and went, signaling that the swim cut-off was just twenty minutes away, Laura Arnez was still in the water. At ten minutes until the cutoff, her husband and five children, who were huddled near the swim exit and nervously scanning the horizon, began to wonder where she was.

For much of the first portion of the swim, Tom Arnez had actually managed to walk along the shoreline and keep pace with his wife, who was easy to track because she was near the very back of the pack. Occasionally she could even hear him shout words of encouragement.

But Laura had ultimately become preoccupied by a glitch that threatened to derail her Ironman pursuit before she even got a chance to climb on her bike.

Like Seth Cannello, she found that her goggles—which covered far more than her eyes, and resembled the eye protectors worn by scientists in their labs—kept filling with water. But unlike Seth, she just couldn't seem to identify what the problem was and make them watertight.

She found herself repeatedly paddling over to the kayakers along the swim course, pulling herself up to her waist, which the rules permitted, and emptying her goggles of water before repositioning them on her face. Then, as soon as she'd get started, they would fill up again.

She knew she was proceeding slowly, and, without looking at her watch, she began to calculate in her mind how quickly she might need to do the bike ride if she took two hours to complete the swim. She also wondered how she could even manage *that*, given the state of her goggles.

Still, one particular thought gave her confidence: She felt none of the familiar twinges of a panic attack. She was calm, as comfortable as she'd ever felt in open water.

Finally, as she neared the halfway point of the swim—or what she assumed was halfway—a volunteer who'd been watching her brought his kayak near and said, "Let me see your goggles."

He looked at her head and partially pushed up the three layers of swim caps that had been riding low on her forehead, just above her eyebrows. He then placed the goggles back on her face, and, for the first time all day, she heard the welcome sound of suction.

With her eyes now clear, Laura began the trek back to shore. She would later explain that she had lost track of how long she had been in the water, and how much time she had left to complete the swim. She was just trying to move forward.

At a certain point, another kayaker, this one a woman in a blue boat, approached Laura and asked her, "What's your name?"

Laura introduced herself, then asked the volunteer, "How long have I been in?"

Laura noticed that the woman didn't answer her question but did assure her, "You'll be fine."

"Will you stay with me?" Laura asked her.

Yes, the woman said, and as Laura began to swim again, taking breaths on her left side, Laura could clearly see that blue kayak. Every time she breathed, it was right there. Laura began to think of the woman as "my kayak angel."

It was 9:17—three minutes before the swim cutoff—when Laura bounded into view from the shore, a blue kayak to her left and another, red, to her right.

Perhaps a dozen red and white caps bobbed behind her, and it was clear that those who were wearing them were on the verge of being disqualified from Ironman Arizona for exceeding the time limit.

Laura herself still appeared to have about seventy-five feet of water to cross—about the length of a standard pool—and whether she would make the cutoff was not at all assured. By now Mike Reilly had left the small riser from where he'd been broadcasting and walked down to the edge of the lake, his wireless microphone in hand.

Along with more than a dozen other volunteers, he was frantically waving one arm repeatedly toward shore, trying to urge Laura and a few other swimmers ahead of her to pick up the pace. Laura, though, appeared oblivious to how close she was cutting it and kept stopping and looking.

She would later explain that she was tiring. But her kayak angel would have none of it. "You've got to keep going," the woman urged her. "You can't stop anymore."

Now, for the first time, Laura heard panic in the woman's voice.

And so, oblivious to the waves of the crowd in front of her or to the time on her watch, she placed her face in the water and began putting one arm in front of the other.

All she could hear now was her kayak angel saying, "Kick, kick, kick."

Laura was so focused on moving forward that she didn't even pay attention to where she was headed—so much so that she feared she might hit her head on the steps.

After what seemed like an eternity, she felt a pair of hands grab her on the left side, and another pair on the right. Tentatively, she found her footing on the stairs, but she did not feel she could stand, at least not without some help.

She then heard someone say, "She's in."

Finally, mercifully, pulling her goggles off her face for good, Laura brought the digital watch on her left wrist toward her face and tried as best she could to focus on the time.

Two hours, 19 minutes.

She was so stunned at how close she had come to missing the swim cutoff that she began to sob.

Later, she would learn that her official time on the swim was 2 hours, 19 minutes, and 17 seconds. In fact, only one other swimmer came in after her—another woman from California, who emerged from the water with just five seconds on the clock—before the swim portion of the event was officially brought to a close.

All told, 2,516 swimmers completed the race—out of a total field of about 2,530. Laura Arnez's swim time ranked her 2,515th.

As her family looked on from the sidelines—not close enough to speak, but close enough to see her—Laura heard a race official say that she looked "horrible." She couldn't stop herself from shaking.

While she desperately wanted to head toward the changing tent, the official would not allow it, and guided her into the same medical area where Seth had been administered to some forty minutes earlier. She, too, was plied with broth, and hot packs were placed under her armpits.

"Sit down," she was told.

"I don't want to sit down," she responded.

Eventually the first-aid team made it clear that they were not going to take no for an answer.

Finally, a race official approached her and asked, "Do you want to continue?"

"Oh, my gosh," Laura said. "Of course I want to continue."

A female volunteer was accordingly drafted to escort her to the changing tent, where she was stripped bare and quickly covered with a dry bra and biking shorts. Laura still couldn't feel her fingers, and apologized for being unable to dress herself.

"We'll dress you," someone assured her, before instructing her to extend her arms outward so she could be assisted in getting on the longsleeved jersey that, she hoped, she would eventually be able to shed along the way.

They then got Laura's socks on, which were white and extended to her knee—the better to keep her warm and aid her circulation—and her bike shoes.

"She only has two minutes," she heard an official outside the tent say.

Moments later, Laura emerged from the tent and was escorted to her bike, which, like all the others, had been arranged in numerical order. She was immediately struck by how few bikes were left. Where once there had been more than 2,500, now there were perhaps a few dozen. And the owners of all the others that were left were done for the day.

"You go, girl, we're all counting on you," the volunteer who'd led her to her bike said as he bade her a brisk goodbye.

As she walked her bike through the archway that signaled the beginning of the 112-mile bike course, Laura said to no one in particular, "We're going to make it, we're going to make it."

But to those watching her from the sidelines, it was not immediately clear how she would manage to do that.

It was now 9:39 A.M.—a full twenty minutes after Laura had come out of the water.

In the worst-case scenario she'd played out in her head before the race, she had tried to think about how she could possibly make up the time if she climbed on her bike at 9:00 A.M.

Now it was nearly forty minutes after that.

She drew a smattering of applause as she made her way past the few spectators who remained in the crowd and headed toward Rio Salado Parkway, where the bike portion of the race would begin.

She was still so dazed that she hadn't realized she'd yet to get on her bike.

"What are you going to do?" a man yelled from the crowd. "Walk the whole 112?"

Laura had heard him, loud and clear.

She didn't have the strength to answer him, but even if she did, she had no idea what she'd say—or, for that matter, what to do next.

CHAPTER 16

Talking to God

Bryan Reece had climbed on his bike at 8:52 A.M.—nearly an hour before Laura Arnez. By this point, Leanne Johnson was eighteen minutes ahead of Bryan, and her husband, Scott, was seven minutes ahead of her. But their race times—or those of any of the hundreds of other riders ahead of him, or, presumably, the hundreds more behind him—were of no concern to Bryan. Like a golfer, he was focused on playing his own game, which was the only thing he could control. There was no sense dwelling on the performances of others.

As Bryan began to ride—the replacement helmet he'd received in the mail several weeks earlier tight on his scalp, and dark glasses shielding his eyes from the desert sun—he contemplated how he might break up the 112 miles ahead into more manageable pieces. The course, which would soon take him out of downtown and into the desert, was made up of three thirty-seven-mile loops. In his mind Bryan divided them further into six 18.5-mile segments.

18.5 miles is cool, Bryan thought to himself as he sipped water from one bottle and then, from another, Infinit, a mail-order nutrition drink with a formula that the manufacturer customized to the preferences of each consumer. *I can ride 18.5 miles. One piece at a time. Like eating an elephant.*

With the lake in which he'd been swimming less than a half-hour earlier still visible on his left, he rode along the right side of the four-lane parkway, the handful of corporate buildings receding behind him and the ASU football stadium once again coming into view on his right.

But whatever sightseeing he was permitting himself was interrupted by the image of a man shivering noticeably, and occasionally wobbling, on the bike in front of him.

As Bryan approached him from the rear, he began to make out the black number 1250 on his white bib. He then noted the man's first name—printed large enough by the race organizers so that the crowd might be able to call it out from the sidelines.

"Seth," Bryan said to himself under his breath.

And then: a flash of recognition. Bryan remembered having met this same Seth during a practice swim on Thursday. Seth learned that Bryan had whipped himself into shape on doctor's orders; Bryan, in turn, discovered that Seth faced a real struggle in cold water.

"Seth from Colorado Springs!" Bryan now cried out, loud enough for any number of riders to hear.

Seth would admit later that he had no memory of getting on his bike. He did recall, however, how he had managed to escape the medical tent: He'd said he needed to go to the bathroom—which, in fact, he desperately did. But afterward he'd apparently made his way to the changing tent instead of returning to medical.

The next thing he would remember was someone pulling up on his left during the competition and saying, "Hey, man, let's go for a bike ride."

Seth, who had prided himself on taking all those bike rides alone, was pleased to see Bryan's (relatively) familiar face.

Now that Bryan could get a better look at Seth, he could see that he wasn't just shivering—his legs appeared to be in spasms.

"I'm cold, I'm cold," Seth mumbled.

"Just keep riding," Bryan urged him. "You'll warm up."

Each man then said goodbye to the other, Bryan reluctantly pulling ahead and leaving Seth Cannello behind to face a future that, at least in the near term, was uncertain.

Tom Bonnette first felt the painful twinge on the left side of his leg, between his backside and his knee, just a few miles into the bike ride and around the time he passed the Old Navy store, part of a relatively new shopping plaza called Tempe Marketplace.

Until that point, all that time he had spent shuttling between hot and cold baths—the setback caused by the family dog notwithstanding—had appeared to have paid off. He'd come out of the water in a relatively brisk 1 hour and 25 minutes—and felt he could have done so even faster had he not made the "rookie mistake" of following a cluster of swimmers as they veered far to the right of the buoy line. He had just assumed they knew where they were going, but they didn't, and he figured he lost about seven minutes on this detour.

"I tell my children and students all the time, 'Don't follow the crowd,'" Tom, ever the teacher, said later. "The crowd was wrong. The crowd is always wrong. When am I going to learn that?"

He had also been rattled on the swim by a seemingly constant rhythmic slap on his feet, which felt like the nip of a fish. When he finally turned around, he realized a man's hands had been brushing his foot as he sought to draft close behind him. Though using a fellow athlete's body to aid one's own performance was not permitted on the bike, there was no such prohibition in the swim. Tom tried to veer a little to the left, and then a little to the right, yet he continued to feel the man's gentle but persistent touch—sometimes as high as his calf and knee.

"At that point, I kicked—hard," Tom said. "He figured it out."

Still, Tom felt he'd had a great swim, and unlike Seth and Laura, he'd relished his immersion in the cold water; it felt like one of his baths, and served to anesthetize his various aches and pains—including the jangly nerves caused by the Morton's neuroma at the bottom of his foot. He'd also felt his adrenaline soar as he prepared to exit the bike transition area and saw one of his daughters, Paige, thirteen, who'd gotten up before sunrise at their Phoenix home to accompany her dad to the race site.

"This is cool!" he thought he heard Paige say as she stood next to her friend Beca, who'd also been there since before 6:00 A.M. Tom was elated; one of the reasons he'd persisted in doing the race, despite his lingering guilt over the financial drain, was to be an example to his children.

But minutes later, as he pedaled his beat-up road bike (reconstructed since his accident) along McClintock Drive, a flat, six-lane road he'd been on before in recreational rides and races, he was in pain. He immediately diagnosed the problem: It was his IT (iliotibial) band, which, among other things, provides bracing support to the upper leg as a person walks or runs. But Tom's left IT band was pulling as taut as a rope, and the feeling was familiar: He had experienced similar shooting pain in his first marathon, years earlier. He wasn't sure this particular flare-up was a result of the bike accident, but its origin was, at the moment, irrelevant.

OK, he said to himself, *yet another stress.*

After that marathon, Tom had read up on IT band problems and learned that the only way to ease its grip was rest. But with more than a hundred miles still to left to pedal, and a marathon to run, how was he supposed to do that?

Over the next few miles, he pulled over to the right side of the road to stretch. He was now in the heart of the Salt River Pima-Maricopa Indian Community, which was largely open, dusty, and sparse, punctuated with sagebrush and cacti in the shape of prickly candelabras, and red rocks looming in the distance.

I've prepared myself for this, Tom kept telling himself. *I've finished marathons with IT band problems, sometimes hopping on one foot. I know I have it in me.*

Still, even if he could fight through the pain and tightness on the bike—which he considered a bit of an open question at this point—he wondered if he could run.

"I didn't want it to be a freak show," he recalled.

But that was a problem to be dealt with a few hours from now. Tom was determined to keep pedaling, even as he reached the main challenge in the bike course: a gradual climb (relatively speaking, considering he was now in the desert) that would last for several miles on a ramrod-straight stretch of the so-called Beeline Highway (Route 87). At the end of that climb, Tom and his fellow riders would have covered the first 18.5 miles of the bike ride, much of it against a headwind blowing across the desert, before turning around to head back toward town—and the start of the second of the three loops.

As he climbed the hill, moving at a pace of about a dozen miles an hour, he noted that the sky was clear and the midmorning sun was growing warm—by midday the temperature would reach about seventy.

It was a beautiful day, and Tom, who was "not a super-religious person," nonetheless found himself in the unusual position of talking to God, expressing his gratitude for weather that could not have been better.

"Thank you for the creative force that's out there," Tom said aloud. "Thank you for getting me here. Thanks for giving me the financial resources, as tough as the economy is on a teacher right now. Thanks for giving me this day."

And then, as the Beeline reached its crest, Tom found himself making that first turn back, at a main intersection with Shea Boulevard. He pulled over again, at the aid station just past the turn, used the orange Porta-Potty and took some sips from his bottle of HEED—a concoction, by a company called Hammer, that served to replace the electrolytes and salt he was losing as his exertion increased along with the desert temperature.

And then he was off again, coasting down that same incline he'd just made his way up, the wind now at his back as his digital speedometer ticked well over twenty miles an hour. At this point Tom had clicked off his conversation with God, but he still had something to say.

"This is fucking awesome!" he screamed, an observation that was followed by a string of other profanities from riders nearby.

As the desert gave way to a handful of gas stations, then that mall, then ASU Stadium and the gleaming glass and steel of Tempe's small downtown, Tom slowed down to make the turn at the intersection of Rio Salado Parkway and the Mill Avenue Bridge—near the swim start and the bike and run transition areas. It was 10:41 A.M. The first third of the bike course, thirty-seven miles, was under his belt and had taken him 2 hours and 6 minutes, at an average speed of 17.2 miles an hour.

As Tom analyzed the data from his bike computer, he felt pleased, all things considered. He was not, he had to acknowledge, going to meet his goal of finishing the Ironman in twelve hours, a target that had effectively moved out of range after his collision with the SUV bumper a week earlier. But he felt confident that he could finish and realize a dream that had been rattling around his head for nearly three decades, ever since he'd first seen highlights of one of the earliest Hawaii Ironman competitions on TV.

With two laps to go, he recalibrated and set two intermediate goals.

One was to finish the entire bike ride in six hours—a little less than four hours from now, which would require him to gain a little ground on loops 2 and 3 but not leave him exhausted.

The other was to carry himself on the marathon—a marathon, he had to remind himself, that would be following a swim and bike ride, each of epic length—in a way that he, his family, or anyone else watching would consider "respectable."

"It was no longer a race to me," he said, later. "But it was an event."

Leanne had been looking for Scott all through the first loop of the bike course. While she couldn't be sure he'd finished the swim ahead of her, she had assumed as much, given that the swim was one of his strengths and decidedly not one of hers.

On their extended Sunday bike rides, she usually ended up passing him. She figured she might today, as well—but certainly not as early as the end of the first loop of the bike course. And yet, as she prepared to make the turn at Rio Salado and Mill to begin her second lap—it was 10:32 A.M., nine minutes before Tom Bonnette would cross the same threshold—Leanne saw a friend from Wilmington, and then Scott just ahead of her.

She had managed, in under forty miles, to erase the seven-minute head start that Scott had as he started on the bike course. Indeed, she'd covered the first loop at a relatively scorching average speed of nineteen miles an hour—faster than what she'd typically ride on a Sunday, when she hadn't started the day with a swim. So far in Ironman Arizona, Scott was moving, on average, about a mile and a half slower than Leanne. Usually they rode at about the same rate.

"Hey, honey," Leanne said as she pulled up on her husband's left.

They talked for a few moments—each reassuring the other that he or she was fine—and then Leanne pedaled off ahead.

Leanne might well have passed her husband farther down the road, but for the fact that he'd had to spend a bit longer than usual in transition—12 minutes and 40 seconds, compared with Leanne's 8 minutes—because his hands were shaking so violently, presumably from the cold water. He couldn't put his socks or bike shoes on without assistance.

Eventually the shaking subsided, and Scott was on his way. But he hadn't mentioned the reason for the delay to Leanne; he couldn't recall something like that happening to him in a previous Ironman. Having competed in four other Ironman competitions, and finished in Florida, he knew that it was inevitable he'd see a few curveballs.

Meanwhile, as she began to put distance between herself and her husband, Leanne found the climb on the Beeline Highway during loop 2 to be more physically challenging, to say nothing of "mentally tricky." The desert winds were picking up even more speed than when she had passed along the same stretch ninety minutes earlier, and were sometimes gusting close to thirty miles an hour. For her and her fellow cyclists, it would sometimes feel as if they were pedaling against an invisible wall.

For the first time all day, she began to tire.

Oh my God, she thought to herself at one point on the second of the three loops, *I can't believe I've got to do this one more time.*

At 11:00 A.M. sharp, the unmistakable voice of Mike Reilly—who was now broadcasting from a platform set up at the intersection, so that he might give some play-by-play—announced, "Now making the turn: Seth Cannello of Colorado Springs."

Seth had wound up recovering sufficiently to cover those thirty-seven miles in just over two hours, at an average pace of 17.4 miles an hour.

He would later credit Bryan Reece's impromptu pep talk with helping quiet his shakes and getting him back in the game.

At some point on the downhill, Seth repaid Bryan for his kindness by zooming past him.

Bryan, a full decade older than Seth, had found himself huffing and puffing a bit on the uphill portion of that first loop. Looking down at his speedometer, he would recall seeing some single digits, including speeds of nine and even eight miles an hour in those headwinds. *So much for that forecast of light breezes*, he had thought.

But as he made the turnaround at the halfway point of the first loop, out by Shea Boulevard, he had been cheered by the sight of Debbie, whose voice was already hoarse from cheering, and of his brother, Bruce, who'd flown in for the occasion from Texas.

After taking a break to use the portable toilets at the aid station there and chatting for a minute or so with his family, Bryan soon found himself "screaming fast downwind," as he later put it. Now his speedometer was indicating that he was going upward of sixteen miles an hour, and when he made the turn at Rio Salado and Mill to begin the second lap—a full eighteen minutes behind Seth—he was pleased.

At 2 hours and 26 minutes, Bryan's first lap was "dead-on my predicted time," he said later.

Though the wind had picked up, he maintained an almost identical pace for the second loop. The third loop, which he began at 1:45—6 hours and 45 minutes after his swim had begun, and nearly four and a half hours after he got on his bike—would feel, to him, like his toughest.

The number of cyclists on the course had thinned considerably, and Bryan had a particularly hard time watching some of those riders just across the median on the Beeline Highway, speeding toward the transition tent from bike to run, while he still had more than thirty cycling miles in front of him.

He also noted, for the first time, that "there was some carnage out there."

"I saw several folks stopped along the side of the road, bent over, stretching or puking, or just laying flat on the shoulder of the road," he would say later. "You began to see people in pain."

In his everyday life, Bryan's disposition was almost relentlessly sunny, and he was always there as a cheerleader to his colleagues at work or his friends at the gym. But now he found his mind drifting into what he would describe later as "some dark places."

Whether it was sixty miles—or fifty, or forty, or, now, thirty—that he still had to bike, Bryan could "never totally forget" that a marathon awaited him at the end of the ride.

At some point on the third loop, when he heard a fellow rider mischievously mention something about the upcoming run, Bryan had thought, a bit uncharacteristically, *Shut up! Not now!*

Moreover, he could not stop focusing on how sore his butt was from all that time in the saddle.

I love my bike, he would remember thinking, *but I want off it right now!*

Still, as he passed the halfway point of his third and final loop, he had to admit to himself: He felt "very good." Almost miraculously, his sinuses had begun to clear for the first time in days, and his back no longer hurt. The calories he was taking in—as many as three hundred an hour, via the customized concoctions he was drinking and occasional bites of his Uncrustables-brand PB&Js—felt just right: enough to keep him energetic and alert, though not so much that his stomach was heavy.

"My training rides were much more painful than that day," he would say later. "The excitement of race day. The adrenaline. It was a great control of my mental state not to get ahead of myself. I just knew what I had to do. I just had to work through each segment."

Bryan would be surprised to learn that his third loop on the bike—which he wound up completing at an average pace of nearly sixteen miles an hour—was his fastest, by at least a half mile.

No one who participated in Ironman Arizona on November 22, 2009, had started the bike segment later than Laura Arnez. (The woman who had finished the swim behind her had managed to get through transition and begin her cycling trek several minutes ahead of Laura.)

Having been reassured by the sight of her getting on her bike, Laura's husband and five children had returned to their hotel—a bit unsettled by her late finish in the swim, as well as her late start on the middle stage of Ironman Arizona, but hopeful that if anyone had the grit to battle back, it was she.

For much of the first loop, Laura would recall later, she was continuously telling herself, *Go, go, go.* With nothing else to shield her from the noonday sun, which hung now in a cloudless sky, she had stripped down to an orange sleeveless bike jersey with white stripes down the side and black tights high on her hips. Her thick brown hair was in a long ponytail that extended from her silver helmet, and her hands gripped the front bars of her bike through black, fingerless gloves.

"I was hauling," she said. "I just wanted to play catch-up."

"I knew I had my work cut out for me, to make up the time."

She completed the first loop in 2 hours, 20 minutes, at an average speed of 15.5 miles an hour, but was well aware that she was in real jeopardy of missing the first cut-off on the bike course. She would have to make the turn at Rio Salado and Mill for the third loop no later than 3:00 P.M., which was less than two and a half hours away.

"Pray for me," Laura yelled as she kept her gaze on the road ahead.

More than two hours later, just after 2:30, Laura's husband, Tom Arnez, had positioned himself with the couple's two youngest children—Mary, nine, and Isaiah, seven—on a median in the middle of Rio Salado. Earlier, he'd taken the family's rented minivan to drop his three older children, Megan (eighteen), Nathan (fifteen), and Matthew (twelve), at a showing of *Twilight* at a movie theater on the outskirts of town. The older children had already spent plenty of time waiting to catch glimpses of their mom along the way—and, with any luck, they'd have many more opportunities to cheer her on later in the day. In the meantime, they hoped a movie might help pass the time and make waiting somehow easier.

Tom and the youngest Arnezes' vantage point was a perfect one: They were able to see the end of one loop, and the beginning of another.

Tom was a man who looked capable of participating in an Ironman himself, his head shaved nearly bare and his physique toned from the marathons and other races he'd been running for years. Yet he now found himself nearly on the verge of tears, as did Isaiah, who'd laid his hand-made sign—2699 GO MOM—on the pavement. Megan had done the same with hers (#1 IRONMOM) and Matthew's (FASTEST MOM OF 5.)

By now, the 3:00 P.M. cutoff had come and gone. And neither Tom nor the kids had caught any glimpse of Laura. Well, he tried to console himself, her finish in the swim had been heroic and inspiring, not just to her family but to the perfect strangers who'd watched it at close range. Everything she'd done today, he knew, would be of help to her in the next Ironman she would surely undertake.

But the reason they'd not yet seen Laura, Tom soon discovered, was that she had passed through this very intersection at 2:28 P.M.—just minutes before they'd taken up their position on the median.

Or, to put it another way, she'd beaten the 3:00 P.M. cutoff by thirty-two minutes.

She was still very much in the race, and might yet be able to call herself an Ironman before day's end.

"Hooray!" the family yelled as this news sunk in. Tom knew that Laura's strongest event in any triathlon, by far, was the run—the sport that had transformed her from a sedentary, overweight, unathletic teen into the dynamo she'd become today.

But before she could get onto the run course, she faced two final hurdles: She needed to reach the halfway point on her third and final bike loop by 4:15 P.M. or once again face automatic elimination; and she needed to be off the bike course, and in the transition, by 5:30.

With Laura out there battling, Tom directed the kids to pack up their gear for another break, before they resumed their sentry post on the median at the intersection near the finish of the bike portion of Ironman Arizona at 4:30 P.M.

This time they were taking no chances. Though they'd spent much of their time away hiking Hayden Butte—a sandy hill with gorgeous views of the lake and desert that sat, however improbably, smack in the middle of downtown Tempe—Tom had made sure that they didn't dawdle.

However exciting Isaiah had found the day, he was still a seven-year-old boy with a typically limited attention span. At present, he was tapping away with his thumbs on his electronic Game Boy.

Mary, meanwhile, was asking her father plaintively, "When will Mom be done with the race?"

A few minutes later, at 4:50, Mary found out firsthand that her mom would not be done with her day anytime soon. Because at that moment— a full forty minutes before the final bike cut-off—Laura pedaled by, the end of the bike course just a few hundred yards away.

"I didn't even recognize her," Isaiah said.

With her stunning comeback on the bike, Laura had now left herself nearly seven hours to complete the marathon. With that amount of time, she could practically walk it, at a rate of sixteen minutes per mile.

"If she fuels up good, she'll be fine," Tom said. "If she got sick and didn't eat, she'll suffer."

In fact, Tom had already determined that there was no longer any reason for concern.

"She already knows she's made it," he said. "I could see it in her smile."

He added: "Now she'll be the one passing people, instead of them passing her."

CHAPTER 17

You Are an Ironman

I t was around mile 3 of the run course that Scott Johnson came upon Lowell Gould, an acquaintance from his town in North Carolina. Though they'd trained a bit together back home, they were not quite friends. But Scott knew Lowell well enough to recognize that Lowell was, at present, woozy and confused, and obviously staggering.

"Hey, man, are you doing okay?" Scott asked.

It was about 4:00 P.M.—forty-five minutes, as it would turn out, after the winner of the race, Jordan Rapp, twenty-three, of Westchester County, New York, had crossed the finish line. Both Scott and Lowell, by contrast, had now been exercising nearly continuously for nine hours, with the end nowhere in sight. Before them lay the lion's share of a marathon—26.2 miles that, like the bike course, were more or less divided into three loops, each just shy of nine miles. Though the participants would be covering a great distance, much of it after a 5:30 sunset, they would actually be staying close to downtown Tempe the entire time: The run course was basically a figure eight that crossed back and forth over each of the three bridges built over Tempe Town Lake, each a little more than a mile apart. While there was a fairly steep hill on the opposite side of the lake, the course was otherwise flat.

The course had been designed to be crowd-friendly—an eagle-eyed spectator on the Rural Road Bridge might see a loved one go by six times—which also served to buoy the participants themselves at the moments when they would likely need it most.

Having just crossed his first bridge, at Priest Drive, on his first loop, Lowell Gould obviously needed a pick-me-up.

"I can't keep pace," he told Scott, as Scott recalled. "I don't know what I'm supposed to be eating. I don't know how to pace myself. Should I be walking or running?"

"Get on with me a little bit," Scott, the Ironman veteran, told Lowell. "We'll get through it."

But what Scott had really been thinking was: *This guy is a mess.*

Tearing a page from the Ironman marathon playbook that Bryan Reece, among others, intended to follow, Scott told Lowell that they would run a bit (maybe for as long as five minutes, if Lowell could handle it), then walk for two minutes. As near as Scott could tell, the idea of running and walking and running and walking hadn't been a contingency Lowell had contemplated.

"When you train for these things, you can go out and run a long distance," Scott would say later. "But on race day, you always have to have a Plan B. The only plan shouldn't be, 'I'll get off the bike and run.' That shouldn't be your whole plan."

Still, Scott could hardly fault Lowell for not being able to think clearly at that particular moment. "Your brain is scrambled," he said. "It's easy to get flustered and not have the mental capacity to figure something like that out on the fly."

Scott told Lowell he had always planned to do a little walking on the run course, which was true—"Just about everyone does," Scott assured him—and he promised Lowell that he'd be able to keep up.

And indeed Lowell would, as Scott remained at his side for the next fifteen miles.

Leanne Johnson was now a full half-hour ahead of her husband on her marathon, and she was cruising. Like Laura Arnez, she considered the run to be, by far, her strongest event. After a much-needed five-minute layover in the transition from bike to run—Leanne would later say that a volunteer's offer to remove her bike shoes for her had been "the best feeling in the world at that time"—she charged out of the transition, bound not just for the Priest Avenue Bridge but, she felt sure, for the finish line.

For the first half of the marathon, Leanne ran at an average pace of just under ten minutes a mile. That would have been considered impressive in any marathon, even one that had not been preceded by a workday's worth of swimming and biking. (By contrast, Lowell and Scott were covering a mile every fourteen minutes or so.) But even Leanne, fresh and fit at the relatively young Ironman age of thirty, had her limits.

Having run without stopping up to mile 13, she suddenly grew woozy. "My eyes were seeing stars," she said, and not because night was now falling around her.

"It was like hitting a wall. I didn't feel good at all. I couldn't function."

Leanne had experienced similar episodes in traditional marathons, but much later in the race. Checking her watch, she saw that she had a little more than six hours left on the clock. She quickly did some math in her head and felt, with confidence, *I can finish.*

But she didn't quite know how she'd be able to run. And so, reluctantly, she began to walk—and would still be doing so more than five miles later as she approached the last eight miles of the final loop.

Seth Cannello reached mile 13, the midpoint of the marathon, about ten minutes after Leanne. All day long, from that moment Bryan had crossed his path at the beginning of the first bike loop, he had only felt better and stronger. If he had to identify a point at which he hit a trough, it was only temporary, and occurred at around mile 90 of the bike course.

It was then that he lost any desire to eat or drink.

I'm so bored, he thought to himself. *I'm tired of being on this bike. This is really long. My legs are really, really tired.*

But a few miles later, these feelings passed, and he began to rally.

This year is finally coming to an end, he thought, taking a moment to reflect yet again on his father's passing and the injuries that had plagued him as he had tried to find time to train for this very moment.

I'm actually here, he marveled.

Now Seth, who had always prided himself on riding alone, decided it was time to get out of himself and help a few others, just as Bryan Reece had done for him.

If he saw a rider struggling ahead of him, he would surge close enough to read the rider's number.

"Keep it up, you're doing good," he would say, calling the rider by name. "Let's keep going."

Like Bryan's, Seth's sinus problems had seemed to disappear amid the day's exertions. (So, for that matter, had Leanne's back and shoulder pains; an Ironman aspirant could experience that kind of healing power, however temporarily.) At the outset of his run, at 4:00 P.M., Seth relished the warm glow of the late-day sun. At the first-aid station, about a mile in, he stopped to squeeze some wet sponges over his head.

Nice and cool, he thought.

He also grabbed some water and Gatorade, but was careful just to take sips. He knew that Ironmen with far stronger digestive systems than his would often develop symptoms mirroring a gastrointestinal flu on the run course as their bodies began to balk at exerting any more effort.

In a further boost to his spirits, Seth crossed paths at one point on his first loop of the marathon with Rob Ladewig, the retired colonel from Colorado who had urged him to take on the challenge of an Ironman. Rob, who at fifty-nine was nearly twenty years older than Seth, was already on his second loop. But rather than be intimidated, Seth was glad he had seen his friend.

As it would turn out, Rob would finish the entire race in 11 hours, 9 minutes, fast enough to earn a qualifying spot in his age group at Ironman Kona the following year.

When Ironman Arizona reached the twelve-hour mark at 7:00 P.M., Tom Bonnette, who'd long imagined he'd be crossing the finish line right around then, was beginning the third and final loop of the run. Though his initial goal was now, officially, out of reach, he felt no less pleased by his progress. His left IT band still painfully tight, he had resolved not to walk at all during the run, and had heretofore met that target.

"I'm not judging people who walk on the Ironman," he said later. "I just couldn't see spending all that money and going out there to walk."

Not that he wasn't tempted. When Tom would later see photos of himself on the run, he would be startled to see the degree to which the IT pain was forcing his left foot unnaturally—and uncomfortably—sideways as he strode.

Still, Tom, who had been hyperactive as both a kid and an adult, was encouraged that his energy level remained high—but not too high. The Ironman book he'd consulted like a bible throughout his training had advised that Ironman triathletes not permit their heart rate to climb above 84 percent of their maximum effort. The heart monitor watch on Tom's wrist told him he was comfortably below that, at 82 percent.

He received what he considered the greatest gift of all as he crossed the Mill Avenue Bridge at about 5:30, at the end of the second run loop, and spied his wife and three daughters cheering to his right.

"Dad-dy!" his youngest, Ellie—clutching a white Starbucks cup filled with hot cocoa—screamed.

Tom, a white baseball cap turned backward over his shaved head, swiveled around as he passed his family—so that he might continue to press forward while still talking to them.

Though his skintight, black sleeveless running shirt and thigh-length tights were drenched in sweat, he didn't look especially tired under the bridge's streetlights, which had just gone on. He certainly didn't appear to have been competing as long as he had, and he was doing a good job of masking whatever pain he was feeling.

When his wife offered him a Gatorade, though, Tom politely demurred. "I'm waterlogged," he explained. "I can't do it."

And then, after flashing a toothy smile and extending a confident wave, he turned back around and soldiered on.

Had he lingered just a moment longer, he would have heard his oldest daughter, Marlee, fifteen, pay him the ultimate compliment.

"I'm extremely proud of him," she said. "I always knew he had it in him . . . I can't wait to tell my friends about his Ironman."

His middle daughter, Paige, thirteen, who was a star of her eighth-grade basketball team, was even more moved and announced, "*I'm* going to do an Ironman now."

———

As Bryan Reece emerged from the bike-to-run transition tent, a volunteer dipped a gloved hand into a baking pan and smeared every inch of his exposed skin, especially his face, with white sunscreen. He now suspected he looked like a ghost, but he had never felt more alive.

Bryan, keeping to his commitment to never run very long without walking, nonetheless covered the first few miles at a pace of about twelve and a half minutes a mile. As he prepared to cross over the Priest Drive bridge for the first time, he once again heard the familiar shouts of his wife and brother; he waved and then proceeded to "dial back" his pace a bit.

"I didn't know what the next twenty-two or twenty-three miles were going to hold, or how my body was going to react," he explained later.

As he checked the time on his watch—it was just before 5:00 P.M., a cushion of seven hours before the final midnight cut-off—he allowed himself to exhale.

If nothing goes catastrophically wrong, he thought, *I should make it. But I don't want to take anything for granted. A lot can happen, and probably will.*

Bryan decided to ease his pace, running for a minute, then walking for a minute. When, during his first loop, he reached the only meaningful hill on the opposite side of the lake—"It was really big," he said later—he walked the entire distance, just as he'd planned. By now his stomach was starting to feel a little odd—for the first time all day, he felt that he couldn't keep anything down—and he wished to take no chances.

Just before 7:00 P.M.—twelve hours after the day's journey had begun—he approached the halfway point of the run and decided he was "ready to get this done." He was running a bit more now—and striding faster when he was walking.

"I was beginning to let my head and heart start to think about the finish line and hearing Mike Reilly call my name," he said later. "It was a very emotional time."

He grew even more emotional as he neared mile 13, when he decided to retrieve the contents of the "special needs" bag he had dropped off in the staging area at Tempe Beach Park before sunrise.

Among the items inside were two Hallmark cards, their envelopes turquoise blue and purple. They had been placed there by Debbie. One had a drawing of a bunny illustrated with phrases like "bounce in your step," "heart of gold," "bushy tailed," and "winning smile."

Reading it, as he began to jog slowly, made Bryan smile.

In the other—which featured a drawing of an exultant child, under phrases like "Kick Butt!" "Ain't No Stoppin' You!!" and "Y-e-e-s!!"—Bryan saw that Debbie had written a personal message to him:

> I know how hard you worked for this—I also know that if anyone can do this, you can!
>
> I believe in every stroke of your swim, every pedal of your bike and every step on your run—you are my Ironman.
> ♥ Deb

Bryan felt a lump in his throat as he placed the cards back in their envelopes and carefully slipped them into the waistband of his shorts.

By the start of the third and final loop of the run, his stomach felt settled enough for him to accept a volunteer's offer of a Styrofoam cup of the steaming chicken broth that—he knew from his time as a volunteer the previous year—was a favorite of the participants in Ironman Arizona.

"It's salty and it's warm and it's different than any flavor you've ever had before," he said later. "I'm pretty sure it's the sodium in it that makes it taste so good. It's a welcome treat."

There had been another note in Bryan's special needs bag. This one he'd written to himself, in the event that he might have become too delirious to remember why he had put himself through all this. As it turned out, his thinking remained quite clear. Still, by mile 21, he decided he might as well read it.

> Keep moving—
> No matter what you feel right now, it is nothing compared to the feeling that is right around the corner.
> While there may be others watching, this is YOUR journey. It has been a long trip—a wild year—but here we are, just steps from something very few can say they have done.

This separates—period. Not better, just separate. Get your name on that list.

Go shake Mike Reilly's hand.

See you at the finish line.

As a final reminder of the essence of the task at hand, he had closed his note with a final piece of advice to himself.

He wrote: "Left. Right. Repeat."

It was around mile 16 of the run, with just ten miles to go, that Seth Cannello turned his left foot a bit awkwardly as it came down, probably atop a small rock. He instantly felt as if he'd sustained a bruise, and perhaps even a hairline fracture, below his big toe. His hips and hip flexors, as well as both feet, had already begun to ache over the past few miles.

"My muscles were just starting to say, 'Enough,'" Seth would observe later. But this pain felt much more serious. "Every time I would take a step now, it was bothersome."

Further aggravating his injury was that he was now running mostly on concrete, which was not something he typically did in Colorado.

Still, he pushed himself forward; by this point he just wanted to be done.

Before long, he realized that he was.

Through the final six miles, Seth ran at a pace of about nine minutes a mile, about a minute faster than he had on the previous six. As he reached the base of the Mill Avenue Bridge for the last time, he was directed by a sign not toward yet another loop of the run but through a parking lot and back up toward Rio Salado Parkway, where he would enter the chute that would carry him to the finish line.

As he did so, Seth became aware that this section of the parkway, in front of the headquarters of US Airways, had been closed entirely to traffic. Bleachers stood on either side of him, filled with screaming spectators, and ahead was an oversize white archway that closely resembled the one at the start of the swim. The arch was decorated with the logos of Ironman sponsors, including K-Swiss and Gatorade. To the left were freestanding signs for Ford and the investment firm Janus.

Seth had always been a quiet, modest man who shunned the spotlight. But now, as he approached the klieg lights—as well as the pounding music that sounded as if it were emanating from a house party and, of course, Mike Reilly's voice over the loudspeakers—he allowed himself a rare display of ego. He began to slow down so that he would be sure to cross the finish line alone—a moment he knew would be captured by an official Ironman photographer.

By now Seth could see Reilly on a small podium to his left. He was wearing an oversize San Diego Chargers jersey—Reilly was a big fan, and the Chargers had a big game that day—as well as a dark blue knit cap with KONA stitched on it. He had no idea that Reilly, worn out not only by the day but by the effects of his flu, had actually taken a twenty-minute break and only just resumed his post.

Had Seth been aware of this, it might have made what he heard Reilly say next even more meaningful.

"Seth Cannello of Colorado Springs," he announced, "*you* are an Ironman."

As Seth passed below the archway at the finish line at 7:39 P.M., the Timex digital clock above his head displayed a final time that he would later find hard to believe: 12 hours, 39 minutes, 19 seconds.

It was then that Reilly added a rare coda.

"You did it!" he told Seth.

A volunteer in an orange Ironman T-shirt with FINISH LINE printed on its back quickly placed a shiny Mylar blanket over Seth's shoulders and began to support him on the left. Another man wearing the same shirt took his place on Seth's right.

Seth's legs appeared as if they were about to buckle under him. Whatever strength had carried him through the marathon seemed to have instantly disappeared.

"I'm dizzy," Seth said, and one of the volunteers at his side asked him, "You want to sit down?"

"No, I'm all right," he assured them.

But his face looked as white as the archway he'd just passed through, and the distant look he'd had at the swim finish had returned as a gold medal on a long orange strap marking him as an IRONMAN FINISHER, 2009 was placed around his neck.

After Seth bade goodbye to his two attendants, he turned left out of the finish area and into the athletes' pavilion inside Tempe Beach Park. To his left were massage tables, and ahead of him platters laden with Papa John's pizza—plain, pepperoni, and chicken. Seth beat a slow, determined path for a plastic folding chair and sat down, eventually agreeing to eat a slice of chicken pizza, the foil blanket still on his shoulders.

After some small bites, he got to his feet, but taking a few steps, he found he could go no further. At that point a medical worker intervened and guided him back across the finish area to the medical tent that had been erected in a parking lot adjacent to the US Airways building.

An emergency medical technician named Diana Padilla helped Seth sit down on the blue carpet outside the tent and propped up his feet on a chair. She gave him a Gatorade to sip. Inside the tent were competitors in far worse shape, lying on cots and tethered to IV bags. When Seth asked the nurse what his pulse was, she said, "It was forty four; now it's sixty-eight."

He had been close to going into shock, she told him, but now appeared to be out of the woods.

That said, he was in no shape to get up and go anywhere right now.

Somehow, Robin, who had been so far back in the crowd when Seth crossed the finish line that she had to settle for seeing him do so on an oversized TV screen nearby, had figured out that he might be in the medical area, and found him there.

"What are you doing?" she asked him.

"I was feeling nauseous," he said, sheepishly.

Robin, the concern on her face obvious, took a seat next to Seth on the mat, and immediately their conversation turned to the mundane.

"Did you pick up my bike?" he asked.

"Yes," she replied, "it's already in the van."

"I don't know how I got on my bike," he said.

"Well," she said, "it did take you seventeen minutes!"

Not only had she watched that scene firsthand, but her father had passed along each of Seth's times, including in transition, in dutiful text messages as he tracked Seth's progress on the Ironman Web site.

Then, as she stared at the medal around his neck, Robin's tone softened considerably.

"I'd like to say he'll have my respect from now on," she said to the EMT. "But soon I'll start teasing him again."

Seth managed a wan smile, the first since he'd crossed the finish line. A few minutes later he said to Diana, "I'm good."

After she and Robin helped him to his feet, Robin ushered him toward the family van, which they'd somehow had the presence of mind to park that morning at a lot immediately adjacent to medical.

Diana later revealed that, as Seth had been getting settled on the mat, speaking very softly, "He told me about his dad. It was emotional for him."

While Seth was in medical, Leanne Johnson came across the finish line at 8:02 P.M. Like Seth, she'd managed to leave plenty of time on the clock, finishing in 13 hours and 2 minutes.

Such a relatively fast final time had seemed unthinkable to her as she'd walked from mile 13 to mile 18. But then, in the crowd, she'd seen Ross and Daradee, the parents of Liam.

"You have one more loop to go," Ross told her. "Be strong. Finish strong."

That, as it turned out, was just what Leanne needed to hear. She began to run again, and the thirteen-minute miles she'd been walking became ten-minute miles in the final stretch.

Leanne had approached the finish area so quickly that her brother and his wife were still on their way there as she ran by them en route, and almost spontaneously they began to run on the sidelines alongside her.

"When I finished, I felt awesome," Leanne said afterward. Still, she had to admit, "It wasn't anything like I imagined. I don't know if I built it up too much. It didn't really sink in. I was just glad to be done."

She wasn't hungry, and though she was sore, she wasn't in the mood for a massage. She just wanted to get out of the athletes' area as quickly as possible and reunite with her brother, the Murrays, and her other friends, none of whom were permitted in the area where the pizza and massages were being offered.

Once she had met up with them by the lake, they told her that they had seen Scott along the run, albeit a while ago and well behind her.

"He was smiling and having a good time," someone added, and they had even gotten a photo of him.

"We were all ready for him to come in," Leanne said later, and they all moved toward the finish line to wait for him.

As Tom Bonnette closed in on the final loop of the run course, he tried desperately to distract his mind from the pain along his left leg and the boredom that was setting in as he ran in the dark. Sometimes he would count from one to one hundred, counting off each time his right foot hit the ground, repeating that ritual over and over.

Tom had adopted this practice for previous races—none as long as an Ironman, of course—and it felt to him almost like meditation.

Occasionally he would say a Hail Mary or Our Father to himself—he was a Catholic—or have conversations with his three daughters, or his wife, inside his head.

As he ran painfully up the small hill to the chute, he saw his ex-brother-in-law, Kevin, along with his fiancée, in the crowd. "He knew I was hurting," Tom recalled. "He just kept clapping his hands, telling me, 'Finish strong, finish strong.'"

The next thing Tom heard was the roar of the crowd on either side of the chute, and then he saw the bright lights and began to wonder how he should proceed.

"Some people high-five," he said later. "Some people ham it up. In my mind, I was sprinting."

He was so distracted by thoughts of how, exactly, he should finish his Ironman that he ran by his family without acknowledging them.

"You looked right at us and kept going," his daughter Paige told him afterward.

"No, I didn't," Tom protested.

But the evidence was there on the video of the moment that Paige had captured with her Flip camera. Her dad was clearly a bit out of it.

What Tom was thinking at that moment was that, with all the lights and loud music, this was what a rock star must feel like.

The one thing he did remember, clearly, was hearing Mike Reilly say his name.

Like Seth, Tom suddenly felt "weird, and kind of light-headed" after crossing the finish line, at 13 hours, 12 minutes, 37 seconds.

"Everyone was looking at me strange," he recalled.

And so, like Seth, he was escorted to medical and lay down in the parking lot, his feet propped up on a chair so the blood might return to his upper body and head.

After a couple of minutes of rest, he felt well enough to eat a piece of pizza.

And then, craving only a Coca-Cola, he was on his way home, the rare participant in Ironman Arizona who would be able to sleep in his own bed.

Leanne had been waiting more than an hour for Scott when, just after 9:00 P.M., her cell phone suddenly buzzed.

The caller ID flashed a number she didn't recognize, and she quickly answered.

She did know the voice, though. It was Scott.

He explained that he was at the bike tent, and that he had already arranged for both their bicycles to be packed up in preparation for shipping back to North Carolina.

He then told her that around mile 18, at about 8:00 P.M., he'd decided to quit the race.

His right hip had just been throbbing too fiercely, a result of overuse. He had begun to feel significant pain on the bike but had hoped to ward it off by taking a prescription painkiller in transition. Whatever relief it had given him had been fleeting. The pain had become so bad that, over the course of these last few miles before he decided to call it a day, he had begun to drag his leg.

"I didn't know if I was causing myself significant damage," he said later. "And I knew I didn't want to be hobbled for the rest of my life."

Still, there had been the matter of Lowell Gould, who'd hung in there with him for miles and was still at his side as Scott weighed his decision.

"Hey, man," Scott had announced to Lowell. "I have to drop out."

With the tables suddenly turned, Lowell now found himself trying to pep up Scott.

But Scott would not be dissuaded from his decision. "I want to finish," he told Lowell. "I just can't finish today. It's not that I didn't train enough. It's not that I messed up my nutrition. I'm just not going to cause myself permanent damage."

And so, however reluctantly, Scott had sent Lowell on his way, advising him, in a final, Yoda-esque bit of wisdom, "Walk when you need to. Run when you need to."

Besides, he reminded Lowell, it was 8:00 P.M., meaning that he had four hours to cover eight miles. "You could walk that if you had to," Scott told him. "Keep focused."

Scott would later learn that Lowell did finish, just before 10:00 P.M.

But as he spoke to Leanne, using a borrowed cell phone, whatever disappointment he was feeling was counterbalanced by elation at the thought that Leanne had met her own goal—the one she'd announced to him after watching his own Ironman finish in Florida—to become an Ironman herself.

"I was so proud of her," he said later. "Words just couldn't describe it."

"As long as she finished," he added, "that was good enough for me."

As she passed through the transition from bike to run, Laura Arnez could barely contain her euphoria.

I did it, she thought confidently to herself. *I'm there.*

That degree of self-confidence wasn't a matter of arrogance so much as the fact that she just knew her body that well—how it had dependably responded in the past, and how it felt now. She could certainly do this marathon in a little under seven hours, which was all she cared about.

As she began her run with a light jog, she ate some of the food left over from her bike ride, including a bagel. As people cheered her on, she thought to herself, *I'm being so rude, stuffing my face!*

"I felt good," she said afterward. "My legs felt fine. My back didn't hurt. It was sore, but it wasn't like death."

Indeed, Laura would later order a photo snapped by the Ironman photographer at this very spot. Her husband would tell her it was one of the best of her that anyone had ever taken.

"You look pretty," he said. "You don't look like you just biked 112 miles. You look so happy."

Near the start of the run, she saw that some volunteers were manning a makeshift massage tent. Laura knew she didn't want to lie down, however much she was tempted, but she asked, "Can you guys just rub my quads with some oil?"

The two women said they were happy to oblige, with each grabbing a leg as if Laura were a Thanksgiving turkey in need of basting. Just the smell of the eucalyptus was calming to her.

As she made her way through the run—initially at a pace of 13 minutes a mile, then 12:40, then, as the finish neared, 11:54—Laura had only one concern. One of her contact lenses had torn at some point, probably on the swim, and she was quite certain that a piece of it remained in her eye. As a result, her vision was a little blurry.

But even that was more annoying than anything else. Whenever she'd hear a song wafting onto the course from the finish line, such as "Shout" or U2's "Where the Streets Have No Name," she'd break into a spontaneous dance. At several points along the way, she'd catch sight of her husband and all five children, and as she'd fast-walk next to them, they'd try their best to keep pace for a few steps.

Just after 10:40 P.M., Laura began her run down the chute, still in the same orange tank top she had worn on the bike, but her helmet had been replaced by a black baseball cap. Her forearms were covered by long black warmers that made her appear as if she were finishing not a 140.6-mile juggernaut, but a night at a cotillion.

As she crossed the finish line, her smile as bright as the spotlights above, she was clutching something in her right hand: a photo of her family standing in a grove of what appeared to be evergreen trees. As it happened, this was the photo they had already decided to use as their Christmas card the following month.

In anticipation of this special day, her husband had had a copy of it laminated, and Laura had placed it with great care with her running shoes.

She wound up carrying it the entire 26.2 miles of the marathon, shifting it every so often from one hand to the other.

Throughout the final loop of the run, Bryan began to do something that he had done at so many triathlons over the past three years, albeit at far shorter distances: He started to thank every possible volunteer with whom he could manage to make eye contact.

"Sorry, you won't get to cheer for me anymore tonight," he'd say as he savored passing each spot for what he knew would be the last time.

Just before he was to cross the Mill Avenue Bridge en route to the parking lot that would take him toward the finish chute, Bryan caught sight of Rudy Garcia-Tolson—"moving doggedly through the night," as he would describe it later.

Bryan stopped cold and applauded.

Rudy had managed to make it through the bike course of the event, which had been his undoing in Kona, and was now, gloriously, on the run.

As he watched Rudy stride on those gleaming prosthetic limbs fastened high on his thighs, above where his knees would be, he was in awe.

I am amazed by this young man, thought Bryan, who was nearly three decades older than Rudy. *I know he's going to make it. I can see it in his eyes.*

But then Bryan remembered that he, himself, had work to do. As he passed Rudy, it suddenly dawned on him that he was in his final mile.

"It is amazing how much better I felt realizing that," Bryan said later. "The legs had energy. The posture got better. I was able to run more. I passed some people. I was going home."

About a quarter-mile from the finish, Bryan saw Debbie and Bruce in the crowd and told them he'd be done soon. They immediately headed off, not necessarily at a faster pace than Bryan but with the benefit of a more direct route, to try to get to the finish before him.

Oh my, Bryan thought a few minutes later. *Here it comes!*

It was 10:45 P.M.—fifteen hours and forty-five minutes after his day had begun. Wearing a red baseball cap that made him impossible to miss and a black LiveStrong shirt, Bryan motored down the chute as if he were Jay Leno, high-fiving every hand that was extended his way from the sidelines.

The last palm he clasped was that of his brother, who had managed to commandeer a prime vantage point inside the VIP tent, just steps before the finish line.

Then they both heard it.

"Bryan Reece of San Antonio, Texas, *you* are an Ironman."

Mike Reilly hadn't even waited for Bryan to cross before he said it.

But as soon as Reilly did say it, Bryan thrust both his fists high in the air, crossed under the arch, and fell into the arms of a volunteer who had pushed her way to the front of the line of so-called catchers, so that she might have the privilege of embracing him first.

It was Debbie.

Bryan held his wife in a tight clutch, his hands wrapped all the way around her back.

As they both wept, Bryan could only muster three words:

"I did it."

Epilogue

As if in a daze, the Reeces shuffled through the finish area as Bryan picked up his finisher's hat, T-shirt, and medal. He then made a purely precautionary detour to the medical tent, mindful of the cardiac history that, however improbably, had put him on the path to this moment. He wanted to get his blood pressure checked, and he wanted a nurse or EMT to reassure him that he was fine.

His pressure, he was informed, was normal, and he looked as great as he apparently felt, his face flush with color.

Bryan doubled back over the finish area to the athletes' pavilion, where he signed up for a massage. Though he was eager to eat a slice of pizza, he decided he wanted the rubdown more.

It was while he was being worked on that he heard a sudden roar from the crowd.

"Rudy Garcia-Tolson," Mike Reilly's voice boomed, "*you* are an Ironman."

It was 11:06, less than an hour before the end of the race, and though Bryan had wanted to tip his red cap to the young man and to see his face, he was not exactly in a position to do so at the moment.

Instead, he would pay tribute to Rudy silently.

Rudy, Bryan thought to himself, *you are an Ironman stud.*

The last of the finishers of the 2009 edition of the Ford Ironman Arizona—a teacher from Sanger, California, named Nicole Olivarez—crossed the

Bryan Reece.

finish line at 16 hours, 56 minutes, 23 seconds. By then, "I'm Too Sexy," by Right Said Fred, and "I Gotta Feeling," by the Black Eyed Peas, were thumping from the speakers at the finish line, and Reilly, his voice as coarse as sandpaper, was in the chute himself, charging up and down, trying to will one more participant in before the midnight deadline.

With less than two minutes on the clock, and a handful of participants still out there on the darkened run course, jogging, walking, and, in some cases, stumbling, their paths lit by the glow sticks organizers had passed out hours earlier, Reilly announced that he had christened 2,399 Ironmen that day, and that "one more gives us 2,400."

Each of the several hundred spectators who remained—many now in ski hats, down jackets, and gloves—had come down to the edge of the stands to bang on the barriers separating them from the chute, and now they peered down it toward the course as the timing clock above the archway flashed: "17:00:00."

"It's in the books," Reilly announced, unable to have welcomed that 2,400th Ironman.

When all the final tabulating was done, those books would show that Scott Johnson was one of only about 140 participants who began the race that day but did not cross the finish line—meaning an impressive 94 percent did. Of those who made it out of the water, all but 117, or 4.6 percent, went on to complete Ironman Arizona. (One of the relative few who did not was the woman who came out of the water after Laura; she never made it onto the run course, or at least not the first checkpoint.)

All of which is to suggest that amateur Ironman triathletes, or "age-groupers," are an astoundingly self-selecting group. On a day like this one, when the weather and course conditions were about as good as at any Ironman anywhere, almost all who actually started the race finished it.

There were about six hundred who had registered for the race a year earlier who did not show up that day, forfeiting most, if not all, of their $525 registration fees. Some were scared off by pre-race jitters; others, like Tracy Tucker-Georges, who'd done severe damage to her knee during that California mud run in June, had informed the organizers well in advance that they'd had to pull out due to injuries received in training. A few others were military personnel who received unexpected deployments to the conflicts in Iraq and Afghanistan. At least one cited a recurrence of the cancer whose remission had prompted her Ironman quest in the first place.

I was proud to see all five friends I'd accompanied from Team Will, the ragtag triathlon group in my town in Westchester County, New York, cross the finish line that night. Our fifty-six-year-old leader, Gary Rodbell, participating in his fifth Ironman on shaky knees he'd feared would give out on the pavement of the run, came charging down the chute after 15 hours, 34 minutes. While Gary is as modest and soft-spoken a man as Seth, he decided to mark what he presumed would be his last Ironman finish, his "retirement race," in a most un-Gary-like way: He dropped to the pavement, steps from the white archway, and executed a quick series of push-ups.

As an encore, he didn't just cross the finish line—he leapt over it, high enough to slap the top of the white archway with both hands. Then he, like Bryan, collapsed into the waiting arms of his wife, Colette.

Gary was preceded by Matt, the local chef; Ghent, a cousin of Will's who had only recently gotten over a case of the flu; and Heather, a native Canadian like Leanne. Not far behind Gary was our friend Paul Epstein, whose family business manufactures duck sauce and supplies Chinese restaurants with chopsticks. He realized as he approached the chute that he was now neck and neck with Rudy.

Having listened to Rudy speak on Friday night, and then having heard many of Reilly's references to him over the public address system, Paul knew that Rudy's finish was going to be a big deal. In fact, as the two men approached, Reilly had stepped onto the finish line with a camera crew to greet Rudy for what would be an impromptu, in-chute press conference. Paul made the decision to hang back a little so that Rudy could cross alone and have his Ironman moment, and then Paul could have his. They ultimately finished two minutes apart.

The following morning at the awards breakfast, Gary was called to the podium to accept a presentation (on behalf of Team Will) for raising the most money for charity of any group that had participated in Ironman Arizona that year:

$370,000.79.

Gary donated it all to the Barth Syndrome Foundation, which is seeking to cure the genetic disorder that had made our friend Will McCurdy, and several hundred other boys and young men around the country and the world, so susceptible to infection and at risk of an early death.

By that point I was already on my way back to New York, having been in Tempe for nearly a week, but Bryan Reece (whose donations for the LiveStrong Foundation totaled $2,000) watched from the audience and reported that Gary had been beaming.

All told, Janus, which had provided the technological support for the athletes to collect their donations, calculated that Gary, Bryan, Leanne, and the forty-four other participants who formally registered their efforts with the organization had raised $1.1 million on behalf of charitable organizations through Ironman Arizona. In recognition, Janus contributed another $47,100.

Though an occasional screech of an ambulance siren could be heard coming from on or near the racecourse during Ironman Arizona, the number of those transported to local hospitals wound up being mercifully small: nearly 20, the race organizers said, for injuries that ranged from dehydration and dizziness to lacerations, including several who collided with other cyclists on the bike course.

Sometimes, though, the call for medical assistance came after the race as some participants' circulatory systems and organs struggled, in the immediate aftermath, to return to a normal state. Even those who appeared so spry at the finish line that they seemed capable of jumping right back in Tempe Town Lake to do it all over again could be afflicted.

Laura Arnez, for example, had ended her race looking as if she'd just taken a run after dropping her kids at school. But once back at her suite at Extended Stay America, she had fainted, however momentarily, while walking through the room's kitchenette en route to the bathroom. As her frightened children looked on, her husband helped her to the bed. There she appeared to have two more brief fainting spells, at which point Tom, over his wife's protests, called 911. It was nearly 2:00 A.M., and she had been up for almost twenty-four hours.

The emergency room doctor who examined her concluded that her blood pressure had dipped and she'd become dehydrated after taking in too little fluid (and food) after the race, her body temperature likely rising during a long, hot, steaming shower. (It was only in that shower that Laura's torn contact lens, a fragment of which had remained in her eye since the swim portion of the race, finally came out.) As a precaution, Laura was kept in the hospital overnight, attached to an IV and various heart monitors.

Laura Arnez.

By midday on Monday she was given a clean bill of health and released. Though the episode had dampened, if only a little, her post-Ironman elation, such feelings didn't last long. On Tuesday, the whole family dragged Laura, sore legs and all, up Hayden Butte, the little mountain in downtown Tempe that they'd climbed without her during her race. She, of course, made it all the way up.

Once back in Sacramento, Laura said she found herself experiencing a level of confidence in herself she never could have imagined. Returning to her gym, she shared her experience and prompted two girlfriends to enroll in triathlon classes. Even Laura's daughter, Megan, a freshman studying software engineering at California Polytechnic State University in San Luis Obispo, had been talking about building up, someday, to a half-Ironman, perhaps after she finishes college.

As for Laura, after experiencing just a brief letdown similar to those that had been predicted at Iron Prayer—Laura likened it to a mini post-partum depression—she quickly rebounded.

"I would like to do another," she said a few months after Ironman Arizona. "Some of the girls are already talking, 'Let's do it in one year or two years.' I say four years."

Her main motivation, as she explained it, was, "I want to redeem myself on that swim."

After celebrating his Ironman triumph back at his hotel room with a Philly cheesesteak that Robin had gone out to get for him at Subway, Seth Cannello slept as soundly as he had in months. When he awoke at 4:00 A.M., about six and a half hours later, he was surprised that nothing really hurt—not his knees, not his hamstrings.

He and Robin were on the road by 4:30 that Monday morning, and she drove the entire trip. Occasionally along the way, his body was seized by the leg cramps and the tightening that he had anticipated. But those aches seemed to melt away when the family van pulled into the driveway and Seth's three daughters, who'd followed his whole Ironman online, raced from the house to hug him.

Within a few months his weight had ballooned—from 156 the week of the race to 182. Normally a scrawny 175, he'd developed his first love handles—"And I don't like it," he laughed. After not exercising much for the few weeks after Ironman Arizona, he now saw his expanding midsection as reason enough to get back on the exercise bike and into the pool.

Asked if he'd experienced any post-Ironman letdown, he replied, "I was just really happy I didn't have to worry about it anymore," and added, "I was really worried I wasn't going to finish."

But the biggest post-Ironman transformation in the Cannello household has been Robin's. Having witnessed her husband's heroic performance in Tempe, she has since shed the ambivalence, sometimes bordering on hostility, with which she had once greeted her husband's Ironman dream.

Along with Seth, she took part in the Austin half-Ironman, and, as her husband boasted, "Robin finished in 7:09! She did really well." (Seth himself had completed that race in a scorching 5:33.)

"It's really funny," Seth observed. "My wife turned into a complete training nut this year. I think she has a much greater appreciation for how difficult a full Ironman is."

Seth Cannello.

Robin lost 20 pounds and looks awesome.

Have you ever seen that movie "Pay It Forward" with Kevin Spacey? I think that is what an Ironman is like. One person does an event and it inspires another.

Robin's Aunt Terise saw what training did for Robin and now she's exercising. Terise thought we were crazy for training so hard; now she's running up to four miles a day. This is a lady that used to refuse to exercise.

As Robin herself explained her change in attitude:

It was really inspiring watching Seth's race. It was exciting. Not every person looks like an athlete that does an Ironman. I thought, even on the ride home, if those people could do it—maybe I could.

Thank God I started with a half. It took a lot of work. I don't know if I could have run a whole mile when I started training. It's hard to remember that now.

This has all done a world of good for me. I feel healthier. You go and watch an Ironman—it changes you.

Robin made a point of saying that Seth had played a crucial role in her training—teaching her, basically, how to ride a bike and then riding alongside her to set a challenging but doable pace.

Was there, I wondered, a full Ironman in her future?

"I do not think so, not right now," she said. "I don't have any actual plans, even for another half. But I'm not opposed to trying it."

Scott Johnson didn't spend much time licking his wounds following his aborted mission at Ironman Arizona. Largely because he had the foresight to quit when he did, his hip had healed well, and on its own, in the weeks following the race. He and Leanne are still happiest when participating, together, in triathlons—including one in Raleigh in early July 2010—but Scott said he learned a valuable lesson in Tempe, in terms of being careful to set a boundary between his wife's goals and his own on any particular day. Intertwining their objectives too closely together, as they had with their hopes of crossing the same Ironman finish line on the same day, had wound up proving potentially perilous.

Scott and Leanne Johnson.

"When I trained for Arizona, that was strictly for Leanne," Scott said. "You can't do it for somebody else. When the chips are down, and you're hurting, you need to be doing a little for yourself."

To that end, in late July 2010, Scott marked another milestone since his life-changing surgery in 2001. He and Leanne traveled to Madison, Wisconsin, so that Scott could compete in the U.S. Transplant Games. He had registered for one swimming event (500 meters) as well as two cycling events, a time-trial, and a road race.

He and Leanne also did a 5K running race there—together.

Having competed in five races at the epic Ironman distance, Scott's experience provides a bit of foreshadowing for those who have finished their first Ironman: They are rarely content until they take part in at least one more.

Compulsive and goal-oriented by nature, the weekend warrior who hears his or her name called out by Mike Reilly at the finish is eager to hear it again, and sometimes again and again. (And some, like German Silva, the New York City Marathon winner, who came up short at Ironman Arizona 2008, are not satisfied until they actually finish such a race; Silva did so at Ironman Cozumel a year later, in a striking 10 hours, 40 minutes.)

But for some, it's not just the execution and completion of an Ironman that can become addictive; the preparation itself has its own rewards, not just in the way it keeps one's body in shape but also because of the endorphins released on a daily or near-daily basis. Many participants have remarked that it can be hard to return to first or second gear afterward, at least over the long haul.

In my own town, several members of Team Will have found themselves surprised to be drawn into this vortex. At Gary's prodding, several of the Ironman Arizona finishers have signed up for Ironman Lake Placid in July 2011, along with Laura, who works with Gary, and another friend, Jaime, a chief technology officer. He completed his first Ironman in Florida in November 2010, with Gary and Paul cheering him on at the finish line, this time as spectators. (At forty-three, Jaime had managed to meet the goal that Tom Bonnette had set for himself but ultimately found elusive: He came in 8 minutes and 10 seconds under 12 hours.) At Lake Placid, the members of Team Will knew they would face technical challenges that did not exist in Arizona, including long, steep climbs on the way up the mountainous bike course and dramatic hairpin turns on the way down—which, of course, made the prospect of crossing the finish line in Lake Placid, site of the 1980 Winter Olympics, all the more appealing.

Before he had even traveled to Tempe to compete in his first Ironman, Bryan Reece had already signed up online for his second Ironman: the same November 2010 race in Panama City, Florida, that Jaime entered.

In Panama City, Bryan experienced some variables that were not present in Tempe—an air temperature at the start of just 40 degrees; a saltwater swim (he swallowed many mouthfuls, which made him queasy), and a bike ride over pavement cracked so badly in spots that, he recalled, "You leave the seat of the bike."

And yet again he prevailed, finishing in 16 hours, 23 minutes, with Debbie, of course, there to greet him at the finish.

That same weekend, Leanne Johnson completed the New York City Marathon in 3 hours, 16 minutes, a personal record by more than six minutes, with Scott there as a cheering spectator positioned alongside the final mile in Central Park.

When Ironman Arizona was staged yet again on the Sunday before Thanksgiving in 2010, I was home in New York, working on this book and disappointed to not be able to be there in person for the first time in two years. (Such events can become a little addictive to watch, too, especially as midnight nears.)

But at least I could watch a live feed via the Ironman Web site, checking in with the Athlete Tracker. Just after 9:00 A.M. my time, 7:00 theirs, I notified my daughter and son that the race was starting. It was then that it hit me: In all of the frenzy I'd been experiencing to meet an end-of-the-year deadline for the book, I'd inadvertently lost touch with Tracy Tucker-Georges.

When last we'd exchanged e-mails, she'd told me that her surgically repaired knee had recovered sufficiently for her to be able to compete in a master's swim race near her home in California on November 22, 2009—the very day, but for that disastrous mud run, that she would have been in Tempe for Ironman Arizona. At the time she'd told me she needed to do some organized athletic competition on that day—something that might simulate just a portion of the Ironman.

What, I now wondered, had happened to her since?

At least part of the answer was now on the screen of my iMac. Wearing bib number 2601, Tracy, now forty-six years old, was competing in Ironman Arizona 2010, according to the Ironman Web site. In fact, at that moment, I could imagine her getting kicked and punched on the swim—and, given her propensity for dustups in the transition area over the years with those who made the mistake of telling her she'd racked her bike wrong, I suspected she might be throwing a few kicks and punches of her own.

Tracy would confirm that I had been dead on in my guess. In stark contrast to the silly Disney songs she was singing in her head throughout the swim to keep herself calm, she got kicked hard several times—once, in the mouth, with such force that she tasted blood. Whenever she would hit someone, however unintentionally, Tracy would try to gurgle, "Sorry." As for her competitors:

> The men, they could care less. They smack the crap out of you. They don't say sorry. One guy was swimming, swimming, swimming, and I punched him in the head. Not on purpose. I said I was so sorry.
>
> He gave me a look like I was the devil woman.
>
> I thought, Screw you, buddy. Then I wanted to smack him again.

Tracy nonetheless survived a swim that at times, at least for her, seemed like a floating boxing match. She came out of the water in 1 hour, 26 minutes, 33 seconds, grateful for the expert instruction she'd gotten from, among others, her husband, who'd once coached swimming.

The bike ride was even more harrowing, on a day that not only featured heavy rains and strong winds but, however improbably, hail. Somehow Tracy stayed on her bike and finished the course in 7 hours, 2 minutes, 40 seconds.

By now her legs and back, surgically mended so many times over the years, had started to betray her. At mile 11 her body told her, *You don't want to run anymore.*

"I always thought people don't walk in the Ironman," Tracy said. "But everybody walks at some point. I saw so many people doing it."

And so she walked the last fifteen miles—as fast as she could, her arms swinging just as hard as in those marathons where she used to walk the entire course. It took her 6 hours, 19 minutes, and 19 seconds to complete the marathon that day at Ironman Arizona, but that wound up being more than fast enough.

She crossed the finish line, to the welcome serenade of Mike Reilly's voice, at 7 minutes after 10:00 P.M.—15 hours and 7 minutes after her day had begun.

There to celebrate her accomplishment were her training partners "Vit Tornado" and "G-Money," who'd also finished the day's race, as well as a first-timer from their group, "Wriggle Worm" (Jeff Wrigley). Tracy even got a congratulatory hug at the finish line from British world-record holder Chrissie Wellington, who'd won the women's portion of the race that day and had then spent hours at the finish congratulating the winners.

It had taken Tracy two years since her sign-up—and nearly $1,000 in registration fees, since she'd received a rebate of only $150 from her first attempt—but she could now, finally, call herself an Ironman.

Long before her Ironman journey had begun, Tracy had struggled with her weight, which had once topped 160 and was of sufficient concern that she had sought out Weight Watchers. She had since slimmed to 127, and stayed more or less at that level.

When she returned home after her Ironman finish, Tracy put her medal around her neck and went to a Weight Watchers meeting, where she stood up to speak to the group, which included several people who were obviously obese and struggling.

"I want you to know, when you don't think you can walk ten steps, that you—we—are capable of things we don't think we could do," she told them. "We shouldn't use the words 'I can't.' You don't know what your body is capable of doing."

Tracy's remarks received a rousing applause, and several of those in attendance came up to speak to her afterward.

Tracy Tucker-Georges.

When I asked her if she'd be participating in Ironman Arizona in 2011, she said, "Hell, no!"

But with the excitement of her Ironman finish still fresh, she was making plans to get a tattoo of a swimmer, cyclist, and runner around her left ankle, complemented by the tattoo of an Ironman "M-Dot" hanging from it like a pendant, atop her left foot.

Though he resides relatively close to the Ironman Arizona course, Tom Bonnette passed on making the trip when the race was rerun a year after his finish. "I stayed home and hung out with my kids and graded papers," he said. "Probably the cold weather, and the rain and hail, had something to do with it."

"I have been running," he added, "so went for a run first thing in the morning and, yes, thought about what I was doing exactly one year earlier. Maybe someday I'll do another."

Perhaps the best news Tom had since Ironman Arizona had nothing to do with swimming, biking, or running.

"I got my raise!" he said. The Phoenix Union High School District, he explained, had agreed to boost his pay to the level he'd expected prior to the budget cuts.

"I only mention this," he added, "because, sadly, the money factor was part of my 'plot.'"

Tom Bonnette.

And what of the noisy steering column in that sputtering van? When he finally got around to getting it looked at, Tom's mechanic rendered a surprisingly simple diagnosis: a filter was clogged, and needed to be flushed. The mechanic didn't even charge Tom for the repair.

While Tom Bonnette had been content to stay away from the finish line that night in November 2010, others felt an almost mystical pull back to the scene.

At the moment Tracy had crossed through the final white archway, Bryan Reece was milling around the same finish area, yet again serving as a volunteer "catcher," as he had in 2008, the year before his own Ironman finish.

And just as he had in 2008, Bryan got up well before dawn the morning after Ironman Arizona 2010, the better to get a good position in line at Tempe Beach Park.

He had flown out from San Antonio to sign up for what he imagined would be his third Ironman, and second in Arizona.

This time he had been motivated to sign up, at least in part, to support his friend Mark Elledge from Fort Worth who, following Bryan's example, wanted to see for himself what all the fuss was about and experience his first Ironman.

As the sun came up, Bryan had already been chatting animatedly for more than an hour with the guy in front of him, a tan, squat-framed man with a blond buzz cut and a Southern accent, his black Under Armour running jacket zipped to the chin to ward off the late November morning chill.

At a certain point, Bryan recalled later, he told the man that he'd begun on his own trail to Ironman as a result of a scare in the emergency room.

"What about you?" Bryan asked.

The man responded that he, too, had been drawn to triathlons and ultimately Ironman for "medical reasons. I had a transplant."

"What'd you have, a double lung?" Bryan, ever the smart aleck, recalled asking, the words tumbling out of his mouth before he could even realize what he had said.

Bryan would later explain that he had done so because of the stories I'd told him recently about Scott, which were fresh in his mind, though the two had never met.

Now they had.

It was Leanne—who was standing alongside Scott, listening to Bryan—who connected the dots. In addition to having all participated in Ironman Arizona the previous year, each knew that the others were characters in this book.

Scott and Bryan would hit it off so well that they would find themselves still talking an hour after they had reached the front of the line and registered for Ironman Arizona 2011. They promised each other that they'd get together then, if not beforehand.

Like Bryan, Scott and Leanne had flown across the country that week just to sign up for Ironman Arizona, so that they might help a friend. Their friend, they told Bryan, was also a first-timer—someone who had once been an overweight heavy smoker who'd begun to turn his life around after he and his wife lost their first child to a heart ailment before he had even turned one month old.

It was then that Leanne and Scott introduced Bryan to Ross Murray, bundled under a brown knit cap. He was now the proud father of a seven-month-old baby girl named Hudsyn.

It had been nearly two years since the day his son, Liam, had died. That same day, of course, Leanne, a perfect stranger, had called Ross, looking to rent his guesthouse. In the example of Leanne and, especially, of Scott, Ross had found a way back to the world of life and the living.

Though never much of an athlete, he now considered himself a triathlete.

"I've lost sixty pounds from my heaviest and I'm an absolute health freak," he said. "I took old bad addictions and turned them into new healthy ones."

On November 20, 2011, Ross Murray would seek to become an Iron-man, comforted by the thought that his friends Scott and Leanne, and now Bryan, would be out there, somewhere, on the course with him.

Acknowledgments

There are many ways in which writing a book is nothing at all like completing an Ironman. As I tap out the first keystrokes of this extended thank-you note, for example, there are no jabbing elbows or ankles coming at me, and I am at no immediate risk of tumbling head over heels over the screen of my laptop—at least no more risk than usual. And yet, like the characters profiled here, your Iron Author (or "Penman," as Bryan Reece came to call me) put in hundreds of hours of preparation without knowing the outcome of this exercise, and I could not have done so without the assistance of many, many people.

The first person at the Ironman organization whom I approached with the idea of an extended narrative about the world's toughest triathlon was Blair LaHaye, then director of communications and now brand specialist for World Triathlon Corporation. I am forever grateful that she was willing to let an outsider peek under the Ironman tent, and that she agreed to be my main point of contact throughout my research and writing. At Ironman, I also thank Helen Manning (who first told me about Seth Cannello), Paul Huddle, Roch Frey, Jimmy Riccitello, and Mike Reilly. I also received crucial early support and encouragement from Casey Cortese, president of the Janus Foundation. It was Casey who first told me about Leanne Johnson (and her quest on behalf of Liam), as well as Scott's incredible life story. Meanwhile, Rob Hephner, a writer himself, made me the envy of my children by chaperoning me on the thirty-seven-mile loop of the Ironman Arizona bicycle course (twice) on the back of his motorcycle. I also thank

Anthony Pedeferri for welcoming me into his home and telling me how his Ironman training very well saved his life after his crippling accident, as well as Nell Martin, Gordon Topper, Tammy Sue Roberts, and German Silva for sharing their stories with me.

Anyone I've met who has completed an Ironman, or aspires to, has been fairly bursting to tell the story of why, and how, and to encourage others to embark on a similar path. That said, it is quite another level of commitment to submit to hours of questions from a journalist and to then permit him to quote from letters and journals and blog posts that are sometimes set in showers or that lament the soreness of one's "girlie bits." I would have no story to tell here if it were not for the generosity and patience of Laura and Tom Arnez; Tom and Shannon Bonnette; Seth and Robin Cannello; Leanne and Scott Johnson; Bryan and Debbie Reece (and, of course, Bryan's brother Bruce); and Tracy Tucker-Georges and her husband, Chris.

My agent, Kris Dahl of ICM, could moonlight as an Ironman coach in her own right, considering the way she cheered me on (and up) at various times when my resolve flagged. Rick Kot taught me so much when he edited my first book, *The Gatekeepers,* and made the process so much fun that I wouldn't allow myself to imagine that he might take me on a second time—and yet he did, and I am better (in so many ways) for it. I also feel fortunate to have been able to work, once again, with Carolyn Coleburn, Viking's formidable director of publicity. Yen Cheong, the book's publicist, brought her own triathlon experience and a natural editor's eye to her reading of my proposal, asking a question early on about the philanthropic nature of Ironman competitors that set me on the path that would lead to Leanne Johnson. Kyle Davis, Rick's ace assistant, was always a reassuring voice on the phone as well as gentle, but firm, about keeping me on task. I also thank Clare Ferraro, president of Viking; Nancy Sheppard, Andrew Duncan, and Ellen Abrams, of Viking's marketing department; Kristen Haff, who designed the moving book cover in your hands, inspired partly by her mother's experience as a triathlete; Nancy Resnick, who oversaw interior and photo design; Noirin Lucas, managing production editor, and Will Palmer, the book's ever-vigilant copy editor.

Paul Epstein could not have possibly known when he invited me to take a swim at our local YMCA, with Gary Rodbell riding shotgun on the drive there, that those few laps would lead to his own Ironman finish at Arizona and my chronicling that same race in a book available on the iPad (which hadn't even been invented yet). But somehow, all these things happened, and I treasure the friendship of Paul and Gary. The rough narrative of this book was composed in the bike saddle on long rides on Sunday mornings throughout Westchester County, New York. Among the many training partners on Team Will who proved a receptive audience (albeit a captive one) were Laura Azar, Jaime Jofre, Frank Julie, Matt Karp, Angelo Mancino, Mike McEvily, Francois Odouard, Heather Segal, John Steigerwald, and Stefan Tunguz. Paul's wife, Leah, a novelist, let me know I was on the right track by reading an early version of several chapters, and Gary's wife, Colette, and Heather's husband, Mark, not only helped keep me sane but also gave me a sense of what it is like to be an Iron Spouse. The McCurdy family provided Team Will with ample inspiration, and a well-stocked clubhouse, too. I also thank Laurie Parkinson, and everyone else at the L Train, for spinning me into sufficient shape to keep up with the people chronicled here. And I thank Blaine Peloso and John Santalone, among many others at Horseshoe Harbor, for providing me a patio table with a view of Long Island Sound where I could review the manuscript.

This project was undertaken and completed outside of my work as a reporter at *The New York Times,* but I got valuable feedback from a number of fellow *Times* journalists. They include Raymond Hernandez, who somehow managed to edit some early sections of the book by cell phone from Washington, D.C., as well as Joseph Berger, Bill Carter, Jack Kadden, Steve Reddicliffe, Liz Robbins, John Schwartz, and Chuck Strum. Rebecca Ruiz proved a quick and thorough researcher. Thanks also to Fred R. Conrad. Outside of work, I got wise counsel from Jon Birger, Jon Danziger, Sarah Jackson, Dave Marcus, Dorothy Michaels, and Bob Victor. I also thank John Firestone and Alessandro Saracino of Pavia & Harcourt in Manhattan. Special thanks to Antoinette Machiaverna for being so encouraging, early on, about the promise of the idea that evolved into this book.

It surely takes a village to write a book while holding down a full-time job and striving to be an engaged husband and parent. My family and I got an occasional, much-needed extra pair of hands during this period from Rachel Posedenti, Amanda Stephen, Susan Sullivan, A. J. and Allison

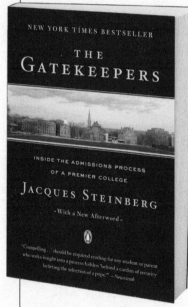